16LIVES

WILLIE PEARSE

Róisín Ní Ghairbhí

D1419892

THE O'BRIEN PRESS

DUBLIN

DEDICATION

County Louth Library Service
ACC No. ... 606.3916
CLASS No. ... 920 PEA
INV. No. 450169634
22/10/15
CATALOGUED
O'Mahonys

Do mo mhuintir agus do mo chairde.

First published 2015 by
The O'Brien Press Ltd,
12 Terenure Road East, Rathgar, Dublin 6, Ireland.
Tel: +353 1 4923333; Fax: +353 1 4922777
E-mail: books@obrien.ie. Website: www.obrien.ie

ISBN: 978-1-84717-267-9

Text © copyright Róisín Ní Ghairbhí 2015
Copyright for typesetting, layout, editing, design © The O'Brien Press Ltd
Series concept: Lorcan Collins
All rights reserved.

No part of this publication may be reproduced or utilised in any form or by any means,
electronic or mechanical, including photocopying, recording or in any information
storage and retrieval system, without permission in writing from the publisher.

8 7 6 5 4 3 2 1
18 17 16 15

All quotations, in English and Irish, have been reproduced with original spelling and punctuation.

Printed and bound by CPI Group (UK) Ltd, Croydon, CR0 4YY
The paper used in this book is produced using pulp from managed forests.

PICTURE CREDITS

The author and publisher thank the following for permission to use photographs and
illustrative material: front cover image courtesy of the National Library of Ireland; back
cover and inside-front cover courtesy of the Pearse Museum/OPW.

Courtesy of the Pearse Museum/OPW: section 1, p1, p2 all, p3, p 4 and 5, p6 top and
bottom, p7 bottom, p8 bottom; section 2, p2 all, p3 top; p4 top and bottom, p5 top,
p8 bottom; Courtesy of Kilmainham Gaol Museum: section 2, p6 bottom, p7 top and
bottom; RTÉ: section 2, p6 top; Courtesy of the National Library of Ireland: section 2,
p1, p8 top; Lorcan Collins: section 1, p8 top left; section 2, p5 bottom; Courtesy of James's
grandson, Noel Scarlett, son of Florence Scarlett, née Pearse: section 1, p8 top right;
section 2, p3 bottom; Courtesy of Dara Ó Conaola, author of *Saol agus Saothar Albert
Power*, and Pacella Uí Chonghaile: section 1, p7 top.

If any involuntary infringement of copyright has occurred, sincere apologies are offered
and the owners of such copyright are requested to contact the publisher.

ACKNOWLEDGEMENTS

Thanks to the series editors: to Dr. Rúan O'Donnell for his trust in asking me to write this book and Lorcan Collins for his generous good-humoured support. Míle buíochas to everyone at St. Patrick's College, Drumcondra, especially my colleagues in Roinn na Gaeilge, for their ongoing collegial support. Thanks to Brian Crowley at the Pearse Museum/Kilmainhnam Gaol Museum and OPW for generously sharing his unrivalled knowledge of the Pearse family and for alerting me at an early stage to many important sources. I was also greatly helped by Brian's important research on Willie's father, James Pearse. A special thanks to Professor John Turpin who wrote to the author with expert guidance on possible sources for investigating various aspects of the art world frequented by Willie and who also provided kind advice at the final stages.

I would like the acknowledge the gracious help of staff in the following libraries and archives: Leabharlann Uí Chriagáin, St. Patrick's College, Trinity College, James Joyce Library UCD and UCD archives, the Allen Library, Special Collections at the Boole Library (UCC), Public Record Office, Kew, Bibliothèque Nationale de France, Archives Nationales de France, National Art Library South Kensington, NIVAL at the National College of Art and Design, Irish Capuchin Provincial Archives, the Archives of the Passionist Community at Mount Argus, and especially The National Library of Ireland. The Bureau of Military History witness statements, an online initiative of the Military Archives and National Archives, and the biography database at www.ainm.ie were invaluable sources of information. The author was also facilitated by the Letters of 1916 Project at Trinity and the Hansard House of Commons debates at www.parliament.uk.

Thanks to Willie Pearse's grandnephew Noel Scarlett and his son Ciarán for hospitality and generous sharing of information about James Pearse and other members of the family, and to Tony Pearse for sharing information about the Pearse relatives in England including a family tree. I would like to acknowledge help given by Alf and Fionnuala Mac Lochlainn on a previous occasion which also proved helpful for this book.

Thanks to Seán Tadhg Ó Gairbhí for reading an early draft and for his expert advice. The extended Ó Gairbhí, Griffin and Lee families provided practical help that allowed me to devote time to the book.

The O'Brien Press have been wonderfully supportive. In the final stages Jonathan Rossney gave invaluable guidance; thanks also to Helen Carr, Kunak McGann, Nicola Reddy and Michael O'Brien.

My interest in the Revival period was sparked by many marvellous teachers, including Hilda Bean Uí Reachtaire, Professor Gearoid Ó Tuathaigh, Dr. Lionel Pilkington and an tOllamh Gearóid Denvir. Many people suggested sources of information or helped in other ways at various times including Dara Ó Conaola, Deirdre Nic Mhathúna, Pádraig Ó Snodaigh, Lorraine Peavoy, Angus Mitchell, Órla Nic Aodha, Ted Garvey, Brian Ó Conchubhair, Micheál Mac Craith, Julian de Spáinn, Therese Uí Ghairbhí and Emer Ní Dhomhnaill. Discussion of the St. Enda's plays draws partly on research completed in collaboration with my colleague Dr. Eugene Mc Nulty for an edition of Patrick Pearse's plays. The participants in a subsequent conference also influenced my reading of the theatre world Willie moved in. Though I do not share all of the conclusions reached by Ruth Dudley Edwards in relation to Willie Pearse, her book on Patrick provided vital initial guidance.

Thanks to all my friends for their interest and ongoing support. And finally to my parents, Máire agus Seán, my brothers Seán Tadhg, Domhnall and Cillian, my ever-patient husband Aidan Lee and our two small daughters, Sadhbh Áine and Nóra: míle míle buíochas for your patience, love, support and inspiration.

16LIVES Timeline

1845–51. The Great Hunger in Ireland. One million people die and over the next decades millions more emigrate.

1858, March 17. The Irish Republican Brotherhood, or Fenians, are formed with the express intention of overthrowing British rule in Ireland by whatever means necessary.

1867, February and March. Fenian Uprising.

1870, May. Home Rule movement founded by Isaac Butt, who had previously campaigned for amnesty for Fenian prisoners.

1879–81. The Land War. Violent agrarian agitation against English landlords.

1884, November 1. The Gaelic Athletic Association founded – immediately infiltrated by the Irish Republican Brotherhood (IRB).

1893, July 31. Gaelic League founded by Douglas Hyde and Eoin MacNeill. The *Gaelic Revival*, a period of Irish Nationalism, pride in the language, history, culture and sport.

1900, September. *Cumann na nGaedheal* (Irish Council) founded by Arthur Griffith.

1905–07. *Cumann na nGaedheal*, the Dungannon Clubs and the National Council are amalgamated to form *Sinn Féin* (We Ourselves).

1909, August. Countess Markievicz and Bulmer Hobson organise nationalist youths into *Na Fianna Éireann* (Warriors of Ireland) a kind of boy scout brigade.

1912, April. Asquith introduces the Third Home Rule Bill to the British Parliament. Passed by the Commons and rejected by the Lords, the Bill would have to become law due to the Parliament Act. Home Rule expected to be introduced for Ireland by autumn 1914.

1913, January. Sir Edward Carson and James Craig set up Ulster Volunteer Force (UVF) with the intention of defending Ulster against Home Rule.

1913. Jim Larkin, founder of the Irish Transport and General Workers' Union (ITGWU) calls for a workers' strike for better pay and conditions.

1913, August 31. Jim Larkin speaks at a banned rally on Sackville (O'Connell) Street; Bloody Sunday.

1913, November 23. James Connolly, Jack White and Jim Larkin establish the Irish Citizen Army (ICA) in order to protect strikers.

1913, November 25. The Irish Volunteers are founded in Dublin to 'secure the rights and liberties common to all the people of Ireland'.

1914, March 20. Resignations of British officers force British government not to use British Army to enforce Home Rule, an event known as the 'Curragh Mutiny'.

1914, April 2. In Dublin, Agnes O'Farrelly, Mary MacSwiney, Countess Constance Markievicz and others establish Cumann na mBan as a women's volunteer force dedicated to establishing Irish freedom and assisting the Irish Volunteers.

1914, April 24. A shipment of 35,000 rifles and five million rounds of ammunition is landed at Larne for the UVF.

1914, July 26. Irish Volunteers unload a shipment of 900 rifles and 45,000 rounds of ammunition shipped from Germany aboard Erskine Childers' yacht, the *Asgard*. British troops fire on crowd on Bachelor's Walk, Dublin. Three citizens are killed.

1914, August 4. Britain declares war on Germany. Home Rule for Ireland shelved for the duration of the First World War.

1914, September 9. Meeting held at Gaelic League headquarters between IRB and other extreme republicans. Initial decision made to stage an uprising while Britain is at war.

1914, September. 170,000 leave the Volunteers and form the National Volunteers or Redmondites. Only 11,000 remain as the Irish Volunteers under Eoin MacNeill.

1915, May–September. Military Council of the IRB is formed.

1915, August 1. Pearse gives fiery oration at the funeral of Jeremiah O'Donovan Rossa.

1916, January 19–22. James Connolly joins the IRB Military Council, thus ensuring that the ICA shall be involved in the Rising. Rising date confirmed for Easter.

1916, April 20, 4.15pm. *The Aud* arrives at Tralee Bay, laden with 20,000 German rifles for the Rising. Captain Karl Spindler waits in vain for a signal from shore.

1916, April 21, 2.15am. Roger Casement and his two companions go ashore from U-19 and land on Banna Strand in Kerry. Casement is arrested at McKenna's Fort.

6.30pm. *The Aud* is captured by the British navy and forced to sail towards Cork harbour.

1916, 22 April, 9.30am. *The Aud* is scuttled by her captain off Daunt Rock.

10pm. Eoin MacNeill as chief-of-staff of the Irish Volunteers issues the countermanding order in Dublin to try to stop the Rising.

1916, April 23, 9am, Easter Sunday. The Military Council of the Irish Republican Brotherhood (IRB) meets to discuss the situation, since MacNeill has placed an advertisement in a Sunday newspaper halting all Volunteer operations. The Rising is put on hold for twenty-four hours. Hundreds of copies of *The Proclamation of the Irish Republic* are printed in Liberty Hall.

1916, April 24, 12 noon, Easter Monday. The Rising begins in Dublin.

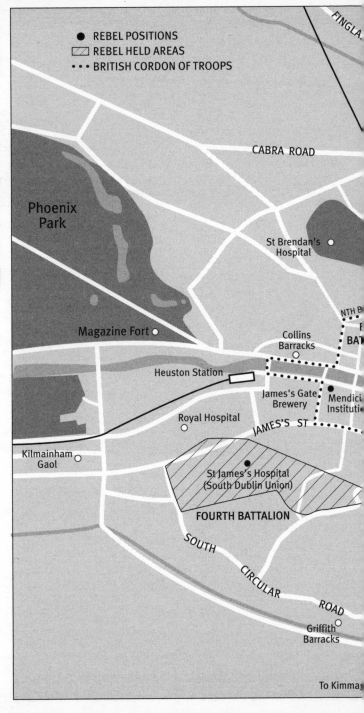

16LIVESMAP

- ● REBEL POSITIONS
- ▨ REBEL HELD AREAS
- ••• BRITISH CORDON OF TROOPS

FINGLA...

CABRA ROAD

Phoenix Park

St Brendan's Hospital

Magazine Fort

NTH B...

BA...

Collins Barracks

Heuston Station

James's Gate Brewery

Mendici... Instituti...

Royal Hospital

JAMES'S ST

Kilmainham Gaol

St James's Hospital (South Dublin Union)

FOURTH BATTALION

SOUTH

CIRCULAR

ROAD

Griffith Barracks

To Kimma...

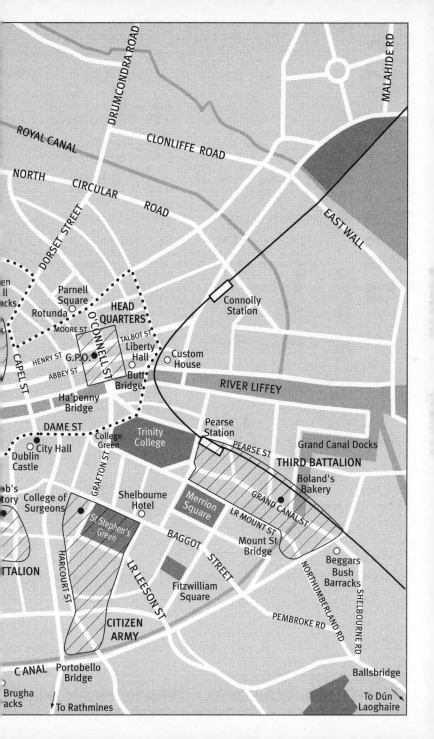

16LIVES – Series Introduction

his book is part of a series called *16 LIVES*, conceived with the objective of recording for posterity the lives of the sixteen men who were executed after the 1916 Easter Rising. Who were these people and what drove them to commit themselves to violent revolution?

The rank and file as well as the leadership were all from diverse backgrounds. Some were privileged and some had no material wealth. Some were highly educated writers, poets or teachers and others had little formal schooling. Their common desire, to set Ireland on the road to national freedom, united them under the one banner of the army of the Irish Republic. They occupied key buildings in Dublin and around Ireland for one week before they were forced to surrender. The leaders were singled out for harsh treatment and all sixteen men were executed for their role in the Rising.

Meticulously researched yet written in an accessible fashion, the *16 LIVES* biographies can be read as individual volumes but together they make a highly collectible series.

Lorcan Collins & Dr Ruán O'Donnell,
16 Lives *Series Editors*

CONTENTS

Introduction

'Yet William Pearse has been sometimes pronounced a
victim of circumstance rather than a victim of destiny or
a victim of conviction. It has been taken for granted too
readily that he followed his brother [...] but there the matter
ends. The matter neither ends nor begins there.'[1]

Willie Pearse led a rich and varied life in the years
before his execution by firing squad on 4 May 1916.
He helped run the family stone-carving firm and was a language activist, a sculptor, an actor, the chairman of a Students' Union, and a teacher before becoming a revolutionary.
Yet if Willie is mentioned at all it is usually in relation to his
brother Patrick, whose key role in the 1916 Rising made
him one of the best-known and most contested figures in
Irish history. Willie is seen as having played only a minor role
in the Rising as his brother's right-hand man; his execution
was particularly controversial and has in some ways become
the defining moment of his life. Often portrayed as having
drifted into revolution in Patrick's trail, and dying, if not for
his brother, then under his influence, Willie has become an
afterthought; a shy, gentle shadow of his dynamic sibling.[2]

In addition to the common perception that Willie's story
was a peripheral one, a lack of obvious source material

may also have been an obstacle for potential biographers. Although there have been a number of short biographical accounts of the younger Pearse brother, his story has never been documented or discussed in detail.[3] Almost a century after his death, this is the first attempt at a substantial biography of Willie Pearse.

Ironically, it is perhaps the relative neglect of Willie and his achievements that offers the most compelling invitation to investigate his life. Willie Pearse's life is not overshadowed by the hagiography or moralising that has so often skewed discussion of the motivations and achievements of Patrick and his fellow signatories to the 1916 Proclamation.

A detailed examination of Willie's life can allow us to revisit an exciting and turbulent period of Irish history from a different angle, on a more intimate canvas. Willie's cultural and political journey is in itself a fascinating one, more nuanced than is commonly acknowledged. An exploration of his life also takes us on a path less trodden into the rich cultural world of Dublin at the beginning of the twentieth century. Such an examination offers a fresh perspective on the artistic and political movements of Willie's time, and on some of the major and minor players in a crucial period of Irish history. Professor John Turpin has noted the (relative) critical neglect of the influence of the art world on aspects of Irish nationalism. It is hoped that this book will encourage others to examine this topic further, to reflect on the responses of art and artists to the Gaelic Revival, and to revisit other lesser known strands of cultural life in the pre-revolutionary period.[4] It may also provide impetus for a comprehensive assessment of Willie's sculptural work.

Chapter One

• • • • • •

1881–1897

Childhood

William James Pearse was born on 15 November 1881 in a room over his father James's stone-carving business at 27 Great Brunswick Street in the centre of Dublin. William, whose name was quickly shortened to Willie, was Margaret and James Pearse's third child: their other children were three-year-old Margaret and two-year-old Patrick. James, who was considerably older than his wife, also had two children from a previous marriage, sixteen-year-old Mary Emily and fourteen-year-old James Vincent. On the night before Willie's birth, his parents had given Patrick a wooden rocking horse called Dobbin. James had toiled at the horse for weeks, modelling it in the evenings when his stone-carving work was finished. If the gift was an attempt to assure young Patrick that his parents' love for him would be undiminished by the arrival of a younger brother, they needn't have worried. In later years, Patrick would recall

LOUTH LIBRARY SERVICE

his delight on the arrival of his chubby little brother. 'What greater thing happened to me than the coming of that comrade?' wrote Patrick. 'Willy and I have been true brothers.'[1] But the excitement surrounding Willie's birth was very quickly followed by a family crisis, as Margaret Pearse became seriously ill following complications related to her second son's birth; she nearly died, and the infant was sent away to be cared for by her uncle Christy Brady and his wife. Thus Willie Pearse spent the very first part of his life on a farm outside Dublin city, where he was fed on cow's milk until his mother recovered sufficiently for him to return to the city and her care. Patrick then declared that as soon as he was big enough, his new brother should have an equal claim to his wooden horse.

Meanwhile, there was political turmoil in Dublin to mirror the drama surrounding Willie's birth. The bitter and at times violent struggle over the rights of tenant farmers in Ireland had radicalised some leading Irish nationalists, and in October 1881 the leader of the Home Rule League, Charles Stewart Parnell, was incarcerated in Kilmainham Gaol along with nationalist leaders William O'Brien, John Dillon, Willie Redmond and the radical Land Leaguer and republican Michael Davitt. In the preceding years, crop failure had caused distress to many Irish farmers and tenants, and the ensuing hardship, combined with the often excessive rents and a lack of rights regarding economic security, had sparked militant agrarian agitation in some places and even a small-scale famine. The salient issues of the 'Land War' of the 1880s – land redistribution and tenant rights – would eventually be resolved through the introduction of a series of Land Acts that went some way to assuaging the farming tenants' grievances, but the struggle for Home Rule in Ireland would take far longer to play out. In June 1886, when Willie was only four years old, a bill called the Government of Ireland Act, more commonly known since as the First Home Rule Bill, would be defeated in the House of Commons, and in 1893 a second bill would be stymied by the House of Lords. At the time of Willie's birth, the two great organisations of what would later become known as the Gaelic Revival, the Gaelic Athletic Association (GAA) and the Gaelic League, which respectively sought to revive traditional Irish sports and the Irish language, had not yet been founded. While he was still a child, the Irish Parliamentary Party, which replaced the Home Rule League, was split due to a scandal involving Parnell's affair with a married woman.

Both James and Margaret's sympathies were with Parnell, though their backgrounds were, at a first glance at least, strikingly different. Born on 8 December 1839, James was an Englishman, and the Pearse family were recorded in the 1841 census as living in London in a shared house in Bloomsbury. James's father, also called James, was a composition maker (a craftsman who made picture frames and decorative ornamental mouldings). The son of a tailor, his religion was recalled as being 'to honour his wife and lovingly to fashion beautiful things out of wood which no one would buy'.[2] Although still in his early twenties at the time of the census, James Snr was already father to three young sons, William, James, and Henry. Willie's paternal grandmother, Mary Ann, was recalled as a devout Unitarian, 'ruling her husband and her three boys calmly and gently, obeyed and reverenced by them all'.[3] Life for the family was not easy, and as a result of her husband's meagre income Mary Ann often struggled to make ends meet. In these early London years the family lived close to the British Museum in Russell Square, and as Victorian society encouraged the intellectual enlightenment of working men, the museum was open to all. Therefore, modest though their circumstances were, the Pearses had plenty of opportunities to appreciate art and sculpture of the highest quality. It is an interesting coincidence that the Pugins – Augustus Charles (who died in 1832) and his architect son Augustus Welby Pugin, leading exponents of the Victorian Gothic style of architecture that would later inspire James – had also lived in the area (although the elder Pugin had died and the younger moved away by the time of young James's birth).

Workmen tended to live wherever jobs were most plentiful, and when Willie's father was young the family moved to Birmingham. James did not speak often of his parents or of his life in England, but when he did his children loved to

hear stories of his childhood and the home which, although it had only two rooms and a garret, was a place of happy memories for him. According to family folklore, William, the eldest son, for whom Willie was named, worked in a gun factory and, at only eight years of age, James went to work in a chain factory. Henry became a picture-frame maker. However, the 1851 census, taken while the Pearse family lived in Birmingham, designates both James and his brother Henry, aged eleven and ten, as 'scholars'. Perhaps James later exaggerated the young age at which he went to work in the chain factory, or maybe the reference to education was a statement of defiance in a household where culture and learning were prized. In any case, young James inherited his own father's creative impulses and rebelled against the grind of factory life. He left his next job, at a printers, after his employer's son struck him. Showing the independence of spirit that he would pass on to his own children, he also left the Sunday school whose reading class had been a source of formal education after his teacher told the pupils not to ask questions. For a boy born into such humble circumstances, a life of drudgery might have seemed inevitable, but James's ambition led him to study drawing at a local art school in Birmingham. He then became an apprentice to a sculptor and, for a time at least, dreamt that he might become a great artist himself. In the end, he was attracted by the revival in Gothic decoration pioneered by the Pugins and still in vogue in church decorating, and decided to become a professional stone carver. The boom in church building in both Ireland and England at the time meant that there was ample work for someone skilled in making ecclesiastical images.

Sometime around the end of the 1850s or the beginning of the 1860s, James Pearse, by then a professional carver, moved to Dublin to become a foreman for the firm of Charles Harrison of 178 Great Brunswick Street (now Pearse Street). Following Catholic emancipation and the cultural upheaval caused by the Great Famine of the 1840s, the Catholic Church in Ireland was undergoing a resurgence. There was a consequent increase in the building and decoration of new churches, which meant that commissions were plentiful for an ambitious young carver. Although working regularly in Ireland in the early 1860s, James Pearse had not left Birmingham completely; he appears on census records there in 1861, and on 28 April 1863 he married eighteen-year-old Emily Susannah Fox in St Thomas's Church, Birmingham. In 1864 James began a three-year contract as one of the principal sculptors for the newly constituted firm of Earley & Powells at No 1 Camden Street, Dublin, a business with links to the Hardmans, a company based in Birmingham responsible for church decoration in the Gothic style in both England and Ireland and closely associated with the very influential Pugin.[4] It was an auspicious time for James Pearse to be involved with Earley & Powells. Such was the rate of church building and restoration at this time that the trade newspaper *The Irish Builder* carried a column in each of its issues dealing specifically with the construction and decoration work being carried out by the various denominations in Ireland. Its pages also allow us to glimpse the milieu that James now operated in. While much of the content was practical information for builders and architects, there was a very definite sense that tradesmen and artisans were viewed as craftsmen and even artists. Various scholarly essays dealt with aspects of the Gothic style as well as the influence of local scenery on architecture, and the tone and content of the paper reflected its readers' desire to educate and better themselves.

Patrick would later recall with, one would imagine, a little relish, that his father had made carvings of princesses with robes and crowns for the 'throne room' in the House of Lords.[5] The Hardman connection was the reason James had occasion to undertake this work: they were contractors for its decoration, with Pugin being the interior designer. James's carving work for the 'throne room' (in reality the Queen's robing room) in the House of Lords was completed in Dublin, then sent to London in 1867, the year of a Fenian uprising in Ireland. The Irish Republican Brotherhood (IRB), known also as the Fenians, sought the overthrow of British rule in Ireland and the establishment of an Irish republic by military action. Although the 1867 'rising' was really no more than a series of skirmishes, the subsequent clampdown and imprisonment of activists, often in appalling conditions, and the songs and poems composed about the events, helped to maintain the tradition of militant nationalism; one of those imprisoned, Jeremiah O'Donovan Rossa, would much later be the subject of a famous graveside oration by Patrick.

James and Emily Pearse, like many city-dwelling people of their era, rented their accommodation and moved frequently. A daughter, Mary Emily, was born on New Year's Eve 1864 in Portobello in Dublin. On 19 December 1866 a son, James Vincent, was born, with the address this time given as 3 Bloomfield Place. Sometime after James Vincent's birth, the entire family converted to Catholicism, and there was yet another move, this time to Harold's Cross. When a daughter, Agnes Maud, was born there on 30 November 1869, she was baptised Catholic. In a letter written at James's request, Fr Pius Devine, Rector of the Passionist Congregration in nearby Mount Argus, would later testify to the impression that James had made on him as a prospective convert. Fr Devine attested to the Englishman's 'sensible objections and difficulties' while under instruction and 'the clearheaded manner' in which he found answers to his questions.[6] Fr Devine had also promised to bring whatever work he could James's way; the Passionists did indeed provide commissions for James, and the family would maintain a lifelong connection with the congregation. Whatever the reasons for James's conversion, or the sincerity of his new convictions, it was a prudent move for a man whose livelihood depended mostly on commissions for church decoration in a country with a largely Catholic population. Meanwhile, another daughter, Catherine, was born to the Pearses in 1871: this child was also baptised a Catholic but, like Agnes Maud, she did not survive infancy. Patrick would later state that James and Emily had an unhappy marriage and that one of their children, of whom James was very fond, died because she had been neglected by her mother. It is not clear if James's second family were even aware that there had been two infants who died, not one.

In 1875 James's mother, Mary Ann, died. She had never visited her son in his adopted city, but as James's work had often taken him to England he had spent extended periods with his own family. He was distressed at his mother's death, writing in a draft for a poem of her 'tender and patient heart' and of how his own heart must burst.[7] The following year, James's wife, Emily, died on 26 July of a spinal infection, aged only thirty, meaning that in the space of seven years, James had lost two infant children, his wife, and his mother. At some stage – it is not clear exactly when – he met Margaret Brady, who was working in a paper shop he frequented. He was clearly smitten by her, recalling in a letter to Margaret herself his own friend's impression of her as a suitable match: 'a grand-looking young woman, dark hair and dark eyes, no nonsense about her, plump and soft, she seems homely yet bright and full of life.'[8] Given that his first marriage was described as unhappy, James's enthusiasm is perhaps understandable. In any case, he certainly did not waste time grieving. Indeed, there was a certain haste about the new romance, a fact evidenced by Patrick's deliberate vagueness about its timing when he wrote of how his parents met in his unpublished autobiographical writings. Emily died in July 1876 and by the following Christmas, Margaret, who had yet to meet James's children, was already addressing her new friend as 'my dearest Mr Pearse'. By the following 18 January, any lingering pretence of formality was gone; Margaret was now 'my own darling', and Mr Pearse had become 'Jim'.[9]

Though both of Willie's parents grew up in large cities, there was a striking contrast in the cultural and social factors that had formed their identities. Born in 1857, with her birthplace given as Clarence Street in Dublin city, and educated by the Sisters of St Vincent de Paul, Margaret Brady was Irish Catholic, and the Bradys had strong ties to the countryside and to Gaelic culture. At the height of the Great Famine, Margaret's father, Patrick Brady, had come to Dublin from Nobber in County Meath along with his siblings and their father Walter. Willie's mother remembered her grandfather as 'a tall old man who wore knee breeches and a silk hat and who spoke Irish'.[10] Though Willie's maternal relatives came from Leinster farming stock, their background was atypical. During Willie's grandfather's youth, the area around Nobber was the last bastion of Gaelic culture in Meath and preserved a rich oral and manuscript tradition. The scholar Henry Morris/Énrí Ó Muirgheasa drew attention to the exceptional nature of the Irish-language community of North Meath when he wrote:

> Even when the last great rout came on the spoken tongue, the poets of Meath continued to sing, and the scribes to write their songs … This is the peculiar glory of the Meath-Oriel district that the literary knowledge of the language accompanied the spoken tongue down to its grave. In most other places the literary knowledge and cultivation of Irish had disappeared many generations before the spoken tongue died out.[11]

Having left North Meath as young adults, Willie's grandfather and his siblings would have had personal exposure to this rich pre-Famine culture.[12] The same North Meath area also had a strong republican tradition, and the Bradys were republicans by more than inclination. Walter's father, another Walter Brady (Willie's great-great-grandfather) had fought in the 1798 rebellion, while one of his brothers was hanged for his participation in the same rebellion and yet another brother was buried in the Croppies' Grave in Tara. (Willie's maternal grand-uncle, James Savage, also fought in the American Civil War.) Given his republican relatives, it is unsurprising that

Patrick Brady (who was recalled as never having said a bad word about anyone) followed radical politics with interest: he was a follower of the radical separatist involved in the Young Ireland rebellion of 1848, John Blake Dillon, and while James Pearse carved statues for the Queen's robing room in 1867, Patrick Brady was supporting the Fenians.[13] He himself had a small farm on the outskirts of Dublin and would be badly impacted upon by the poor harvest of '79, but luckily his business interests in the city were more successful.

On 24 October 1877, James and Margaret were married in the Church of St Agatha near the North Strand, and moved into rented rooms above James's workshop at 27 Great Brunswick Street. The children were born in quick succession: Margaret in 1878, Patrick in 1879, Willie in 1881, and, lastly, Mary Brigid in 1884. Space was restricted, as other rooms were let out to subtenants, and for some time the family slept in one room. Though their home was in 'town', with Trinity College nearby, the young Pearses maintained a strong connection to country life through the Bradys. They visited their farms with their mother; Uncle Christy and grandfather Patrick had horses and cows, while Aunt Margaret had chickens. Willie, along with his brother Patrick, 'loved all helpless creatures, and though naturally quiet and gentle they were filled with righteous indignation, often with great anger, at even the semblance of cruelty to an animal'.[14]

Aunt Margaret (in fact their grand-aunt) brought with her

the songs and lore of her Gaelic childhood and nationalist background. She told stories of the Fenians, 1798, and
Robert Emmet, and sang 'Déirín Dé' ('Dán an Chodlata'),
the haunting Gaelic lullaby about the rhythms of country
life. She was a regular visitor until she died when Willie was
entering his teens. At a time when Irish was not part of the
national school curriculum, the children's relationship with
Aunt Margaret meant they had a personally felt sense of cultural continuity with what would later be summed up in
Daniel Corkery's famous phrase 'the hidden Ireland'. Nonetheless, even though her influence on Patrick was profound,
it is debatable whether Margaret left a similar impression on
his brother. Willie would later take part with some enthusiasm in various aspects of the Gaelic Revival but, unlike
Patrick and many of his peers in the art scene, he never drew
directly on Gaelic sources in his own creative work. However, the militant republican themes of the songs and stories
of Aunt Margaret would find echoes in political activities
undertaken by Willie in his later years.

The seriousness with which Willie's father, James Pearse,
approached his sculptural work is reflected in his book collection, which included richly illustrated antiquarian volumes
about European art and sculpture as well as contemporary
journals on architecture and art. This artistic backdrop meant
that the home Willie grew up in was in many respects an
unusual one. Although visitors to the family home were few,

those who came were often artist friends of James's who were passing through Dublin. We don't know if Willie eavesdropped on his father's conversations on art with these friends, but it seems likely he was privy to their discussions as the family accommodation was compact, particularly in Great Brunswick Street. In any case, the rhythmic sound of the carving in his father's workshop below their accommodation would have been a constant reminder of his creative endeavours. Though he never fulfilled his dream of becoming a famous sculptor, James Pearse achieved considerable success as a businessman. The slogan on the stationery for his business, *Labor omnia vincit* (Labour Conquers All), could be seen as his personal manifesto. It summed up the manner in which he had overcome the poverty of his childhood to achieve a comfortable existence and a richer cultural life.

In his professional career James was not afraid to try new enterprises, and in 1877 he had struck out alone in business as an ecclesiastical and architectural sculptor. A few years later he formed a partnership with his foreman Edmund Sharp that lasted until around 1888, when both Sharp and Pearse decided to work independently. The firm of Pearse & Sharp was awarded a first-class award at the 1882 Dublin Exhibition, and they secured prestigious commissions, including that of the sculptural group 'Éire go Bragh' for the National Bank on College Green. The various firms James was associated with worked on commissions for churches throughout Ireland, including carving work for St Joseph's Church in Berkeley Street in Dublin, the High Altar for St Aidan's Cathedral in Enniscorthy, and the pulpit and communion railing for the Star of the Sea Church in Sandymount. Though he was often dependent on designs made by others, there is no doubt that there was some merit to Patrick's boast that, 'If ever in an Irish church you find, amid a wilderness of bad sculpture, something good and true and lovingly finished, you may be sure it was by my father or one of his pupils.'[15]

As Patrick remembers him, their father was an introspective figure who would sit for long periods in gloomy silence and then unexpectedly come to life with a perfectly timed comic intervention to leave his family shaking in laughter at the dinner table:

By some old convention or instinct we never made any noise once his big dusty figure had come into the room. He was big, with broad shoulders that were a little round; he was very silent, and spoke only once or twice during the course of a meal, breaking some reverie to say something kind to my mother or something funny to one of us; otherwise whether we were by ourselves or one of our rare visitors was there, [he was] sitting a little abstracted, always a little lonely we thought, a little sorrowful at times indeed, but [occasionally] he would in order to please my mother rouse himself to exercise the rare social gift that he had, and then my mother's face would flush with pleasure and we would laugh in pure happiness or join shyly in the conversation.[16]

Usually undemonstrative and reserved, James would occasionally embrace his children, but he always made a point of kissing them goodnight, and in letters he asked Margaret to embrace the 'kiddies' for him. The extended family of grand-uncles and grand-aunts provided a network of Brady relatives for Willie and his siblings to socialise with. Though Margaret Brady's sister Catherine and her husband, John Kelly, died young, the Pearses remained close to their children, Mary Kate and John Kelly, and to their other cousin Mary Kate Brady, who was Willie's age.

Grandfather James Pearse visited Dublin when Willie was very young, and was recalled by Patrick as a 'little white bearded man, quizzical and original, who spent all his time making bird-cages of rare woods, and carving them exquisitely; he left us about twenty of them when he went back to England'.[17] Their grandfather seems to have been much loved by his middle son: notwithstanding his long absence in Ireland, James cried when his father died. Uncles William (Bill) and Henry (Harry) also visited Dublin, and the family maintained connections with other relatives in England and later with cousins in Canada.

James sometimes needed to be away on business, and it seems Willie missed his father at these times; in one letter, written after Willie had injured his arm during some mishap,

Margaret wrote: 'Willy's arm is just all right. He calls his dada still', the brief comment a hint of a close relationship between father and son.[18] James missed Margaret on these occasions, writing long letters and always eager for news of 'the kiddies'.[19] He was not afraid to voice his affection and joked in an intimate way with his young wife in his correspondence home.

In 1884, as the business prospered, the Pearses moved to a house in Newbridge Avenue, Sandymount. This was a definite signal that the family were now financially comfortable. Despite his success, however, James was not ashamed of his own impoverished past. 'You must not forget the garret!' he would caution his children as they listened to his stories of childhood deprivation.[20] But while James's reminiscences might have passed on a sense of responsibility for the poor to his children, they lived at a certain remove from the poverty that was rampant in Dublin at the time, even though Great Brunswick Street bordered on areas of extreme deprivation. While living in Sandymount, Patrick and Willie decided they would sell apples from the house orchard in order to help poor children. They were beaten up by their would-be beneficiaries.

The children from James's first marriage were, initially at least, involved in the lives of James's second family: Mary Emily helped with the care of the younger children, and James Vincent got on particularly well with Willie's sister Margaret. On a trip to England he insisted that a special toy, a mechanical bird, be brought home to Willie, though his father had planned to give the gift to the young boy in the house he was staying in.[21] But because of the age gap between James's two families, the children from his first marriage – Mary Emily in particular, who was twenty when Mary Brigid, James's last child, was born – spent a limited amount of time with his second family. Mary Emily married Alf McGloughlin, the son of James's old friend John McGloughlin, on 5 July 1884. At the wedding breakfast two-year-old Willie, the godson of the new groom, asked for apple pie. Patrick, in an early example of brotherly loyalty, 'felt wounded when they laughed at him'; he was 'always wounded when Willie was slighted or ill-used'.[22] Alf and Mary Emily initially made their home at 33 Glengarriff Parade and a daughter, Margaret Mary, was born to them on 6 August 1886. The Pearse family got on well with Alf, but his marriage to Mary Emily was not to be a happy one.

By the late 1880s and early 1890s James Pearse's business was on an upward trajectory. The firm he founded would eventually boast of being the largest employer of skilled ecclesiastical decorators and craftsmen in Ireland, and he had achieved the means that allowed his children access to a wealth of culture and knowledge. Despite being largely self-taught, through his own passion for knowledge James grew to 'know most of English literature well'.[23] His extensive book collection included an atlas, French and Hebrew grammar books, a handbook on law, a book about the mistreatment of native American

Indians, several dictionaries, and a handsome edition entitled *The World's Great Men.* There were books about art, religion, history, and politics, and he was the owner of multiple volumes of Edward Gibbon's *The History of the Decline and Fall of the Roman Empire*. His four volumes on the life of Gladstone include a section on the Government of Ireland and Land Purchase Bills of 1886. James was interested also in literature, and he seems to have enjoyed the historical novels and poetry of Walter Scott as well as the complete works of Shakespeare and Charles Dickens's *David Copperfield*. Though there was a family Bible, James's attitude to religion was intellectual and sceptical. It is noteworthy that in his library James also found room for a copy of the Koran as well as Mackey and Peck's *Lexicon of Freemasonry*.[24] By any evaluation, therefore, the young Pearses had an unusually broad selection of reading material at their disposal. As well as inheriting his father's interest in Dickens and Shakespeare, Willie was able to avail of his father's numerous art books to further satisfy his curiosity about a world that had been first opened up to him through James's carvings and sculptural murals. His older half-brother, James Vincent, who began attending the nearby Metropolitan School of Art at the age of thirteen, provided another channel of influence. It was no surprise that Willie would turn to the formal study of art at an early age.

Among the other interesting – and, for the time, quite controversial – items in James's collection of books were biographies of the radical journalist and politician John Wilkes and the reformist William Cobbett, both published by the Freethought Publishing Company, in which he had invested money. Pearse Museum curator Brian Crowley has noted that James was an admirer of Charles Bradlaugh, who headed the Freethought Publishing Company and was a leading secularist, feminist and confirmed republican.[25] The radicalism of Bradlaugh, Wilkes and Cobbett is discernible in James's understanding of Irish politics. Based on general principles rather than ancestral sympathy, his feelings on Irish nationalism were nonetheless strong enough for him to take an occasionally proactive stance. In 1886 he published a pamphlet entitled 'A reply to Professor Maguire's pamphlet "England's duty to Ireland" as it appears to an Englishman' in response to a bigoted diatribe against Home Rule. James's piece was well-written and carefully researched, showing him to have been articulate, well-read, and possessed of a lawyer-like ability to argue logically from empirical evidence and to both pose and answer a series of questions with style and humour. His knowledge of Irish history (he acknowledged Thomas D'Arcy McGee's *A Popular History of Ireland* as one of his sources) allowed him to comment with some authority on the Elizabethan conquests and the Act of Union. There was also a practical edge to the pamphlet's arguments: speaking with some pride in his role as a tradesman, James alluded to the economic collapse of Dublin after the Union. This public statement of his political convictions was risky for a man in his position: when James acknowledged what he perceived as the courage of the Parnellites and defended Michael Davitt from the aspersions cast upon him by Professor Maguire, he was taking a stand which could very likely have lost him friends and customers. Although he happily described himself in the pamphlet as a British subject, his espousal of 'the inalienable right to be free and self-governed, which the very constitution of England sanctions, which the lives of reformers and patriots of all times sanctify' would find echoes in the lives and deaths of his two younger sons.[26]

The radical edge to James's politics also informed his thinking on religion, to an extent that would probably have alarmed Fr Pius Devine, on whom he had made such a favourable impression. His religious doubt had caused him profound spiritual distress before he decided to become an atheist. However, in this matter the Pearse children followed their mother and her devout – though never sectarian – Catholicism. As very young children Willie and Patrick acted out the Mass, with Willie's duties consisting of 'ringing a tiny bell and moving a large book from side to side of the bedroom altar'. Patrick, in a signal of an emerging dynamic, played the priest. As a child Willie had an acute sense of right and wrong, and was very sensitive to anything pertaining to sin. This meant that even if he did not feel like doing something, he did not hesitate to do it if he felt 'there was even a shadow of wrong in his not doing it'. This sense of duty remained a life-long characteristic.[27]

Willie's half-brother, James Vincent, became a stone carver like their father. James's letters suggest James Vincent accompanied him on visits to England, and family lore recalls that the latter had, initially at least, social status as the son of the owner of the Pearse business. However, James Vincent is rarely mentioned in Pearse family memoirs or reminiscences, despite the fact that he would have provided an attractive role model for his artistically inclined half-brother, Willie. Details are given in Patrick's unfinished autobiography for the wedding of Mary Emily Pearse and Alf McGloughlin in 1884, but none are given for that of James Vincent, although he married Cork-born Mary McCasey. When James Vincent and Mary's eldest daughter, Emily Mary, was baptised in 1888, the family were residing at 64 Eblana Villas, very close to the Pearse business premises on Great Brunswick Street. Another seven children would be born to the family. When a son, another James Vincent, was born in 1892, Willie, still a child himself, was a godparent, along with Mary Brigid. By now, James Vincent and Mary were living in a house in Great Clarence Street (later Macken Street), within easy reach of the Pearse family. However, it is possible that work for the family firm often took James Vincent away from Dublin: two of his children were born in Cork, although all were baptised in Dublin.

What is clear is that the predominant part of Willie's childhood was spent in the company of his siblings Margaret, Patrick and Mary Brigid. As children Patrick and Willie used to dress up in girls' clothes and head off to the area around the Custom House along with one of their female cousins. In *The Home-Life of Pádraig Pearse*, Mary Brigid also described how the young Pearses and their cousins took part in plays written by Patrick, the initial inspiration for Willie's lifelong interest in the theatrical world. From an early stage, it seems, Patrick was the wordsmith and Willie the performer. Their forays into acting included Willie taking part in a home-produced melo-drama, *The Rival Lovers*, alongside Patrick, his sisters, and Mary Kate Kelly. They also performed a verse play called *The Pride of Finisterre*. Later still, a homemade theatre provided much entertainment: Patrick wrote plays performed with cardboard figures against scenery drawn by Patrick and set up by Willie. The children's interest in history was evident: one play, espe-cially written for Willie by Patrick, was set around the Battle of Clontarf. This interest in theatre was unsurprising – the Queen's Theatre was just up the street from the Pearses' work premises in Great Brunswick Street. James Snr too delighted in recitations and there were talks illustrated by magic lan-tern shows given by him and by brother Patrick. Mary Brigid recalled Willie acting as her father's very efficient '*aide de camp*' at these social events. The Pearse children enjoyed sporting activities like tennis and boating as well. There were also the normal travails of childhood, such as illnesses: while the family were living in Sandymount, Willie caught scarlet fever from Patrick after kissing his sick brother.

It is not clear if Willie was a pupil at the Miss Murphy's school that his brother Patrick and sister Margaret attended. It seems that Mary Brigid, who was a delicate child, was taught for some period at home, and Willie may have been tutored alongside her.[28] In 1891, at the age of nine, Willie commenced attending the Christian Brothers School in Westland Row, along with Patrick. Here, unusually at a time when only a few hundred students in Ireland studied the subject for examination purposes each year, the Irish language was taught as part of the general curriculum. Patrick and Willie were thus equipped to take a leadership role when interest in Irish classes for adults blossomed in the early years of the twentieth century.

The brothers were also involved in the usual childhood scrapes and misadventures. In one instance Patrick 'lost his temper with great effect' when Willie was about to be punished for a minor misdemeanour in Westland Row. It was recalled that Patrick's 'violent protests soon changed matters for the better, and Willie was never molested again'.[29] But while Patrick excelled as a student, Willie was less conventionally academic and his examination results were very modest. Whatever the reason, it was obvious that the young boy's interests lay elsewhere and, in 1897, aged only fifteen, he followed in his older half-brother's path by registering for evening classes at the Metropolitan School of Art. He was not yet a man, but a new chapter had begun in Willie's life.

Chapter Two

• • • • • •

1897–1905

The School of Art

The Metropolitan School of Art that Willie began attending in 1897 had an entrance just to the side of Leinster House in a corner of the complex of buildings which housed the National Museum, the National Gallery and the National Library. The School formed part of a network that had been founded across the United Kingdom in the nineteenth century in order to give the working class an opportunity to learn about and practise art.[1] Around the same time that he entered the School of Art Willie began his apprenticeship at the family business,[2] where he worked alongside his father and brother as well as a large staff, many of whom were ordinary labourers. Though Willie was not yet sixteen, enrolment at such a young age was not unusual, and some of his fellow students were even younger. The school was easily accessible: the Pearse family were, for the time being at least, back living in Great Brunswick Street, and it was only a ten-minute walk to Kildare Street. In all, Willie would attend the Metropolitan School of Art on both a full-time and part-time basis between 1897 and 1912, mostly in the evenings, but also as a day student. Mary Brigid also attended for a short time, and she and Willie participated in a shared social circle. The School of Art was not simply a place of instruction for Willie, but also a creative and social hub which would in time influence not only his art, but also his politics, his close friendships and his social life.

While attending the School of Art, Willie was being mentored by his father and James Vincent. Some of the craftsmen working for the Pearse family firm were talented artists in their own right; Willie could find inspiration at home. There are references to James Pearse's 'pupils', suggesting that his remit as owner of a sculpture business extended to mentoring in a more formal artistic sense. As we have seen, James Vincent had been working as a sculptor for some time while supporting his rapidly growing family, and Mary Emily's husband, Alf, was a talented architectural draughtsman who had recently worked on the design for the new Portrane Asylum.[3] The Pearses and McGloughlins were by now leading figures in Dublin stone-carving and architectural design.

Though some of those enrolled at this time found the School of Art to be an uninspiring place, where students had to complete tiresomely routine exercises, Willie at least had the opportunity to meet contemporaries of a similar artistic disposition. Students came from diverse social and religious backgrounds: both male and female and of varying ages, they comprised a mix of young ladies, artisan workers and aspiring artists, some attending full-time and some part-time. A young man called Albert Power, who was a student at the School throughout Willie's long attendance, was to become a lifelong friend. Both young men shared an aptitude for modelling, as sculpture was then commonly known. However, Albert was more talented than Willie and would always enjoy greater success. Among Willie's other contemporaries was a young woman called Beatrice Elvery, who would also remain a presence in Willie's life, though her political views would later diverge from his. Elvery recalled her own growing patriotic feelings:

> From the time when I started going to the School of Art, I had found it almost too easy to become romantic and emotional about Irish politics ... It was difficult for a young susceptible person not be swept away in a flood of patriotism, but to be really involved in this movement it was necessary to have a great hate of England and everything English.[4]

The suggestion that there was an overwhelmingly nationalist atmosphere at the School of Art and that students had to have a hatred of England to be 'really involved in the movement' is not borne out by the facts. If anything, the School of Art was remarkably pro-British, and many of the gentry, as well as members of the social and military network associated with the Dublin Castle-centred administrations, attended the annual prize-givings. In any case, Willie was half-English himself. It is true, nonetheless, that several of Elvery's (and Willie's) later contemporaries at the School of Art became deeply interested in Irish culture and sympathetic to the nationalist cause despite coming from a Unionist or Anglo-Irish background. This was true, for example, in the cases of the painters Kathleen Fox and Lily Williams, and the English-born artist Cesca Trench (Sadhbh Trinseach).

But despite his long commitment to formal artistic training – fifteen years in all – Willie's cultural horizons were not limited to art. Given their exposure to the Gaelic culture of their relatives, it was unsurprising that the young Pearses would be drawn to the Gaelic League. This had been founded in 1893 with the aim of promoting the Irish language, which was seemingly in terminal decline, and by the end of the nineteenth century had become a major cultural force, with branches throughout Ireland and abroad. Willie joined in the autumn of 1898, just as it was entering into a period of rapid expansion.[5] His brother Patrick was already one of the League's rising stars, and around the time of Willie's enrolment, Patrick had been elected as a member of the *Coiste Gnó* (Executive Council).[6] Willie had also been participating for some time in the New Ireland Literary Society, which had been founded by Patrick and some of

his friends in order to advance the discussion of Gaelic literature among their peers. The young members of the society
met in the Star and Garter Hotel on D'Olier Street and held
weekly social and cultural evenings that attracted many visitors, including supporters of the Gaelic League and eminent
scholars. Meetings featured readings from the society's manuscript journal, debates and lectures, and although the Pearse
sisters gave musical performances, the main events seem to
have been run solely by the young men. Patrick, unsurprisingly, was president. In his membership of both the Gaelic
League and the New Ireland Literary Society, Willie was following his older brother's example, but was an active member
of both organisations in his own right. On 15 February 1898
he took part in a debate organised by the New Ireland Literary Society on the motion, 'That the Milesian Invasion of
Ireland as Recorded by the Bards is a Myth'. This relatively
obscure subject must have been challenging for a sixteen-
year-old with limited access to Gaelic scholarship. Willie
argued against the motion with Patrick's friend Eamonn
O'Neill, while Patrick and JJ White made the case in support. Willie's side won. The following week Willie gave a
presentation entitled 'Cúchulainn and the Red Branch
Cycle', which focused on the various warriors of the Ulster
Cycle of Gaelic literature, especially Cúchulainn. The script
of this paper has been identified as written with 'Patrick's
fine Gaelic hand'.[7] But the possibility that the paper had

some input from Willie should not be discounted. On the night itself, the reaction to his presentation can be gauged by the fact that a vote of thanks, proposed by a visiting Mr T Hayes from the Central Branch of the Gaelic League in a 'warmly appreciative speech', was 'passed with acclamation'[8].

It is noteworthy that two leading Irish artists, John Hughes and Oliver Sheppard, played an important role in the renewal of interest in Cúchulainn (the major figure in the Ulster Cycle), that took place at the turn of the twentieth century. Hughes was working on a sculpture inspired by the famous warrior around this time, and the writer and artist George Russell noted in 1898 that legends associated with Cúchulainn were 'beginning to exercise their enchantment over Mr Hughes'.[9] At the time of Willie's enrolment in the School of Art, modelling was taught by Hughes. Willie did not begin his study in this area until 1900, but it is likely, given the family interest in sculpture, that he would have been aware of Hughes's work. Meanwhile, though he was still based in England at this time, Oliver Sheppard, who was later Willie's teacher, had exhibited his sculpture, 'The Training of Cúchulainn' to much acclaim in the Royal Hibernian Academy (RHA) exhibition of 1897. Sheppard's dramatic sculpture depicted the boy Setanta (Cúchulainn) in a dynamic pose, preparing to throw a spear while being watched over by his determined female nurse-warrior, the half-naked Scáthach. Art historian John Turpin has stated that this sculpture of Sheppard's could have been construed as a 'patriotic political image stressing the nobility of fighting for one's country', especially as there was growing interest in commemorating the centenary of the 1798 rebellion the following year.[10] Willie, as an aspiring artist, would surely have visited the exhibition. It is possible that Willie's paper on Cúchulainn was influenced, or even written, by Patrick, but it is equally likely that the interest shown by both brothers in the themes and imagery of the Ulster Cycle came from both artistic and literary sources; that is to say, that both Willie and Patrick had their own particular channels of inspiration. And in years to come, Willie's connections with Sheppard would make the sculptor a major influence on Patrick. For now, the positive reception given to Willie's Cúchulainn presentation, his victory in the debate against his brother's team, and his chairing of another debate on 22 March, all suggest that the younger brother was developing an interest in Gaelic literature and a flair for public speaking.

The School of Art formed an important part of the city's cultural life and visitors, including Patrick, frequently dropped by, particularly during evening classes.[11] Regular student exhibitions were covered in some detail by the press and glimpses of the evolving atmosphere in the school — and of Willie's own progress there — are to be found in school records and newspaper reports of the annual prize-giving ceremonies. Academic sessions ran from autumn to summer and the prizes were presented, with much ceremony, in the January after each academic year. The prizes for 1897–98 were presented in January 1899 by the Lord Lieutenant, George Henry Cadogan, and Countess Cadogan. The Lord Lieutenant was the official representative of the British monarch in Ireland, although the office was mainly of symbolic importance as the Chief Secretary played a more central role in exercising British rule. The 1899 prize results show that 'William J Pearse' had mixed success in his first year, achieving a pass in Art Geometry and a first in Elementary Freehand. The Lord Lieutenant's speech ('received with applause') alluded to the fact that 'in all parts of the Empire attempts were being made to improve technical education', a reminder of the political context in which the School was governed.[12] Count George Plunkett, the Director of the National Museum of Science and Art (and father of Joseph, who would be among the leaders of the Rising) also spoke. Plunkett gave Willie and his contemporaries another reminder of the provincial status of the School (and of Ireland) when he stressed that the prizes awarded were for 'no merely local competition' but rather involved students from 'throughout the United Kingdom'.[13] Whatever about the whiff of provincialism in such statements, there were several advantages to the Dublin school's status as one of a network within the United Kingdom. Many of the teachers who taught in the School of Art in Dublin had received their training in England (and elsewhere), while students also had the opportunity to spend time studying in London, something Willie certainly did, though it is not clear when. On 10 January 1900 prizes were presented for the 1898-99 session. We can presume that Willie was present, as he was a prize-winner. On this occasion the headmaster, Mr James Brennan, stated that the 'province of the School of Art was to give a sound education in all the branches of art which might be allied to industry, and not to the production of tenth-rate artists'. This practical focus was an enduring theme at the school network, which was as much concerned with craftsmanship as it was with aesthetics. William J Pearse was listed as achieving a first in Advanced Freehand and a second both in Elementary Perspective and Elementary Science Geometry. Meanwhile, Willie's friend Albert Power achieved two firsts, in Model Drawing and in Shading.

The Pearse family business had by now greatly expanded and by early 1900 the family were living in Sandymount, initially in St George's Villas, and later in another house called Liosán. But tragedy struck when on 5 September 1900, Willie's father James died suddenly at the age of sixty of a cerebral haemorrhage while visiting his brother Henry in Birmingham. Arrangements were made to bring his body back to Ireland, and some of the family travelled to accompany the coffin on the lonely journey home across the Irish Sea. James's passing was reported in the press, where he was acknowledged as 'one of the leading ecclesiastical sculptors in the city ... the pioneer of modern Gothic art as applied to Church work, in this country'.[14] While some commentators have read Patrick's account of his father's reserve as indicative that James Pearse was an emotionally distant figure, James's affection for the children of both his first and second families is evident in his correspondence, and a relative who visited Willie's sister Margaret in her old age formed the impression that she was greatly proud of her father and was very close to him – closer even, perhaps, than with her mother.[15]

Through his interest in carving, Willie would have had an additional bond with his father. Though he had only just begun the formal study of modelling, it was already clear that, like his father, Willie's talent lay in sculpture rather than in drawing or painting. He achieved a first in Elementary Modelling for the session ending in summer 1900. The prize, awarded officially in early 1901, must have been a bitter-sweet triumph for Willie following his father's death, but it was obvious by now that the young man had found his *forte*. Willie would later say that 'anyone who carves becomes so fascinated with it that he would regard painting as a waste of time'.[16] His surviving sketches and paintings show only a modest talent and, while some of his contemporaries suc-cessfully utilised a variety of artistic media, Willie always concentrated on sculpture. It was also around this time that Willie, named for an English uncle he barely knew, began to express the Irish aspect of his identity: when he received a book as his prize for success in the school's special competition in 1900, he signalled his ownership by signing it 'Uilliam Mac Piarais'.[17]

Meanwhile, there was further disruption in the Pearse family when Willie's godfather and brother-in-law, Alf McGloughlin, left his wife, Willie's half-sister Mary Emily. Following a scandal involving a servant, Alf abandoned his family to go to America, where he remarried twice and had further children. Willie would never see him again.[18] The friendship between the McGloughlins and Pearses went back a long way: Mary Emily had known her husband since childhood, and her father-in law, John, had taken in James Pearse and his first family during her mother's final illness. Now the three McGloughlin children were without a father. Mary Emily worked as a midwife in various places, particularly in Fanad in Donegal, though she and her children maintained a close relationship with the Pearses. Her son, also named Alf, attended the School of Art and would live with the Pearses for a long period, becoming particularly close to Willie.

As a consequence of the passing of the Agriculture and Technical Instruction (Ireland) Act of 1899, the School of Art came under the aegis of the Department of Agriculture and Technical Instruction in 1900. The new department was based in Dublin and its vice-president, Horace Plunkett, played a leading administrative role. The new independence available to the Metropolitan School of Art through the 1899 Act meant that greater attention was given to the cultivation of an Irish style of art. Speaking at the 1901 prize-giving ceremony, Plunkett welcomed the new act and looked forward to 'developing any peculiar artistic sense the Irish people may possess'.[19] Plunkett, more famous nowadays for his pioneering role in the advancement of the co-operative movement, was originally a unionist but became what is now termed a 'cultural nationalist' with a strong interest in the role of the Irish language in Ireland's overall development. By this time the idea of an indigenous Irish style of art had already begun to take hold, and native craftsmanship was being championed in Ireland and further afield. Lady Aberdeen, a notable supporter of local arts, had encouraged cottage or convent-based industries such as lacemaking following her husband Lord Aberdeen's first brief period as Viceroy in 1886. The nascent Arts and Crafts movement associated with William Morris had always placed an emphasis on the independence of the artist and on a spirit of co-operation. The movement was also influenced by the writings of John Ruskin, an art critic who believed in social reform and the dignity of labour. Though he died a year before Willie's enrolment at the School of Art in Dublin, Morris's ongoing influence on Irish artists was profound; his socialist espousal of artists' collaboration and guilds had an important impact on the social networks that Willie would later join. The other Plunkett who spoke at the 1901 prize-giving ceremony, Count George Plunkett, touched on another of the artistic debates of the day, railing against what he regarded as a contemporary 'rage for cheapness' and stating that 'drawing and art are fitted to make pupils judges of the beautiful; for to be always seeking the useful does not become free souls'.[20] This tension between the utilitarian desire to produce artefacts of commercial value and the pursuit of art for art's sake formed part of the impetus for the now-burgeoning interest in Irish crafts, and would be of particular interest to someone like Willie, who through his father's business would operate where the commercial and artistic realms of sculpture overlapped. Willie's father had epitomised the new mobility between artisan craftsman and artist sculptor, but there was still some snobbery about artisans, as well as a legitimate concern about the artistic merit of much church architecture. A series of newspaper articles written by Robert Elliott in 1902 was critical of the men carving 'Gothic saints' who could not have felt they were 'expressing anything noble about art, or humanity or religion.'[21] The Pearses, if they had read the articles, may have felt a personal slight at Elliott's intemperate comments. 'The pity of it,' complained Elliott, '[is] that tradesmen should have the art of the country under their usurping heels.'[22] When Patrick later claimed in his unfinished autobiography that James Snr's ecclesiastical sculpture was 'good and true and lovingly finished', there may have been an element of wounded filial pride in his summary of his father's talent.

Willie Pearse is not listed as a prize-winner in the results booklet published in January 1902, which referred back to 1901, but he was certainly registered as a student for the 1900–01 session. One reason for this could be that, as well as grieving for his father, there was also the matter of the family business to take care of. Although several commentators state that Willie took it over, this is unlikely; Willie was only eighteen at the time of his father's death.[23] James Vincent's grandson, Noel Scarlett, believes that during the administration of James Snr's estate (he died without making a will), his widow, Mrs Margaret Pearse, took control of the family business, already called Pearse & Sons. It was Patrick, the elder son of the second marriage, who acted as administrator of the estate in 1901 (probably because he studied law). With Mrs Pearse's involvement, a new dynamic was initiated. James Vincent's daughter Florence recalled her father's sense of hurt at being 'put on a timesheet' (i.e., losing the privileges he had enjoyed as son of the owner and being treated like an ordinary employee). However, surviving paperwork and family memory as well as sculptural inscriptions suggest that Willie and James Vincent worked together in the business, while Patrick was also involved for a time at an administrative level. It seems that Willie had been helping out even before his father's untimely death, participating in work carried out in St Eunan's Cathedral in Letterkenny. The hard-to-please critic Edward Martyn had praised the work done by Irish artists in Letterkenny in an article in *The Leader*, though he was not aware of the Pearses' involvement. It has been asserted that Willie assisted his father with work on altars in churches in New Ross and in Castlebar, but given that the inauguration dates for these altars are after James Snr's death, the James in question is more likely to be James Vincent. Noel Scarlett understood from relatives that Willie had respect for James Vincent's skills as a carver, and that his grandfather had helped Willie on occasion, especially with one particular sculpture of the dead Christ.[24]

In the early years of the new century, Pearse & Sons was a thriving business and occupied premises at 160, 162 and 163 Townsend Street as well as the original 27 Great Brunswick Street. It was attracting major commissions, and company stationery boasted that they employed 'a larger staff' and 'a higher class of artists' than any other firm in Ireland. As well as taking staff photographs and images of completed works for marketing purposes, it was also among the first businesses in Dublin to use a telephone. Pearse & Sons' work could be found in churches all over Ireland, and the firm's notepaper stated that since its establishment in 1877, it had built over 1,500 altars. Aged nineteen, Willie was described in the 1901 census, perhaps with a certain aspiration and familial pride, as a 'sculptor master'. Things did not always go smoothly under the Pearse brothers' stewardship, however, and in April 1902 a priest from Bonane near Kenmare wrote to Willie to complain that the dimensions for work he had commissioned were incorrect. Though the market for church decoration was in general decline due to the fact that, as a result of the previous century's boom, most parishes now had the churches they needed, there was still, initially at least, a certain energy in Pearse & Sons. The firm exhibited a High Altar, a baptismal font, a statue of the Sacred Heart and other works at the 1902 Cork International Exhibition, and their catalogue entry claimed proudly that all of the work had been executed on their own premises by Irish artists.[25] While father James had often, though not exclusively, worked from the designs of others, many of the commissions carried out by 'Messrs Pearse and Sons' were noted as being of their own design.

The first altar that Willie sculpted himself was for the church in Foxford, County Mayo. The Pearses were always supportive of one another's ventures, and Willie's progress on the altar was watched proudly by his mother, Margaret.[26] The close ties with relatives that had characterised the Pearses' childhood continued, and Catherine Kelly's orphaned children, Mary Kate and John, lived for a time with the Pearse family. A family photograph featuring Willie, Mary Brigid and young John Kelly reminds us of the longstanding friendship between the cousins and of their closeness in age. Aspects of the character of Sighle, an orphaned girl in Patrick's later play, *The Singer*, may be partly based on the Pearses' close relationship with Mary Kate. In *The Singer*, Sighle, who is brought up by her aunt following the death of her own mother, cries that 'they put my mammy in the ground', the pathetic cry an unusually realistic note in an otherwise stylised dialogue. In the play the two brothers of the house take great care of the young orphan.

However, further tragedy was about to strike the Pearse and Kelly families. On 14 November 1902, the day before Willie's twenty-first birthday, John Kelly, who had just left the Pearse home at Sandymount Avenue to cycle to work, was hit by a bread van being pulled by a horse on the corner of Tritonville Lane. He was brought to the City of Dublin Hospital on nearby Baggot Street but died on arrival. When Patrick, writing a poem for Willie in May 1916, referred to the two brothers 'standing together' through 'all the glad years, all the sorrowful years', the sorrowful ones mentioned surely included the opening years of the new century. In the space of a few years, Willie had lost two family members to sudden death while his brother-in-law Alf, of whom the younger Pearses had been fond, had deserted his half-sister.

Things were also changing at the School of Art. While it still enjoyed strong links with Dublin Castle, some of its staff and students were beginning to assert a more nationalist identity. From 1902 the teacher of modelling was Oliver Sheppard, a Tyrone-born Protestant who had studied under French sculptor Édouard Lanteri in London. Lanteri was an influential figure who advocated a change from stylised neoclassicism (that is, the use of forms from Greek and Roman sculpture) to a more naturalistic approach.[27] Like Lanteri, Sheppard favoured realism, a preference that influenced the style adopted by his students, including Willie, who owned a copy of Lanteri's seminal text, *Modelling: A Guide for Teachers and Students.* Though the male figures he modelled for exam submission were still classically posed (the statues in the nearby museum were used as models), Willie would eventually turn to more realistic sources of inspiration, including children at play. For now, though, his everyday work of ecclesiastical commissions curtailed his ability to devote time to developing his own artistic career.

The modelling classes Willie attended were held in a room that could only fit about a dozen, and the genial Oliver Sheppard knew his students very well. His friendship with Willie extended beyond the classroom: he brought at least one commission the way of the family firm, and they shared a deep interest in Gaelic literature and art. As well as the already mentioned 'The Training of Cúchulainn', Sheppard's sculpture included 'The Bard Oisín and Niamh', one of the first modern Irish artworks to draw on Gaelic mythology, and 'Isle of Destiny' (later known as 'Inis Fáil'). The latter work, first shown at the 1901 RHA exhibition, showed a young boy and an older woman in a pose which suggested Gaelic strength and nobility – and the potential for action. But Sheppard's interest in Ireland went deeper than artistic influence: he was an intimate friend of the famous Fenian John O'Leary, who sat for Sheppard's bust of him (exhibited in the RHA in 1904). O'Leary gave Sheppard political pamphlets, including one on Fenianism.[28]

During this period, Willie became increasingly active in the Gaelic League, eventually teaching an Irish class in the School of Art and in Blackrock.[29] Given that Willie's gentle and unassuming personality was noted by many contemporaries and commentators, it is somewhat surprising to see that he was a central figure in a controversy in the School of Art in early 1903. Willie, along with a Michael Fitzgerald and Joseph Kelly, signed their names in Irish on the anatomy class register of 3 February 1903. Though individuals like Hughes and Sheppard were interested in Gaelic culture, the fundamental ethos of the school was still British. The signing-in-Irish issue was brought to the attention of Count Plunkett and the following day, he asked that the registrar, Mr Tilly, be instructed 'not to admit to any class any student who does not sign his name in very legible English writing and the same spelling as that which is used on the Register'. Willie and his friends were the ultimate victors in the matter; on 23 February, it was decided that all students 'no matter in what language they sign their names, shall append their registration number'. In other words, as long as a student wrote their correct registration number, they could use any spelling variation they liked.[30] Using the Irish language in public discourse was becoming a political issue: Fr Brian Ó Críocháin in County Sligo, a member of the Gaelic League for whom Willie had carried out some decorative work, was involved in a campaign some time later to have letters addressed in Irish delivered by the Post Office; and in May 1905, in the first of two similar cases, Patrick represented Niall Mac Giolla Bhríde, who had been fined for having his name in Irish on his cart. It is noteworthy that Willie had taken the first stand in asserting a place for the Irish language in everyday life, though Patrick's legal cases drew more public attention.

Despite the demands of the family business, and with the support of Patrick, Willie continued to pursue his artistic development. A surviving drawing shows that he was in Paris at some stage during Lent 1903. The drawing is described as a *croquis* (a quickly drawn rough sketch) and it is of an adult male nude (perhaps female; Willie's drawing skills were modest!). Live nude models were not usual at the School of Art until the arrival of William Orpen as a guest teacher a few years later, so Willie's sketch is an early indication of his open-mindedness. Buoyed, perhaps, by their victory for language rights, Willie and some of his fellow students began making plans for an organisation which could further express their burgeoning sense of national identity: a Gaelic Society for the School of Art. The Gaelic League was still in its period of rapid expansion, and across Ireland young men and women were getting involved in classes and *céilithe* (or social gatherings). A more dynamic figure than has been acknowledged previously, Willie was among those who organised events for the newly formed society in the autumn term of 1903. Willie's contemporary at the School of Art, Thomas King Moylan, later described Willie as the society's 'moving spirit'.[31] A letter Willie wrote to Fr Edward Gibbons on 31 October 1903 provides information on the role Willie envisaged for the new society (although aspects of the style in this letter, and in particular the idiosyncratic use of dashes, suggest that Patrick himself may have had a guiding role in its drafting). Though the wording was a little gauche – Willie lacked the smooth and articulate writing style of his brother – the letter shows that he shared some of Patrick's powers of persuasion:

> We are now about making arrangements to start things with our society at the School of Art. I want to get a good list of names for papers, lectures etc. Would not you be able to do something for us? What is your strong point? Perhaps you would be able to give us something about Irish poetry or anything at all touching the movement would be of great interest to us – History? Music? Archaeology? – Scripture! The drama! I am sure you could do something good for us in one or other of these (or perhaps all if you put your mind to it!) ... I don't know how you could manage coming up here for the night – from your college – But I presume you could manage it. Of course, you could, if you would like to,

stay at our place for the night or so – I would not like to put you to trouble or expense and Mrs. Pearse and all here would only be too glad to have you stay with us. Of course you shall fix your own date and all.

Mise, le mórmheas, beannacht
Uilliam Mac Piarais, Wm J Pearse [32]

Fr Gibbons, who was only two years older than Willie, was to become a regular visitor to the always hospitable Pearses. Based in a school in Navan at this time, Fr Gibbons was a man of literary aspirations and radical politics; he wrote poetry and would later become a shareholder in *The Republic*, a newspaper published by IRB member and political radical John Bulmer Hobson. Gibbons's sister Kitty would marry Seamus O'Doherty, who was a member of the IRB at the time of the Rising. It is not clear how Willie became acquainted with Fr Gibbons, but many young priests were drawn to the Gaelic League, and of course, the family business meant that Willie regularly met with members of the clergy. Nonetheless, it is telling that one of the first clergymen that Willie is recorded as knowing was the particularly radical Fr Gibbons. They enjoyed an enduring friendship and a piece of Willie's sculpture remains in the Catholic church in Kinnegad where Fr Gibbons was a curate. Willie, along with Patrick, also knew the radical Clondalkin curate, Father Michael Traynor.[33]

While Willie continued to work at Pearse & Sons in Great Brunswick Street, the family had moved house yet again. By October 1903 they were living at 39 Marlborough Road, a salubrious residential road in Donnybrook. Meanwhile, at the School of Art, a significant minority of students were becoming more attracted to the expression of Gaelic identity. (The use of Gaelic themes and support for the Union were not mutually exclusive; fascinated by Cúchulainn though he was, John Hughes would later be responsible for a giant monument to Queen Victoria.) In summer 1904 Richard Willis, a talented teacher and artist, was appointed as headmaster. As a former examiner in the Science and Art Department of South Kensington, who also oversaw the development of Manchester Art School as the premier teaching centre in England, Willis arrived with impeccable credentials. He was multi-talented, excelling not only in painting and sculpture but also in enamelling, stained glass, wood-carving and design. He was also a strong supporter of the Gaelic League who spoke Irish fluently. Willis played an important role in advancing the Gaelic identity of the students at the School of Art; during his tenure there were large attendances at bi-weekly Irish classes. Willie was among those who took part in a *scoraíocht* (or *soireé*) held at the School of Art on St Patrick's night in 1905, a jolly event with convivial company and dancing. Continuing to participate with enthusiasm in social and cultural events organised by the Gaelic League, though his prowess as a fluent speaker of Irish was obscured by his natural modesty, Willie was known for a time for his wearing of a kilt and Gaelic dress, a habit not uncommon among some of his artistic and literary friends.[34] Lectures, cultural *soirées* and day trips organised by the Gaelic League provided countless opportunities for socialising with like-minded contemporaries from a wide range of social and religious backgrounds. Photographs of a day trip to Omeath in County Louth show a well-dressed Willie at ease in a varied company that included the feminist academic Mary Hayden as well as a local butcher.[35]

By now, the League had hundreds of branches throughout Ireland and scores more wherever the Irish diaspora had settled. Its democratic and non-sectarian basis for membership provided a dynamic and enduring social and cultural network that would also bring Willie into contact with more radical nationalists in the years ahead. Willie organised a further, very elaborate *scoraíocht* in the School of Art on Friday 28 July 1905, again under the auspices of the Gaelic Society. Among the twenty-two separate items on the programme of entertainment were songs, sketches and musical performances. The very well-attended night was a huge success; Willie was obviously an effective events manager and popular enough to call in many favours. *The Freeman's Journal* reported that 'encores seemed to have been the order of the evening' and that the members and visitors 'seemed to thoroughly enjoy themselves'.[36] Willie and Fr Gibbons were among the many performers, the Gaelic class choir sang, and there was dancing until the small hours. *The Freeman's Journal* acknowledged Willie's central role as general manager of the evening's entertainment, stating that 'Mr Pierce [sic] spared no efforts to make the event a most successful one and right well he succeeded.'[37]

Less than three weeks later, Richard Willis died suddenly of heart failure while he was on holidays in Gaelic-speaking Ballinaskelligs, County Kerry, on 15 August 1905, a little over a year after his appointment. Described on his tombstone as a 'great and a good man', an inscription in Irish acknowledged his contribution to art and the Irish language. With his death, the emphasis on the Irish language which had been encouraged within the School of Art during his short time as headmaster lessened almost immediately.[38]

• • • • • • •

Chapter Three

1905-1908

An Exciting Place To Be

Though now a central figure in the School of Art's Gaelic Society, Willie was still busy working in Pearse & Sons. In 1905 they were responsible for the High Altar and Lady Altar in St Joseph's Church, Terenure, as well as substantial work in St Columba's Church, Drumcondra (though it is often hard to know the extent of Willie's involvement in particular projects). Though Willie's family firm had boasted in the 1902 Cork Exhibition catalogue that their work was executed on their own premises and by Irish artists, aspersions were still being cast on ecclesiastical sculpture. In 1906 Robert Elliott's articles criticising the takeover of church art by 'tradesmen' were collected and published as a book. The writer Edward Martyn, a generous and effective patron of the arts but a specialist in contrary diatribes, wrote in the preface how ecclesiastical art had been 'debased' by the trade architect and sculptor.[1]

But even with the demands of the family firm, Willie was able to visit France on study tours. The Power family recalled that Albert Power and Willie visited the studio of celebrated sculptor Auguste Rodin in France around 1904.[2] Rodin's sculptural style, with its understanding of individual character as well as a sense of passion and movement, would have reached Willie through Sheppard, an admirer of the French master. The Paris visit brought the two young men to the epicentre of the international sculptural world. Willie was in Paris again in early autumn of 1905, and Patrick published a poem in Irish in *An Claidheamh Soluis* (the Gaelic League newspaper, of which he was editor) on 9 September bemoaning his absence. The poem challenges the common perception that Willie was a mere follower of his brother. In this extract, Willie's life in Paris is shown as cosmopolitan and exciting, while Patrick's is unchanging:

Anseo in Éirinn
Dom féin, a bhráthair,
Is tusa i gcéin uaim
I bPáras áigh

Mise ag féachaint
Ar chnoc is cuan
Ar thráigh Bhinn Éadair
Is ar thaobh Shliabh Rua

Is tusa go réimeach
I bPáras mór
Na ríbhrugh n-aolda
Is na dtréanslógh ...

[Here in Ireland
Am I my brother
And you far from me
In gallant Paris

I beholding
hill and harbour
the strand at Howth
and Slieverue's side

And you victorious
In mighty Paris
Of the limewhite palaces
And surging hosts ...][3]

The 'Páras áigh' or 'gallant Paris' alluded to in Patrick's poem was a world away from leafy south Dublin. The extent of Willie's immersion in his new experiences is further hinted at by Patrick's demand that his brother should occasionally think of familiar places. While the placenames cited in the poem had associations with the *Fiannaíocht* literature (the cycle which features the Gaelic warrior hero Fionn Mac Cumhaill), they also recall places which Patrick and Willie frequented together. The two brothers led active lives: they went boating with friends at the seaside villages of Howth and Dún Laoghaire, rowed on the Liffey near Chapelizod, and later in life would go swimming off the Bull Wall with their nephew Alf, Mary Emily's son. There were indoor pursuits as well: Willie and Patrick owned a magic lantern (which projected images) and most intriguingly of all, made humorous recordings on what some accounts refer to as a 'cylinder' and others a record. One recording, which would now be of huge historical interest, featured Patrick making a speech about the Irish language to Alf, Mary Brigid and Willie. Sadly, it went missing sometime in the 1930s, but the fact of its making reminds us, as does the Pearse brothers' use of the magic lantern, that Willie, Patrick, and Alf were keenly interested in the latest technology. Willie himself was able to use a camera.[4]

One of the more interesting commissions completed by Pearse & Sons at this time was a memorial to the late Irish Parliamentary Party MP Dr JE Kenny – one of those incarcerated with Parnell at the time of Willie's birth in 1881 – which was unveiled in Glasnevin Cemetery in the summer of 1905 by IPP leader John Redmond. After reuniting the party following the split over Parnell in the early 1890s, Redmond had been extolling the necessity of Home Rule for Ireland in speech after speech in the House of Commons. However, after the Government of Ireland Act 1893 (the Second Home Rule Bill) was vetoed by the House of Lords, there was little real momentum; even if a Home Rule bill passed the House of Commons (which could only happen if the Liberal Party was in power, as the Conservatives implacably opposed it), it would be thrown out by the Conservative-dominated House of Lords. There was also renewed Fenian activity in the early years of the twentieth century, albeit on a scale that was barely noticed by most people: in 1905 two Northerners, Bulmer Hobson and Denis McCullough, founded the republican Dungannon Clubs in Belfast and set about reinvigorating the now moribund Irish Republican Brotherhood.

For now, the attainment of Home Rule remained a vague aspiration, which allowed a broad spectrum of nationalist opinion to muster together in wider cultural activities such as the Gaelic League and various commemorative projects. One important and often forgotten strand of Ireland's cultural revival at this time was the promotion of Irish industries and renewal of interest in Irish-made goods. This emphasis on self-reliance was also reflected in a renewal of interest in local craftsmanship.

As in England, such activities were often organised under the benevolent patronage of the monied classes, and the Arts and Crafts Society of Ireland was founded by the Earl of Mayo in 1894. The Lord Lieutenant and Chief Secretary, and a long list of luminaries from the Catholic and Protestant gentry and clergy, attended the 'At Home' event, a *soirée* organised by Countess Grosvenor, who hosted the third Arts and Crafts exhibition on behalf of the Arts and Crafts Society of Ireland in 1904. The momentum from the new Arts and Crafts Society and from the Gaelic Revival in general led to a renewal of interest in Irish craftsmanship at the School of Art and also the foundation of several new artistic organisations around this time, including An Túr Gloine (1903) which focused on stained glass, and the Dún Emer guild (1902), which showcased Irish crafts. Another important group was the Young Irish Artists, founded in 1905; though several of his contemporaries at the School of Art were active in the group, Willie would exhibit with them only in their 1909 exhibition. Neither was he associated with the Túr Gloine or Dún Emer guilds. Willie does not appear to have taken part in the social scene associated with Lady Aberdeen's championing of the Arts and Crafts movement. He told Fr Gibbons that he attended the first two Arts and Crafts exhibitions as an interested visitor but claimed he had no other involvement with the Arts and Crafts Society of Ireland and apparently knew little about them.[5]

The need to develop a native art tradition, including a sacred art tradition, was keenly felt by another recently founded organisation, the Irish Art Companions. This was founded in 1904 by Mr Charles Tindal Gatty, an English antiquary who had previously run as an Irish Home Rule election candidate. Irish American nationalist Thomas Hughes Kelly was also involved. Gatty was a personal friend of George Wyndham, the Conservative politician who was Chief Secretary for Ireland between November 1900 and March 1905.

The Art Companions were soon playing an active part in the artistic life of Dublin and elsewhere, aligning themselves from the start with the cultural nationalism of the Gaelic League, an organisation that shared their co-operative spirit. In addition to their group exhibition at the 1904 Arts and Crafts Exhibition, they took part in the Gaelic League's Oireachtas Competition in 1904, in the Industrial Section. Momentum was generated by a Gaelic League–sponsored 'Industries Conference' which Gatty attended in February 1905, where initial plans were made to form an association to foster Irish industry which would avoid 'political and contentious discussions of any sort'.[6] The Art Companions' own opening exhibition, opened by the Countess of Fingal, in late April 1905 attracted much interest, and later that year they participated in the League's 1905 Oireachtas Art Exhibition. While the Companions' initial focus had been on the collection and sale of the work of cottage industries and craftwork, their mission soon expanded to include the sale of all kinds of crafts and art, and the founding of a central depot to store and exhibit works was now mooted. This was later opened under the management of Tipperary-born Gaelic League activist Pádraig Ó Glasáin at 28 Clare Street, a few minutes' walk from the School of Art. Willie Pearse was among those who sold art under the auspices of the Companions.[7] Given their special interest in sacred art, it was natural that the Irish Art Companions should draw the attention of Willie, even if he is not recorded as participating in exhibitions from the outset. However, a draft for a notice, perhaps intended for insertion in a newspaper, survives among Willie's papers and seems to indicate that he played a role in instigating or advancing the sculptural section of the Companions:

> It is proposed that a meeting of a number of art workers be arranged to consider that a sort of 'Guild' or 'Union' with the object of supplying so many workers to form a working staff for a new pottery industry in Dublin. It is suggested that a number of practical sculptors, modellers, designers, colorants (for painting) come together and a general sketch of the scheme will be laid before them. The services and advice of a practical man whose [sic] spent many years in connection with a pottery business is ... [draft tails off here] [8]

The allusion in Willie's draft letter to a 'practical man with a connection to a pottery business' is a reference to Gatty, who had expertise in pottery as well as business interests in Irish gypsum, used for making plaster. The Art Companions' depot was one of the elements which helped to foster a spirit of mutual co-operation between many of those involved in native crafts and Irish-inspired art. The artists prominent in the new sculptural section of the Companions came from both Catholic and Church of Ireland backgrounds, and included Joseph Carré, Gwendolyn Herbert, Joseph Hanrahan, Lydia

'Lilla' Vanston and Mervyn Lawrence. In April 1906 Charles Gatty declared that the Art Companions wanted 'a re-evaluation of this country in the estimation of its own children'.[9] Like many in the cultural and artistic movements at this time, they were looking to the future, as they sought to turn their backs on what they perceived as the stagnation of Irish cultural and political life.

Given the draft letter, it is strange that Willie is not mentioned in a 1907 essay discussing the sculptural section of the Companions.[10] Perhaps he was unable to participate due to work commitments or was not as well-known as the other sculptors. Meanwhile, Willie continued to be active in student affairs at the School of Art. In April 1906 he told Fr Gibbons that the Royal Hibernian Academy had accepted one of his pieces for exhibition. Willie claimed, with characteristic modesty, that it was 'very rough, hardly worth sending, but it is good to make a beginning'.[11] The piece referred to was 'Úna', a sketch model for a study in marble, which Willie exhibited at the Academy. It is hardly a coincidence that Patrick's increased interest in the development of Irish art coincided with the exhibition of Willie's 'Úna' model in the RHA's annual exhibition, which ran from March through May 1906. On 5 May 1906, Patrick published an article entitled 'The Art Revival' in *An Claidheamh Soluis* in which he declared that there was now such a thing as an Irish art movement. Patrick's predictions for the direction this new movement were reflected in the subject matter and staging of the plays he would pen some years later:

> It will be an open air art and not an esoteric thing ... It will bear to English art and to recent Anglo Irish art respectively the same relation that a Middle Irish nature poem bears on the one hand to a story in the Family Herald and on the other to one of the sicklier plays in the Abbey Theatre.[12]

Willie was serious in his desire to 'make a beginning' and immediately after the start of the 1906–07 term in the School of Art, he exhibited 'Úna' again, this time at the Oireachtas Arts and Crafts Exhibition in early August 1906 at the Technical Schools in Rutland Square. Significant figures like Jack B Yeats, William Orpen, Jack Morrow, Beatrice Elvery, and members of An Túr Gloine as well as the Art Companions were among the large number of Irish artists who exhibited.

But 1906 brought further sadness for the extended Pearse family. During that year Willie's niece Emily Mary, the eldest daughter of James Vincent, died. While family tragedy never seemed far away, Willie's home life was increasingly comfortable. By late 1906 the Pearse family were living at Cúil Chrannach in Leeson Park near Donnybrook Village, an address which once more reflected their secure middle-class lifestyle.

On 11 August 1906, Patrick published an article in *An Claidheamh Soluis* dwelling at length on Oliver Sheppard's sculpture 'Inis Fáil' which, though created and exhibited

some years before, was now exhibited anew at the Oireachtas. 'Inis Fáil' depicted a half-naked woman and a naked boy
standing erect over a fallen figure. Patrick's political reading of the sculpture was printed as part of his review of the
Oireachtas Art Exhibition:

> Though the world run red with blood, the cause of that
> Woman shall triumph. Mark next him who lies prone – the
> victorious vanquished, crowned in death. This is a genera-
> tion that has fought and fallen – but the woman of destiny
> blanches not: 'I have my memories … and I have my hopes.'[13]

Patrick identified in the boy's expression and stance 'the
growing of a great resolve ... He will fight the fight – win
it, it may be, or failing gloriously go serenely to his death.'[14]

This political reading of Sheppard's sculpture would find
echoes in Patrick's later writings – and in the 1916 Proclamation. But despite Sheppard's deep interest in Irish history and
Gaelic literature, and his friendship with leading Fenian John
O'Leary (who died in early 1907), he was happy to take an
organisational role on the committee for the artistic section of
the gigantic Irish International Exhibition held in Dublin the
following year.[15] Because of its undertones of imperial display
(exhibits included a 'Somali village' and Indian conjurers) the
exhibition was heavily criticised (and even the subject of a
suggested boycott) by the Gaelic League, the Sinn Féin League
and the General Council of County Councils. Nonetheless,

sketch models for statuettes by Willie, and work by his friend Albert Power and others, are listed in one version of the exhibition catalogue as being shown as part of the 'Arts and Crafts' subsection of the 'Home Industries' display at the exhibition. Although criticising the lack of representation of Irish raw-material producers at what was an international exhibition, the *Freeman's Journal* on 17 August specifically mentioned that the Irish Art Companions had founded a factory at Ringsend for making plaster from Irish gypsum, a reminder of the close ties between Irish art and Irish industry at this time.

While the Irish International Exhibition was in full swing, the Pearse family firm took part in an elaborate Language Procession from Stephen's Green to O'Connell Street and Smithfield on 9 June 1907. The Gaelic League had urged 'all creeds, classes and citizens, of every shade of politics' to take part, and among those involved were delegations from the GAA, Sinn Féin, and education and temperance movements.[16] Most of the numerous historical *tableaux* (staged pictures with living actors, a format pioneered by Alice Milligan and the nationalist women's group Inghinidhe na hÉireann) were non-political, depicting scenes from heroic literature. But there was also an overt political dimension, with one banner stating 'Beidh Éire fé réim arís' ('Ireland will once again prevail') while the participants also included several '98 clubs and the Wolfe Tone and United Irishmen Memorial Committee.[17] The International Exhibition and

Language Procession staked their competing claims to the public imagination and to public spaces, but it seems that nationalist politics was still a broad church in the everyday life of those who attended or participated in both events.

Following the success of the 1906 exhibition, the 1907 Oireachtas Arts and Crafts exhibition was held in the more rarified environs of the RHA buildings on Abbey Street. The statue of Parnell by French sculptor Augustus Saint-Gaudens, ultimately destined for erection in O'Connell Street, was the centrepiece of the exhibition and drew much comment in the newspapers. Unusually for Willie, who often favoured child studies, his exhibition sculpture 'Éire' also had a broad political theme, depicting a nude figure that Willie's friend Desmond Ryan later recalled as symbolising young Ireland 'arising cleansed through the waters of the new Gaelic inspiration'.[18] Willie also showed his 'Design for the O'Mulrennan monument': RJ [O']Mulrennan was a noted Gaelic scholar and activist who had died the previous October. Among the visitors to the exhibition were the Lord Lieutenant and Lady Aberdeen. They may have been particularly interested in the Parnell statue, being, after all, long-time sympathisers with Home Rule. Lord Aberdeen had been appointed by the Liberal government elected in early 1906; as the Liberal Party had a huge majority in the House of Commons, there was no urgent need for them to win the support of the IPP, whose strategy had been to vote with the Liberals in return for concessions on

Home Rule. While the IPP continued to press for Home Rule, they had no leverage and so their goal remained out of reach.

As the new term commenced in 1907, the School of Art was still big enough to be socially diverse, but small enough that most students were acquainted. There were 192 day students and 178 evening students; those whom Willie knew well included the nationalist-minded Kathleen Fox and Margaret Crilly. In the 1908 report, the headmaster, Mr James Ward, alluded to 'the public interest in the matter of Irish industries'.[19] For Ward, the aim of the School of Art was not just to instruct students but also 'to make workmen better workmen, to educate the public in art matters, and so to create a more extended taste in all kinds of art, especially as applied to industries, and the common things of everyday life, including even manmade goods'.[20] The correlation between art and industry was still a significant concern in the Gaelic Revival: this was the reason that the Art Companions frequently exhibited their artwork at exhibitions of 'industry'. In May 1907, the Companions exhibited work at the Aonach na Bealtaine exhibition of Irish industries in the Father Mathew Hall in Church Street. The Aonach was opened by the Countess of Fingal, who was presented with a bouquet by Patrick's goddaughter, the Gaelic speaking Síle Bairéad[21]. There were strong links between the temperance, industrial and language movements, and the Irish bishops had stated their support for Irish goods as early as 1902. Meanwhile, the operators of the Father Mathew

Hall, the Capuchin Friars in Church Street, were also part of the overlapping networks that the new Irish artists frequented. Fr Aloysius was personally involved in the Aonach, while Fr Augustine had been head of the Gaelic League in Cork and among the founders of Coláiste na Mumhan, a summer school for learning Irish. There was also another, more immediate, connection between the Capuchin Friars and the Pearses: Willie's father, James, was responsible for the altar and reredos in their Friary in Church Street.

The same year also saw the amalgamation of Cumann na nGaedheal, an umbrella nationalist organisation founded by journalist and nationalist Arthur Griffith, with the Dungannon Clubs, which had been founded by Hobson and McCullough. The amalgamated organisation adopted a name already in use by Griffith, Sinn Féin, and retained his suggested policy of a political grouping which would abstain from participation in the Westminister parliament. Soon Sinn Féin would be sponsoring their own Aonach.

As well as being featured in the Aonaigh, the Oireachtas art exhibitions, and the prestigious RHA exhibitions, Willie's sculpture was part of the modelling class section of an exhibition by students of the Metropolitan School of Art from St Stephen's Day 1907, and he received a School Prize for his modelling work on 20 February 1908. Willie's old friend Albert Power was the winner of the more prestigious Taylor Prize. Willie had considered entering for the Taylor Prize, a sign that he had growing, if occasionally faltering, confidence in his own work. On the previous weekend a huge monument to Queen Victoria designed by Willie's old teacher John Hughes was unveiled outside Leinster House, very close to the entrance to the School of Art, with much fanfare and military ceremony. The political messages of Hughes's monument differed from those of Sheppard's 'Inis Fáil', which had so excited Patrick Pearse. The lower part of the plinth for the Victoria statue included a (Boer) war memorial, a depiction of a female figure, Erin, gazing with pride and sorrow on a dead soldier.[22] From then on, the monument formed a frequent reminder to Willie and his fellow students that Ireland's role was to honour their benevolent British rulers and to support Britain militarily.

Willie's work featured again at the 1908 RHA exhibition: this time his exhibit was 'Cailín na Carraige', a statuette in plaster which was priced at £5. It was modelled on ten-year-old Mabel Gorman, who lived near the Pearses and who was to become an important model and friend for Willie. Although Willie's letters to Mabel do not survive, her extensive correspondence to him (from 1908 to 1912) is largely extant and offers intriguing glimpses into his day-to-day life and personality.[23] Willie had a good rapport with Mabel and they clearly had fun together: when Mabel went to boarding school in Monaghan she wrote that meeting the nuns 'is not quite all the same as you and I pictured it' and she also alludes to Willie standing on his head. She hoped that

Willie ('Mr Pearse') will 'write often' and occasionally signs herself 'Mabs'. In one letter, written from boarding school, she stated that he was 'right about homesickness' and recalled 'the night we went to the pantomime and had such lovely tea in the DBC [a well known café] and I thought of myself eating all the lovely chocolate cakes'. Mabel's regular references to Willie's studio (at this time in Great Brunswick Street) remind us of the importance of sculptural work in his life at this time. Another young girl, Eileen Byrne, also posed for him. The *croquis* (a quick sketch for later use) of an adult from Willie's 1903 Paris trip shows that he sketched from the nude; his completed child sculptures include both clothed figures and nudes. However, there is no evidence and no reason to believe that Willie had anything other than a platonic relationship with Mabel or any other model.

A letter written to Fr Gibbons in April 1907 asking him to give a talk at the School of Art shows that, despite his obvious passion for his art and his boldness in considering entering for the Taylor Prize in the previous year, Willie needed reassurance:

> I want your opinion – a candid criticism – of my Cailín-na-Carraige. There is nothing like a proper criticism! Sometimes I would like to ask anyone – the man in the street to come in and give his opinion – or better some little child.[24]

Willie's craving for an honest appraisal of his art, independent of convention or fashion and undiluted by the kindness of friends, is further hinted at in this letter when he states that children 'are our best critics: they do not flatter or try to say "nice things". They say what they think, in their own way, and their tastes have not been warped by "rules", schools, principles etc!'[25] Willie was in a creative mood, with his head filled with ideas, and he wrote to Fr Gibbons that he was going into one of his 'annual fits of activity – I mean activity of mind, at certain times ideas and subjects, I mean designs etc come to me all in a heap, whilst at other times I have not an idea in my head!'[26]

Willie's 'fits' of activity now had an outlet in a dynamic Dublin arts scene whose members overlapped with those active in the world of the literary revival and in various nationalist organisations. As Mary Colum recalled of this time:

> Dublin was an exciting place to be for young nationalists and Dublin ... bristled with movements of various kinds – dramatic, artistic, educational; there were movements for the restoration of the Irish language, for reviving native arts and crafts; for preserving ancient ruins, for resurrecting native costume; an array of political movements; here, too, were the theatres and the tearooms and pubs which corresponded to the café life of the Continental city. In the centre too, were the headquarters of the clubs and societies, some at war with each other, but all exciting and somehow, focused together towards one end – a renaissance.[27]

• • • • • • •

Chapter Four

1907–1909

Distinguished Company

Since their childhood forays into drama, both Willie and Patrick had maintained their interest in Shakespeare, and Willie attended Shakespearean plays as often as he could. The brothers often acted out the quarrel scene from *Julius Caesar*, with Patrick as Brutus and Willie as Cassius. Willie was also interested in opera and attended performances as often as circumstances allowed. For the actress Máire Nic Shiubhlaigh, who knew Willie well, 'his interest in the theatre was profound … He gazed at the stage and at actors with a kind of awe.'[1] However, even though Willie knew many of the actors connected to various branches of the Gaelic League, he does not seem to have had any substantial involvement in the annual productions of plays in Irish at the League's Oireachtas festivals. Willie's first documented involvement with theatre followed the foundation of the Theatre of Ireland (or Cluicheoirí na hÉireann, as they were officially known) in 1906.

This company had been set up by a group who had seceded from the National Theatre Society of Ireland (a group closely connected with the newly established Abbey). The new organisation was also part of a dynamic network of amateur theatre groups founded in the early twentieth century, which included the Cork Dramatic Society and the Ulster Literary Theatre. For Máire Nic Shiubhlaigh, the desire for independence and for a truly nationally minded theatre was the reason for the split with the Abbey and the National Theatre Society group. She also recalled that Willie was among the first to offer his services to the newly formed Theatre of Ireland, and Patrick spoke at the foundation meeting on 6 May. Though Patrick's participation lessened after a time, he did publish a series of articles on the development of Irish and Gaelic drama coincident with the new group's foundation. As was the case with art, Willie's participation would be on a practical level, whereas Patrick's connection with drama was – at first at least – more on a theoretical level. Nic Shiubhlaigh does not state exactly what Willie's involvement was (he is not listed as an actor in her own account) but later ventures show he had an aptitude for stage design and choreography. In the following years many of those Willie met through the Theatre of Ireland would play important roles in both his creative and political life.

The Theatre of Ireland's members came from diverse backgrounds, united by their interest in the aim proposed at the founding meeting: 'to carry on dramatic work in Ireland, to produce plays in English and Irish and the masterpieces of foreign dramatic authors'.[2] The committee included Gaelic League scholar Eoin MacNeill, writer Pádraic Colum, and future revolutionary Countess Constance Markievicz. The creative side of the Theatre of Ireland featured various siblings from the radical and bohemian Walker/Mac Shiubhlaigh family, whose father Matthew was a radical journalist. Not for the first time, Willie was involved in a creative endeavour in which politics and culture were intertwined. Though Willie, like Patrick, did not drink alcohol, his involvement in the Theatre of Ireland meant that the vibrant social life he already enjoyed through his participation in the Dublin art scene and in the Gaelic League was further enriched. In these years, many people in Dublin attended the theatre at least once a week. Mary Colum, a writer and critic who was friendly with the Pearses, recalled that regular theatregoers, 'the habitués, or nearly all of them, knew one another and the audience was a sort of social gathering. Between acts one drank tea, chatted to one's friends, discussed their work with the authors.'[3]

When the Ulster Literary Theatre visited Dublin in March 1907, the Theatre of Ireland organised a reception, and important contacts were made with the Morrows of Belfast, who would continue to feature in Willie's life in the years ahead. Fred Morrow, who was skilled in stage management, his brother Jack, who designed scenery, and another Morrow brother, Harry, who wrote plays, all now became involved in the Dublin operation. The Morrows had much in common with the Pearses: they belonged to the same artistic world as Willie, and their family was involved in an interior decorating business. Jack Morrow was also an avowed nationalist who had contributed political cartoons to Bulmer Hobson's short-lived nationalist newspaper *The Republic*. Though he was still based in Belfast at this stage, his path would cross with Willie's again.

Cultural activists from the North had a particular influence on the Dublin scene around this time. Bulmer Hobson, the republican Quaker, IRB activist, and co-founder of the Ulster Literary Theatre, moved to Dublin in 1907. Alice Milligan, well known in Dublin in the early years of the new century as a writer and producer of plays and pageants on Gaelic themes, was a Methodist from a Unionist family in Tyrone, who had previously edited the radical nationalist magazine *Shan Van Vocht*. Like Máire Nic Shiubhlaigh, Milligan was a member of the radical women's cultural and nationalist organisation Inghinidhe na hÉireann, who had for some years been enacting *tableaux vivants* or 'living pictures' in theatres, parades and outdoor spectacles. These carefully choreographed and extravagantly costumed spectacles had a long-term influence on the subject matter and staging of the emerging new Irish drama. Belfast-born author and activist James Cousins was a

committee member of the Theatre of Ireland and typical of
the people Willie was meeting in the forward-thinking circles
he frequented. Cousins was a writer, editor and feminist who
married the suffragette Margaret Gillespie, a friend to James
Joyce. Deeply interested in mysticism, Cousins was an avowed
vegetarian and president of the Irish Vegetarian Society. It
may have been under Cousins's influence that Willie and
Patrick dabbled in vegetarianism for a time and took their
meals in a vegetarian restaurant on College Street, eventually quietly giving up, as 'their lives became a misery', the
food 'not strong enough for their vigorous constitutions'.[4] It
seems vegetarianism attracted the politically conscious, and
this restaurant would later be frequented by members of the
IRB and the Citizen Army.[5]

The motivated, flexible and creative people with whom
Willie worked and socialised displayed a can-do attitude:
they travelled, embraced opportunities, supported one
another's enterprises, and believed in the power of art and
imagination. Willie's circle included Catholics, Protestants,
an agnostic (Jack Morrow) and Estella Solomons, who was
Jewish. Many of these creative contemporaries of Willie's
– like Máire Nic Shiubhlaigh, Oliver Sheppard and Jack
Morrow – also had close connections to radical separatist
politics. In this way they were curiously reminiscent of Willie's father, James, who was a supporter of radical politics and
art. Most of Willie's wider group were deeply idealistic and

sought the imaginative representation of a national identity which had been reignited by the cultural activities of the Gaelic League. Through their various exhibitions, plays, meetings and friendships, the halls and cafés and municipal buildings they frequented were slowly being appropriated by a movement which, though it was often known as 'Irish Ireland', also embraced the wider worlds of art and literature. There was an office for the British Army two doors down from Willie's private studio at the Pearse family business in 27 Great Brunswick Street, but unlike some other young Irishmen seeking escape and adventure through army postings abroad, Willie had every reason to stay at home.

Around this time, though busy with his League work and with *An Claidheamh Soluis*, Patrick found his attention being drawn increasingly to education. The air of possibility in Dublin was infectious, and by the spring of 1908 he was fine-tuning plans for a new departure – a bilingual school teaching in both Irish and English. Despite the rigors of his full-time post as newspaper editor, Patrick's plans began to take shape quickly. Both Willie and Patrick had been helping and encouraging their sister Margaret in a school she was running from the Pearse home, ensuring that the schoolroom was bright and artistic as well as assisting with teaching duties. But Margaret's school was soon sidelined as Patrick's latest project advanced.

St Enda's College/Scoil Éanna eventually opened its doors

in September 1908 and soon became an important part of Willie's life. Advertisements placed widely in the nationalist press emphasised the school's child-centred approach and its family atmosphere, as well as the prominent place that it would accord to Irish language, history and culture. Although Margaret's own school had to be jettisoned, she threw her support behind the new venture and, along with Mrs Pearse, helped to nurture the homely atmosphere for which the school was to become known. Patrick had rented a property, Cullenswood House, on respectable Oakley Road between Rathmines and Ranelagh, to house the new school. A Georgian mansion surrounded by gravelled paths, lawns and trees, it was also well connected by tramline to both the city and its outlying suburbs, and the Pearse family would soon take up residence there.

Patrick secured a strong core group of teachers, the most important of whom was poet, playwright and future Rising commandant Thomas MacDonagh, whose literary interest at this time was also focused on theatre. The Pearses' wide contacts in the cultural world meant that eminent scholars and writers, like Eoin MacNeill and Pádraic Colum, gave guest lectures. Many of the school's pupils were the offspring or close relatives of the movers and shakers in cultural nationalism. The teachers and visiting lecturers were young too, and were driven by the same sense of purpose and the same striving for the articulation of identity that had animated Patrick in founding his school, and Willie in his participation in the Irish art world. As Mary Colum recalled:

> Almost everything significant in the Dublin of that period was run by the young; youth, eagerness, brains, imagination, are what I remember of everybody. There was something else that was in all of them, a desire for self-sacrifice, a devotion to causes; everyone was working for a cause, for practically everything was a cause.[6]

It was unsurprising that, like his sister Margaret, Willie should offer his support for Patrick's new venture, and he was among the welcoming party who greeted the first pupils on 7 September 1908, the day before classes began. Though he did not take up his part-time post as art master until 22 September, he was an important member of staff at St Enda's from the beginning.

In addition, he kept his more pressing day job in the family business. An account book for 1907 to 1909 refers to 'James and WJ Pearse', which suggests that James Vincent was still involved in the business (as it seems unlikely that their father's name would be listed eight years after his death). Pearse & Sons was still a significant operator in the world of monumental carving. While the boom in church decoration was over, account books and letters show that the firm was still getting work all over Ireland. Years later, Dr Patrick McCartan stated (in supporting documentation for a pension application for Mary Brigid) that during this period she had been wholly dependent on Willie.[7] Although McCartan's statement has to be viewed in its context – the success of the application depended on proving that Mary Brigid was dependent on Willie and not Patrick – it nonetheless forms an important reminder of Willie's role at the family firm. While accounts about Patrick refer – correctly – to Willie's supporting role at St Enda's, it is important to note that Willie was, at this particular time, a breadwinner for the family in his own right who also found time to generously support his siblings' educational ventures. On the other hand, though Patrick had a definite gift for fundraising, his own project of a school began – and ended – in debt, and his income from *An Claidheamh Soluis* ceased with the end of his editorship in 1909.

As he combined his work in the family business with part-time teaching, Willie continued to pursue his own development as an artist, particularly in the early years of St Enda's. He was still attending the School of Art, and it is clear that this aspect of his life was central to others' perceptions of his identity. Former pupils of St Enda's recall him as being different and artistic, and his gentle and amenable demeanour is also noted. Among the earliest arrivals to the new school was Pádraic Óg Ó Conaire, who thought Willie at first sight to be a little strange because of his long black hair, and recalled his low, gentle voice. Milo MacGarry, who came to St Enda's during the second term, recalled a 'gentle, lovable character, deeply attached to his elder brother ... [and an] artist more than anything else'.[8] Willie's bohemian appearance also made an impression on Desmond Ryan, a pupil who would eventually become a close friend of both Pearse brothers:

> I remember well the first appearance he made in St Enda's as a drawing master. He gave us, with his quiet, nervous manner, his flowing tie, his long hair brushed back from his forehead in an abundant curve, the impression of an artist first and last ...[9]

Along with Willie, in his semi-detached role as part-time teacher and artist, Mrs Pearse, Margaret, and, to a lesser extent, Mary Brigid were instrumental in creating the family-like atmosphere for which the school became known. St Enda's was, by most accounts, an exceptionally happy place, with one pupil recalling that 'everywhere there was an atmosphere of intimacy ... everything was so different there.'[10] Classes were small; at one stage, there were as few as seven to ten boys in each class group. Students had their own garden and voted for their own council and school officers. It is perhaps not all that surprising that one boy, having been removed from the school to Clongowes by his mother, ran away to return to St Enda's.[11] In an era when educational establishments were noted for strict discipline and conformity, the pupils in St Enda's enjoyed considerable freedom and it seemed to some visitors that in the relaxed atmosphere the boys ran wild. Although St Enda's had a Catholic ethos, it was also, unusually for the time, a lay school.

Willie's role was initially that of art master; in later years he also taught history and geography. His influence (and Patrick's own interest in art) would soon be evident in the school's growing collection of engravings, casts and sculptural work. Artwork by and belonging to James Snr and Willie was displayed alongside paintings by Beatrice Elvery and George Russell; a drawing by Jack B Yeats; stained glass by Sarah Purser; and a mural depicting figures from Irish history and literature by Edwin Morrow, yet another of the talented Morrow brothers. All of this artwork was to inspire and influence Patrick deeply. He based a short story, and later a play, on Elvery's painting 'Íosagán' (of the child Christ), which hung in the main classroom in Cullenswood. He also used an image of her powerful allegorical work 'Éire' as a cover for an edition of *An Claidheamh Soluis*. 'Éire' showed various ghostly historical figures and martyrs behind a cloaked woman who is sheltering naked figures and holding a child who is reaching out from the image. Meanwhile, a phrase from *The Táin* reproduced in the decorative mural by the Morrow brothers which hung over the entrance to Cullenswood House described the esteem in which Cúchulainn would be held beyond his death and was a daily reminder of his famous deeds.

The new school was, for the time, a radical venture, and it had plenty of interesting visitors. Many were women, quite a few were Protestant, and all were politicised. On 22 October 1908 the Presbyterian poet Ella Young paid her first visit to the school, accompanied by Maud Gonne: both were deeply involved in feminist and nationalist organisations, including Inghinidhe na hÉireann. The Gifford sisters, accompanied by journalist Mrs Dryhurst, also visited. The Gifford girls were all involved in nationalist causes of one type or another, while Grace Gifford was a fellow student of Willie's at the School of Art. Meanwhile, the emphasis on art was reflected in a school visit to the National Gallery on November 8th.

Willie's sociable nature and undoubted organisational skills were soon put to use at St Enda's. In addition to his many other roles and responsibilities, he arranged fort-nightly get-togethers or *céilidhe*, which generally involved the whole St Enda's school community, along with invited guests, gathering around the stove in the refectory. These were 'a happy and informal mingling of concert and debating society where subjects of a literary and general interest were discussed'.[12] Sometimes there was dancing. If a dramatic presentation was part of the evening, the *soirée* took place in the Study Hall. Willie recited ballads, such as 'Roddy McCorley', a ballad of the 1798 rebellion written by Ethna Carbery. Sometimes, after a call for 'Roddy McCorley', Willie 'with great pomposity came out and pulled the legs of his

The Pearse family. Left to right: Patrick, James Snr, Margaret Snr, Mary Brigid, Willie and Margaret.

Left, both:
William James
Pearse was born
in Dublin on 15
November 1881.

Pearse siblings. Left to right: Patrick, Willie, Margaret and Mary Brigid.

Willie and Mary Brigid Pearse. To their left is their young cousin
John Kelly, who lived with the Pearses until his untimely death at the
age of sixteen.

The Pearses on a family outing.

Above: Detail from the Burke Memorial, attributed to James Pearse Snr.

Left: A *croquis* or quick sketch completed by Willie in Paris in 1903.

Above: Artists Kathleen Fox, Una Duncan and Willie Pearse in the Metropolitan School of Art, with Albert Power to front.

Right: Willie's '*Cailín na Carraige*'.

Above left: 'Memories' by Willie Pearse. **Above right:** Willie's sister Margaret with his niece Florence Pearse, the daughter of James Vincent.

Willie (bottom left) and Patrick (top right) with friends on a Gaelic League outing.

audience with "Napoleon's Farewell to St Helena" [giving] a bow, a smile [and] with waving tie and mock woebegone face resuming his seat among the revellers ...'[13] At the end of the first term there were two special *céilidhe* on 8 and 12 December. Such events, curated by Willie, helped to hone further his undoubted networking and events management skills. Through Willie's influence, Patrick was still channelling art to convey his growing nationalism, and the Christmas edition of the *Claidheamh* featured a picture of a warrior by Edwin Morrow.

In 1909 the Gaelic League led a vigorous nationwide campaign to have Irish made a compulsory entrance requirement of the new university which was about to be established under the 1908 Irish Universities Act. The League's campaign now galvanised hundreds of thousands of cultural nationalists into political activism, and several of those in the Pearses' circle – and Patrick himself, through the pages of *An Claidheamh Soluis* – provided leadership. Noting the public excitement on the issue, Douglas Hyde wrote that such 'deep and widespread interest in public affairs' had not been seen 'since the time of Parnell' and friends of St Enda's were among those who spotted the wider political implications of the campaign and its opponents.[14] For Hyde, 'nothing short of this [i.e., a university with compulsory Irish as an entrance requirement] will bring home to the Gaelic Irishman that after three or four hundred years he is at least ceasing to be the underdog in Ireland'.[15] He noted that the Universities Act was the 'biggest piece of Home Rule ever conceded'.[16] Even as the Home Rule issue was stagnating at Westminster, the League's campaign resulted in thousands of ordinary Irishmen and women becoming radicalised on the language issue. The politics of national identity were entering a new phase.

Dublin at this time was still an intimate city, and the centre of town was a popular residential area. Willie lived in places – Great Brunswick Street, Sandymount, Rathmines – where he could traverse the city quickly by walking, by tram, or by cycling. The slower pace of transport meant that chance meetings and personal encounters were relatively frequent. Mary Colum asserted that between 'Abbey Street and College Green, a five minutes' walk, one could meet every person of importance in the life of the city at a certain time in the afternoon'.[17] In addition, the artistic, and especially the theatrical, world frequented by Willie was a place of mutual support and convivial social interaction. Interested friends would drop by casually to studios and rehearsals, and there were refreshments and musical interludes where people could chat. Those who participated formally and informally in the many theatrical, political and artistic organisations would meet casually in places like the University at Stephen's Green (later Earlsfort Terrace), the National Library, the National Gallery, or the many events and outings organised by the Gaelic League.

From its inception, St Enda's was an important meeting place as well.

In the second term, theatre took an even more prominent role at St Enda's. Teachers like Thomas MacDonagh, Tomás Mac Domhnaill and Patrick were, like Willie, keenly interested in drama, to the extent that all three wrote plays. Edward Martyn and Alice Milligan were among the guest lecturers to visit the school; as seen before, both had deep links to the art, theatre and political worlds. Students were taken on trips to the theatre, including the Abbey. During that first term, for example, the boys and staff had attended Thomas MacDonagh's play about a future revolution, *When the Dawn Is Come*, in the Abbey Theatre in October, as well as works by Rutherford Mayne and Seumus O'Kelly in November. While the themes of MacDonagh's and O'Kelly's plays were radical and overtly nationalist, Willie's own taste in theatre was eclectic. At Christmas time, at the singsongs he organised in St Enda's before the holiday break, Willie would arrange for students to act out a scene from whatever Shakespearean play they were studying, and was painstaking and enthusiastic in his preparation of the young actors. Through Willie's progressive approach to teaching, the students learned about the drama in a hands-on way instead of depending on written texts as was then usual.[18] And St Enda's brought new opportunities for Willie to promote his work: in 1909 *An Macaomh*, the school magazine, featured a photograph of Willie's statuette of a young girl, 'Memories', which was kept in the school. The statuette was naturalistic and charming, showing a seated girl in childish dress, lost in thought. Willie was obviously happy with this work as he exhibited it later at the 1911 Royal Hibernian Academy (RHA) Exibition and at an Aonach.

Patrick had plans to turn the interest in theatre of the St Enda's community into something more tangible, and in early 1909 intensive preparations began for dramatic performances at the school. The plays chosen, *An Naomh ar Iarraidh* ('The Lost Saint') and *The Coming of Fionn*, were respectively written by leading Revivalist scholars Douglas Hyde and Standish O'Grady. Willie and his nephew Alf were soon busy building the stage and painting the scenery.

That same month, the Students' Union in the Metropolitan School of Art made a foray into theatre, and again Willie was a central figure in the new departure. St Enda's pupils attended the staging of the Students' Union's production of another Fenian Cycle–themed play, Alice Milligan's popular *The Last Feast of the Fianna*, in the School of Art on 12 March. The Students' Union had even borrowed some props from the St Enda's plays. This production seems to have been the occasion for a rather overlong speech given by Patrick. According to Desmond Ryan, as Patrick's erudite speech 'thundered on and on', Willie 'came out and with a firm word in his brother's ear, stopped that nonsense'.[19] When necessary, Willie was not afraid to express his opinion of his brother's occasionally overenthusiastic oratory. Ryan reported that:

> His brother was to a large extent a brake on this recklessness
> of Pearse, for Willie never scrupled to tell him the truth, even
> about a bad speech, and was capable of the reproach 'Pat you
> made a rotten speech this evening. You repeated yourself and
> dragged on and on until the poor people were bored stiff!'[20]

It also seems that Willie alone could influence his brother:
Ryan noted that Patrick listened 'courteously to all critics
and went on doing as he liked until Willie lisped his fierce
word'.[21] Though Patrick certainly had a more forceful personality, he obviously held Willie's advice in high esteem.
That said, Máire Nic Shiubhlaigh, who knew Willie well, felt
that he 'seemed to be overshadowed by his brother. He agreed
to his every decision and seldom put forward an argument of
his own'.[22] The important word in Nic Shiubhlaigh's statement, however, is 'seemed'. Later in her discussion of Willie's
personality, she corrects the common perception of Willie as
the diffident underling and draws attention to the mutually
influential relationship between the brothers:

> But Willie's deference was not born of lack of character. To
> those who knew them the most remarkable thing about
> these two was the similarity of their views on all subjects.
> This, with the admiration they lavished on each other, made
> them almost unique. What P.H. thought, Willie believed;
> whom Willie liked, P.H admired.[23]

The Students' Union staged two more plays at a social function in the School of Art on Thursday 18 March, the day after St Patrick's Day. Willie took centre stage, playing a doomed lifeboat worker in the first play of the night, *The Storm*, which was written by Willie's fellow artist, the young Hugh Barden. The play was produced by Fred Morrow and the cast included some of Willie's fellow students, including Willie's nephew Alf. Harry Clarke, already an acclaimed artist but not yet famous, took part in the second play performed that evening, *Paid in His Own Coin*. These performances proved hugely successful. The *Freeman's Journal* critic was particularly gushing about the 'two little gems of plays', even suggesting that WB Yeats and his National Theatre Society should seek actors among the students of the Metropolitan School of Art. Crowded audiences and critical acclaim meant that the Student Union's plays were restaged for three nights in the Abbey Theatre in late April, when the pupils of St Enda's attended. In the intervening weeks Willie had been busy with the school's dramatic work. He barely had time to draw breath after the triumphant initial performances of *The Storm* and *Paid in His Own Coin* before facing into the performances of *An Naomh ar Iarraidh* and *The Coming of Fionn* at St Enda's on 20, 21 and 22 March 1909. These were the first of many plays performed by the school's students and community, and as there was no suitable hall at Cullenswood, Willie and Alf used their creative skills to convert a corrugated iron shed beside the school into a theatre. The result impressed theatre-lover Joseph Holloway:

> The proscenium was excellently and ingeniously worked into the shape of the hall and the opening was of semi-circular shape, with a head forming the key and festooned curtains falling in graceful folds from the centre and on each side. The drop curtains were divided in the centre and pulled to either side to disclose the stage.[24]

Willie came up with the colour scheme for the stage and modelled the head in the centre of the proscenium, while his old friend Albert Power helped to paint the scenery. The concern for presentation extended to the beautifully illustrated programme for the two plays, designed by one of Willie's pupils, Patrick Tuohy. The costumes, including some monks' habits, were also impressive. A photograph of the pupils acting in the play, which was taken for publicity purposes, shows dramatic poses that are reminiscent of the stylised figures of James Pearse's and Willie's own ecclesiastical sculptural work.

The inaugural theatrical performances at St Enda's, held in the early evening in an improvised theatre, were exciting social occasions on the Dublin cultural scene. Over a hundred and twenty eminent literary guests attended the third performance on 22 March. Joseph Holloway recalled the convivial gathering, where the Pearse brothers shone as hosts in their beautiful new school:

Wm Pierce [sic] presided over the tea and Mr Pierce made himself generally useful in making everyone at home, in a beautiful room newly decorated by the Morrows of Ulster Literary Theatre and Theatre of Ireland fame. After tea the company strolled about the College grounds for a little while and I noted what a distinguished company had come – Stephen Gwynn (who by the way has his son at St Enda's), Edward Martyn, P. Colum, John McNeill, Mary Hayden ... Mr and Mrs Standish O'Grady, Miss Agnes O'Farrelly and her brothers and sisters. When we were all seated for some time Yeats came into the shed late and found it hard to procure a seat but nonetheless had a great chat with O'Grady.[25]

In his diary Holloway also noted the presence of 'some friars in their habits and some priests in ordinary everyday attire'.[26] One of the friars present on this particular day, Fr Augustine of the Capuchin Friars of Church Street, would later make an appearance in the great political drama that would secure the Pearse brothers a place in history.

The evening was a triumphant success. For Holloway 'there was a strange fascination about the crude boyish playing'; the actors 'chanted their words in a style outside nature' and 'created an impression not easily forgotten'.[27] He mused that the torches gave an 'element of danger to the scene not wholly peaceful to the minds of the spectators'.[28] Following the play Standish O'Grady stood on a chair and held forth to the packed audience on how people should live like

Fionn and his companions. A piper accompanied O'Grady's rousing speech and the entire audience rose to its feet when he finished with the rallying cry of the Gaelic League. For Holloway: 'Each and all felt as they left the hall that they had just witnessed a unique and inspiring show and one that promises great hope for the Ireland of the near future.'[29] It would not be the last time that the vision depicted on a stage spilled over into reality.

As soon as the excitement about the school plays died down, Willie began to focus again on his artwork. In March 1909 he had exhibited his sculptural work 'Páiste Óg' ('A Young Child') at the RHA exhibition, one of only seventeen sculptures exhibited that year. In late April he took part in the third exhibition of the Young Irish Artists, which was held at the Leinster Lecture Hall in Molesworth Street. It was an auspicious occasion. Willie's old teacher and friend Oliver Sheppard was there; so too was the artist William Orpen, who had been a guest teacher at the School of Art since 1907, and the ubiquitous WB Yeats. Opened by the Earl of Mayo and visited by the Aberdeens, the crowded exhibition had a congenial atmosphere, with little groups of friends 'feeling their way, both individually and as a group' to a 'distinctive mode of expression'.[30] There was also a cartoon of Máire Nic Shiubhlaigh drawn by Grace Gifford, while Beatrice Elvery exhibited her 'Íosagán' painting, which usually hung in St Enda's. Willie exhibited a bust sculpture, whose name is not documented, while his friend Albert Power showed a statue of Cúchulainn.

But despite his increasingly busy life in the spring of 1909, Willie found time to keep in touch with his child model Mabel Gorman. On 16 May 1909, Mabel wrote from St Louis Convent boarding school in Monaghan thanking him for a 'lovely parcel', and Willie regularly sent young Mabel small gifts, such as plasticine, pictures, and chocolates.[31]

The script for the next dramatic performance at St Enda's was penned by Patrick himself. The outdoor pageant *Macghníomhartha Chúchulainn* ('The Boy Deeds of Cúchulainn'), which depicted some episodes from the Gaelic epic *Táin Bó Cuailgne*, was performed in the grounds of Cullenswood on 22 June 1909. Teacher Tomás Mac Domhnaill arranged the musical score, and articles in *An Macaomh* state that Willie and Alf were responsible for the costumes, grouping and general production. Alf made Cúchulainn's chariot, while student Eamon Bulfin made the spears, and the young Connemara boys Pádraic Óg Ó Conaire and Colm Ó Neachtain made the shoes. As usual, the energetic artistic friends of Willie's and Alf's, including Albert Power and Patrick Tuohy, were on hand to help out.

Oliver Sheppard was in the audience: he and his wife Rosalind were frequent visitors to St Enda's, as was Máire Nic Shiubhlaigh, who came with others from the Theatre of Ireland to help with preparations for the various pageants. *Macghníomhartha Chúchulainn* was imaginative and ambitious, featuring a huge cast and ending in dramatic fashion with a seemingly real horse-drawn chariot circling the school playing field three times. The specially designed and dyed 'sumptuous costumes' were admired by writer Stephen MacKenna.[32] The play – a pageant – had a powerful visual impact, and the elaborate costumes and choreography echoed the imaginative *tableaux vivants* embraced previously by Alice Milligan and the Inghinidhe. The play proved a uniting experience for pupils and staff and a powerful vehicle for impressing the visitors, of whom there were many. There were over five hundred guests in the playing field, including, as Patrick noted proudly, 'most of the people in Dublin who are interested in art and literature'.[33] Many of these visitors were from Willie's theatre and art circles: James Cousins later wrote a poem about pupil Frank Dowling's portrayal of Cúchulainn in the pageant. Though it is not clear if she was among the audience at *Macghníomhartha*, Sarah Purser, the artist and famous hostess of Dublin literary and artistic *soirées*, attended at least one of the St Enda's pageants, finding it a 'very creditable and interesting performance'. Her connection with St Enda's was probably made through Willie or his circle: rather surprisingly, she later remembered that Patrick left no personal impression on her and that she should not have recognised him.[34]

While Patrick instigated the St Enda's plays, Willie always had an important creative role in their staging and 'discussed every detail with Pádraic in the course of long nightly talks'.[35] The plays were generally acclaimed critically, and Willie (along with Patrick, Thomas MacDonagh and Alf McGloughlin) deserves credit for the imaginative and sensitive productions, all the more as the actual play scripts can seem lacking in dramatic potential. Patrick's interest in Oliver Sheppard's sculpture, particularly the 'Inis Fáil' sculpture whose imagery he had discussed so excitedly in 1906, is an important source for the images and themes which occur frequently in his dramatic work. Both men drew on the Ulster Cycle and address ideas about chivalry and the nobility of fighting, and use images of Setanta/Cúchulainn to suggest the ancestral authority of the young person who goes out to fight. The nakedness of Sheppard's heroic figures is also reflected in the portrayals of some of Patrick's dramatic heroes. Clearly Willie had a vital role in providing Patrick with a bridge to Sheppard's artistic responses to Gaelic literature; Patrick's articles on Irish art and on the imagery of Sheppard's sculpture coincided with Willie's first RHA and Oireachtas exhibits. The Cúchulainn-inspired work of Willie's fellow artists Albert Power and Edwin Morrow provided additional channels of influence, as did scholar George Sigerson (who, by coincidence, was Mary Brigid's doctor).

Even though the school term began in mid-September of 1909, Willie spent at least some of that month in Paris. On 30 September his address was the Hotel Jacob on Rue Jacob in the Latin Quarter, the epicentre of the Parisian artistic world.

The impressive halls and statuary of the renowned École des Beaux-Arts were just around the corner from the rear of the hotel, while on the opposite bank of the Seine, the even more impressive Louvre was only a ten-minute walk away. The Académie Julian, a more democratic rival to the École which Oliver Sheppard and a young Constance Markievicz had visited, had its sculpture classes just a short walk away from Willie's hotel in the other direction. Another well-known academy was the Académie Colarossi, while the Académie de la Palette and numerous private ateliers were also situated nearby. This was at least Willie's third visit to the French capital, and given his hotel's location (and it seems to have been the same area he frequented on previous visits), it seems likely that he attended, or at least visited, one or more of these academies, which together sustained a lively, if transient, artistic community. A page in one of Willie's surviving notebooks has phrases in French, offering a further hint that he attended at least some classes or lectures during his trips to France.

Whatever the case, and however long his stay, Willie would have found plenty of stimulation while in the Latin Quarter. The streets surrounding Rue Jacob had long been a hub for artists and writers. Irish writers including Yeats, Synge and George Moore spent extended periods in Paris, and Oscar Wilde died in the nearby Rue des Beaux-Arts in 1900. Yeats's muse, the Irish nationalist Maud Gonne, spent several years in the French capital, and Willie's former teacher John Hughes had been living in Paris since 1903. At the time of Willie's 1909 visit, cafés provided a vibrant social outlet for the city intelligentsia and some of the more renowned cafés, such as Café La Palette and La Clé des Prés, were very close to Willie's lodgings. Meanwhile the celebrated Café de Flore, which had long attracted leading artists and poets, was only a few minutes' walk from the hotel. Despite all these attractions, it seems Willie may have found time to leave the lure of the French capital's rich artistic scene: one of his notebooks includes an (undated) rough sketch of some Romanesque mouldings from Toulouse Cathedral. Desmond Ryan recalled that Willie 'reserved a special affection for the quaintness of costume, the diversity, the eccentricity and the vividness of the student quarters of Paris'.[36] However, he was not there too long: a letter from Mabel Gorman on 11 October, asking 'Mr Pearse' if he had enjoyed himself in Paris, shows that he was back in Dublin by that date.[37]

The camaraderie of the Paris ateliers was echoed in the spirit of communal endeavour now animating the Dublin art scene. While the Aberdeens were sympathetic to Home Rule and shared the democratic and feminist leanings so prevalent in Willie's circle, the dynamic that had them deferred to as patrons of the Dublin art scene would ultimately prove incompatible with the spirit of self-reliance epitomised by the new Aonaigh.

Chapter Five

• • • • • •

1909-1911

Changing Times

Back in Dublin, Willie's star was rising in the art world. By the time of the art exhibition which was part of the week-long 1909 Christmas Sinn Féin Aonach in the Rotunda, 'William Mac Piarais', Albert Power, Joseph Carré and Oliver Sheppard were noted as 'well-known artists'.[1] The popular and well-attended Aonach, a fair dealing in Irish goods organised by Sinn Féin, featured many figures later known for their political and military actions. The dedicated art section was under the charge of Countess Markievicz; Gaelic Leaguer, piper and radical nationalist Éamonn Ceannt was involved on the organising committee; and Michael O'Rahilly, a leading Gaelic Leaguer, was also heavily involved. The Aonach, like the campaign for compulsory Irish, was a sign of the changing times. Up until now, events such as this (like the Arts and Crafts exhibitions) had generally been organised under the patronage of those closely associated with British rule in

Ireland. Now, under the leadership of the Gaelic League and Sinn Féin, cultural exhibitions, processions, and concerts were being organised by a more diverse range of activists, with a broader representative basis in industry, workers' organisations, cultural and educational organisations, and the temperance movement. Many radical nationalists, including IRB activists, were able to network – and recruit – from this wider social and political world.

In 1910, St Enda's was again filled with theatre. The first performances of Patrick's latest play, *Íosagán*, took place on 5, 6 and 7 February, preceded by a performance of Pádraic Colum's *The Destruction of the Hostel*. The audience entered the improvised theatre by the light of Chinese lanterns and, following some music and an address by Patrick, the actors for the Colum play marched in, led by a piper. Willie, as choreographer, presumably held some responsibility for the carefully created atmosphere, and the spectators were deeply moved by *Íosagán*. Set in Connemara, it was a religious play that drew its language and inspiration from the Ros Muc area where Patrick had a holiday cottage. Willie visited the cottage regularly with Patrick and others, including at various times Desmond Ryan, the Dowling brothers, Milo MacGarry, and his mother and sisters. The family, including Willie, also holidayed in Killarney and, in a reminder of both their comfortable background and adventurous spirit, a surviving photograph shows Willie and other members of the family pony-trekking. On one Ros Muc holiday, Mary Brigid, never the most robust of characters, appears to have had a mental breakdown, and her health, both mental and physical, must have played on Willie's mind. However, both brothers seem to have been exceptionally kind and patient with her, despite her sometimes volatile behaviour and her politics: John Dowling, who attended St Enda's and had ongoing connections to the Pearse family, stated that Mary Brigid thought of herself as 'English'.[2] Her plays teetered on the brink of being stage-Irish, and she was deeply uncomfortable in the presence of Connemara Gaelic speakers. Willie and Mary Brigid appear to have gotten on well, though, perhaps finding a bond through their common interest in acting and art. At a *céilí* in St Enda's on 17 February 1910, the two siblings acted out scenes from Richard Brinsley Sheridan's *The School for Scandal* in the course of the evening's entertainment, with Willie playing Sir Peter. This February *céilí*, presumably organised as usual by Willie, also featured a performance of Alice Milligan's *The Last Feast of the Fianna*, with Máire Nic Shiubhlaigh as Niamh, and a reading by Thomas MacDonagh from his latest play *Metempsychosis*.[3] Milligan, Nic Shiubhlaigh and MacDonagh were all advanced nationalists, but while Willie was their friend, his own politics at this stage are a matter of conjecture.

Willie was making plans that would allow him to pursue his interest in theatre on his own terms. Sometime in late 1909 or early 1910, along with Mary Brigid,

Alf McGloughlin and others, he founded an amateur drama society called the Leinster Stage Society. Willie was the driving force of the new society, which viewed itself as a serious outfit; in a letter published in *The Irish Times* in 1911, he claimed to be 'personally responsible for most of the affairs of the society'.[4] The Leinster Stage Society had its own stationery and a busy schedule that involved, as was the case with many other amateur groups at the time, performances in major theatres. On Friday 27 and 28 May 1910, the society performed in the Abbey Theatre, and Willie headed the cast in all four plays, acting as Napoleon in his nephew Alf's *The Countess of Strasbourg* and as Fionn in O'Grady's *The Transformation of Fionn*. There was input from his St Enda's friends in the latter play: pupil Eamon Bulfin played a warrior and Tomás Mac Domhnaill composed the music. The Abbey performances also included two plays by Mary Brigid, *The Message* and *Over the Stile*.

Meanwhile, there was yet another revival of the Students' Union productions of *The Storm* and *Paid in His Own Coin*, which were staged in the Abbey from 31 May to 4 June 1910 as part of an alternating programme that included new plays by TK Moylan and Alf McGloughlin. The artistic vision of Willie and his friends found renewed success: Harry Clarke's posters for the performances were much admired, as were the plays themselves. But Willie was unsure of his own ability as an actor. Máire Nic Shiubhlaigh recalled that 'he was terribly aware of the unsuitability of his speech, and though he worked hard to perfect it, his voice never completely became his servant … At rehearsals he obeyed every command with humility. Often he would draw one aside and whisper: "Do you think I was good? I'm doing my best."[5] TK Moylan recalled Willie as 'rather absent-minded, was as likely as not to forget his lines or walk on the stage without some essential hand prop'.[6] However, there was encouraging feedback for Willie in his reprised role in *The Storm*: the critic from *The Irish Times* stated that 'William Pearse … acted uncommonly well'.[7] Alice Milligan's *The Last Feast of the Fianna* was also restaged as part of the week's programme featuring Willie ('Liam Mac Piarais') as Oisín alongside Rosalind Sheppard (wife of sculptor Oliver) as Niamh. The usual mix of religions prevalent in Willie's social circle was evident in the cast: Rosalind, like her husband, was a Protestant, as was Ethel Rhind, who played Gráinne.[8] Willie also played the eponymous character in his nephew's play *The Fugitive*, which had a more obvious political theme, dealing as it did with the Jacobite and Williamite tensions of 1690.

On 19 June Willie travelled with the St Enda's students, his brother Patrick, and Thomas MacDonagh to Castlebellingham in County Louth, where *Macghníomhartha Chúchulainn* was once more performed at a huge *feis* supported by Sir Henry Bellingham. Willie enjoyed the outing and was recalled as being 'in his element arranging and seeing to

the transport of our costumes and our stage equipment'.[9]
The attendance at the *feis* spanned the usual eclectic range
of social groups who, as we have seen, interested themselves
in Gaelic culture at this time, from advanced nationalists to
pillars of the British establishment, ranging from Countess
Markievicz to a colonel and two army captains, who were
friends with Lord Bellingham. The soldiers might have been
bemused had they seen the St Enda's contingent later on that
evening. On returning home by train to Amiens Street station, the pupils marshalled themselves behind the St Enda's
banner while carrying their props of homemade spears and
battle-axes borrowed from the school museum. A crowd
gathered and sang 'Who Fears to Speak of '98', prompting
MacDonagh to joke that 'they expect us to lead them against
the Castle'.[10] Such a proposition was still a laughing matter.

The Pearse monumental sculpture business appears still to
have been in operation that summer, with Willie accepting
a new commission worth seventy pounds (the Mulrennan
monument), in a letter written from Great Brunswick Street
on 15 July. But an era was coming to a close; the family
business was sold in 1910, making £500. To provide a more
suitable home for St Enda's, a lease was taken on a new property, the Hermitage, a country mansion in Rathfarnham, as
Patrick felt that Cullenswood was too much in the 'suburban
groove'.[11] Sidney Gifford later gave a comical description of
Rathmines at this time:

The district resembled a waxworks museum. The people who surrounded us were lifelike but inanimate models of distinguished English people. It was a deadly atmosphere where any originality of thought or independence of action was regarded as eccentricity or lawlessness … Its residents seemed to typify the flunky Irishman; with their strange, synthetic English accent, their snobbery and their half-hearted desire to be a ruling caste.[12]

It seems that capital from the sale of the business was used to fund St Enda's, and James Pearse Snr's books and artworks were taken to the school. However, the move to Rathfarnham would prove to be financially injudicious. The family still held on to Cullenswood and, in addition to the increased debt involved, the move to what was then considered the countryside lost the school many day pupils.

It is also unclear what the dissolving of the family business meant for Willie's half-brother, James Vincent. The 1911 census recorded him as 'James Pearce', and described him as a 'stone carver' rather than the 'sculptor' of the 1901 census. In 1911 he was living with his wife Mary and their surviving seven children in Verschoyle Place in Dublin, just south of the river. Their tenement house was shared with two other families, the nine members of the Pearse family occupying just two rooms, a stark contrast to the fortunes of Patrick and Willie. By 1912, only two years after the sale of the family firm and while still in his forties, James Vincent Pearse was dead, of cancer of the neck.[13] Willie's sister-in-law Mary, left alone to support the family, lived out her days in a tenement, turning – perhaps not surprisingly – to alcohol for solace. James Vincent never became involved in the numerous dramatic or artistic ventures at St Enda's or in any of the other family activities, which is unusual considering that Willie in particular must have known him well as they both worked for the family firm. It appears that he did not share his half-brothers' nationalist sympathies, but then again, neither did Mary Brigid. His death is not mentioned in Patrick's writings or in Mary Brigid's's reminiscences, and though Margaret refers fondly to James Vincent in an article whose focus is on Patrick and Willie, the reference is to the older brother of her childhood and not to the grown man. While he must have played an important part in Willie's life, the third Pearse brother seems destined to remain a bit of a mystery.

At some stage prior to the dissolving of the family business in 1910, Willie considered applying for an unnamed position at the School of Art. A draft letter of application survives, which hints at Willie's sense of being frustrated in his dreams of embracing his creative impulse:

> I am a practical worker in marble and stone and besides my work at my place of business at Brunswick Street I execute some small commissions on my own responsibility – so that I am not an amateur but one with the earnest intention of pursuing my craft as a sculptor.

It is for this reason that I would be anxious to obtain the appointment that I ask for – as up to the present I have not been able to do justice to myself or my work – my time being too much divided between this or more places or things.

Of course, I know I have not much to boast of in awards or results of examining – as I did not make a practice of sitting for these examinations, and this for more than one reason.

Firstly, my temperament would not allow me to go thro' such things with any degree of comfort or success. And I never saw sufficient reason to do violence to myself by so doing. Besides I have had so much to do both at school and at my work here that I never felt inclined. Of course things might be different if I was under service to you.[14]

Willie's statement that he 'never saw sufficient reason to do violence to myself by so doing' (i.e., entering for competitive awards) is interesting, suggesting that whatever about being nervous, Willie knew his own mind. However, to think of sharing these reasons in a letter of application (albeit a draft) was surely naïve and counterproductive. The letter suggests that Willie's life was in transition and his statement that 'up to the present I have not been able to do justice to myself or my work' suggests that the letter was drafted when the closure of the family business was envisaged. Willie was awarded a studentship at the School of Art for 1910–11 (which was renewed the following year), and it is likely that this was the subject of the draft letter. His studentship covered his fees and gave him a stipend.

By early September of 1910 Willie was back teaching part-time at St Enda's in Rathfarnham. He was also teaching art on Saturdays in St Ita's/Scoil Íde, the girls' school which was formally established by Patrick in Cullenswood after St Enda's moved to Rathfarnham. Willie was a diligent and good-humoured teacher, easily moved to laughter, and seems to have had a particular bond with pupils. Desmond Ryan recalled that:

> As a teacher he was most painstaking. He acted consistently on his brother's maxim that the office of any teacher is to foster the characters of his pupils, to bring to fruition whatever glimmering of ideals and goodness they possessed rather than to indoctrinate them with their master's prejudices or drive them through a course of studies like so many tin soldiers.[15]

Although not yet teaching full-time, Willie played an increasingly important role in the everyday life of St Enda's:

> If the school was made and upheld by Padraic, Willie's common-sense advice upon many occasions, his unwearied attention and management during the Hermitage period, his service as a teacher had an incalculable part in making the venture the success it was. Indeed second is a doubtful word, for the long intimacy between the pair resulted in a

perfect co-operation and harmony which could only come from a thorough understanding.[16]

While most of the credit has, rightly, gone to Patrick for his innovative ideas on education and student freedom, Willie was responsible for introducing a certain amount of routine, and is credited with making 'the young wipe its boots on the mat and keep its fork in its left hand and answer all bells promptly'.[17] Willie's practical input is evident from the various school notebooks he kept where small loans to students and advancement of money for train fares home were noted. His gentle personality and his interest in sport played a crucial part in the creation of the friendly and respectful atmosphere between staff and students, although his temperament meant he sometimes had problems enforcing discipline with his students.

In addition to the school plays, Gaelic games provided an informal opportunity for Willie to bond with students. He liked hurling and often played handball matches with the older students, supplying prizes for the tournaments that he organised. Willie's insight into the dynamic among students was put to good use when the pupils were losing interest in hurling: he mobilised the influential boys and asked them to help him to revive the game. The teams had considerable success, particularly in the early years. The nature of Willie's personality can be seen in an instance where he was hit by a ball during a handball match with student Kenneth

Reddin, whose family had close links to the school. Reddin was wracked with worry:

> I had hurt Willie Pearse, the artist, the gentle Willie Pearse, who wouldn't hurt anyone. I had hurt him. I had insulted him. I went into his room and told him so. I said that after all he was my Arts Master and that what I had done was an insult.[18]

But Willie was not fazed:

> Arts Master? said Willie. I wasn't your Arts Master in the handball alley today. You were mine and you taught me a sharp lesson. Next time I'll keep my ears pinned back like a rabbit.[19]

Despite occasional struggles with discipline in the classroom, Willie had a natural understanding of children, as is demonstrated in his friendship with his child model Mabel Gorman, who was by now a day student in St Ita's. He prepared conscientiously and thoroughly for the classes he taught, planning the subject of each weekly class well in advance. His ability to empathise with a child's imagination is discernible in the lecture notes Willie prepared in 1910. It seems he was undergoing formal training as an art teacher in the School of Art around this time and the notes may have been pitched as an introduction to art for his young students. Given that he did not usually commit his ideas to paper, the lecture notes are important as an insight into his understanding of art and artists.

Willie first of all outlined his belief that 'it is an elementary instinct in children to draw' and that in deciding to draw or paint 'our best instincts call out for the beautiful ... Our senses cry out for pleasant and beautiful surroundings.'[20] Despite his self-professed lack of knowledge of the Arts and Crafts movement, many of the sentiments expressed by Willie echo their foundational ideas:

> For our ordinary comforts the rough stones or bricks would be quite sufficient to keep out the rain and wind – But still we like nice wallpaper and some good furniture. In fact our best instincts call out for the beautiful. We all take pleasure in looking on beautiful things. Beautiful houses, beautiful pictures, beautiful flowers, beautiful people. And this must be right. Otherwise we would be like the animals of the fields ... But remember the smallest child even before he or she comes to the age of reason notices with delight the bright winged butterfly, the dancing sun rays and the rippling water.[21]

Emphasising the importance of nurturing 'the child's power of observation', Willie was able to frame his ideas in language and examples readily understood by his young pupils:

> You all know very well what a house is like, yet if you make a drawing of it and take it to father he might think it was

a rhinoceros or an elephant who forgot his trunk. I wonder how many of you would make a proper drawing of a watering can or a cup or saucer you see so often. Mind you, I don't blame you for this at all – it is only natural. We go along and see things but we are thinking of other things – eating apples or cycling or playing. But our power of observation must be trained. Some time, look carefully at a leaf or flower, note the characteristics of such, how it differs from a motor car or such and then go away and try and draw it. This would be one of the best drawing lessons you could get.[22]

Such an emphasis was unsurprising in the son of an artist and, indeed, Willie's powers of observation extended beyond aesthetics to astute readings of behaviour and motivation. Surviving correspondence shows Willie to have been especially aware of the needs of the 'special cases', the boys who needed extra coaching or those whose exceptional talent needed nurturing and encouragement. Young Patrick Tuohy, encouraged by Willie, entered the School of Art and subsequently achieved great success as a painter. David Sears, who knew Willie as a teacher for six years and as a friend towards the end of that period, later said:

He had exquisite tact in dealing with the boys, with whom he was a great favourite. He won their esteem by taking their reasonings and ideals seriously and trying to convince them when they were wrong, but treating them as equals in the argument. When he had thus shown them that an idea was wrong, and perhaps ridiculous, they were disarmed by the tactful manner of his doing it. It was the same with our essays. Everyone knows how hard it is at first to set our inner selves down on paper. But we soon lost all fear of him and wrote quite freely.[23]

During this first term in the 'new' St Enda's in Rathfarnham, closer ties were made with Na Fianna Éireann, the radical nationalist boys' movement which had been founded by Bulmer Hobson and Countess Markievicz the previous year. Fianna branches had quickly appeared throughout the country, and while ostensibly similar to the boy scouts, the Fianna leadership made no secret of their political intent (many Fianna members would later play key roles in the Rising). A class in code-signalling took place in St Enda's on 20 November 1910, and three days later Con Colbert – a leading figure in the Fianna – began running military foot drills. Eight Fianna *cathanna* (battalions) were organised on 28 November 1910; the number of companies alone would suggest that there was extensive involvement by pupils. While Patrick, Alf McGloughlin, and Eamon Bulfin were named as *taoisigh* (or leaders) of the St Enda's Fianna in *An Macaomh,*[24] Willie, perhaps significantly, was not. How and when he did become involved is not clear, but a member of the Fianna pipe band later recalled that he and fellow band members accompanied

Willie on scouting expeditions on many occasions.[25] This later engagement with the Fianna would have drawn Willie into further contact with Countess Markievicz, in whose home the Fianna pipe band practised, and with Bulmer Hobson. At this time the Fianna were being promoted in *Irish Freedom*, a radical nationalist newspaper whose first edition was issued in November 1910. Officially edited by Patrick McCartan and featuring substantial input from Bulmer Hobson, it was managed by Seán MacDiarmada from the end of 1911. All three were senior IRB members. The first editorial in November 1910 stated it was 'not for an Irish party, but for national tradition – the tradition of Wolfe Tone and Robert Emmet, of John Mitchell and John O'Leary'.[26] In case there was any doubt about the paper's stance, the editorial also stated that the 'independence of Ireland' meant standing 'for the complete and total separation of Ireland from England and the establishment of an Irish government. Freedom can take but one shape among us – a republic',[27] the writer claiming that it was not possible 'to make Ireland a nation by an act of the English Parliament'.[28] In the same edition, a piece by 'Art' stated that 'the history of the world proves that there is but one road to freedom and that is the red road of war'.[29]

The radical Daly family of Limerick and republican tobacconist and senior IRB member Thomas Clarke of Amiens Street were also regular advertisers. In reality the paper was a mouthpiece for the IRB, which Bulmer Hobson, MacDiarmada and Clarke were determined to re-invigorate. *Irish Freedom* also provided an influential organ for the revived Wolfe Tone and United Irishmen Memorial Committee. This committee, which had come about initially to fund the building of a monument to Wolfe Tone, would, in the years to come, provide a convenient front for leading IRB figures including McCartan and Clarke. Patrick began attending Wolfe Tone clubs from this same year of 1910: the clubs were forums for nationalist debate, and another, more localised, public front for the IRB. It is noteworthy that the Irish Art Companions advertised in the first issues of *Irish Freedom*. However, it is not clear what input, if any, Willie had in this decision. Those associated with the sculptural guild had varying political views: Lilla Vanston, for example, was a rector's daughter with a knowledge of Irish, while Joseph Carré was an English-born sculptor and actor.

Willie's involvement in the Dublin art scene meant that he still had one foot in a cultural *milieu* framed by the old world of patronage and the Dublin Castle social set. Sheppard, Power and the Art Companions, including Vanston and Carré, exhibited at the 1910 Arts and Crafts Exhibition which was opened by the Lord Lieutenant in early November. Connections with the Castle did not preclude artistic sympathy with Ireland's lost nationhood: as noted before,

Sheppard's work in particular was often politically charged, and Vanston's exhibit at the 1910 exhibition, 'The Lament of Banba', was based on a goddess who symbolised Ireland. Sheppard had executed memorials to the 1798 rebellion some years previously, and at the unveiling of one of these, in Wexford Town, real-life pikemen had assembled to salute those commemorated in Sheppard's sculpture. This blurring of the lines between commemorative practice and shows of nationalist pride and strength would emerge as a salient feature of nationalist life in the years to come.[30] Interestingly, though he signed his work in Irish and occasionally gave Irish names to sculptures, Willie's artwork was, with the possible exception of 'Éire', non-political. That December, his statue of Mater Dolorosa was among the decorative additions to St Andrew's Church in Westland Row, which were admired in an article by Edward Martyn.[31]

That same month saw the second of two British parliamentary elections in 1910. The Liberal Party, historically sympathetic to Home Rule, was returned as the minority government, supported by the seventy-four members of the Irish Parliamentary Party. The IPP, led by John Redmond, held the balance of power once more and were keen to use their leverage to advance Home Rule. Their position was more favourable than ever before, as the Liberals were intent on removing the House of Lords' veto over public bills introduced in the House of Commons. This veto was a live issue during both elections, as the Conservative-dominated House of Lords had used it to block the Liberals' so-called 'People's Budget' of 1909. Anticipation grew in Ireland that the conditions would soon be favourable for the introduction of a Home Rule Bill.

The IPP envisaged a Home Rule settlement that would devolve power to Dublin, though with some continued representation in Westminster. Ireland would still remain part of the United Kingdom under a British monarch. On 4 February 1910, the *Ulster Herald* cited John Redmond's statement that while the desired outcome of Home Rule was an Irish parliament, Westminster would retain 'an over-riding supreme authority over the Irish legislature, such as it possesses today over all the various parliaments in Canada, Australia, South Africa and other portions of the Empire'. Westminster would retain control of imperial taxation, the army, customs, and foreign relations. That same month, Dublin-born Edward Carson became leader of the Unionist Parliamentary Party at Westminster. While Carson led a party organised on an All-Ireland basis, the unionist population was particularly concentrated in northeast Ulster, where the Ulster Unionist Council (founded in 1905) provided local leadership and momentum. Ulster unionists, many of whom had links to the sectarian Orange Order, were implacably opposed to even the limited form of self-government being discussed by Redmond, believing that Home Rule would involve domination by the Catholic Church and that, given the close market links between northern industries and the rest of Britain, it would disadvantage them economically.

Patrick's interest in militant republicanism was growing, and on 6 March 1911 he gave a talk about Robert Emmet under the auspices of the Wolfe Tone Committee. The 1911 census, conducted at the beginning of April, shows Willie (this time 'Liam Mac Piarais') proudly described in Gaelic as a 'dealbhadóir' (sculptor). Willie's nephew Alfred McGloughlin (by now a 'tarraingteoir' or draughtsman) was also living in St Enda's. Willie's assertion of his Gaelic identity did not necessarily make him a republican; Lady Aberdeen also signed her name in Irish on occasion.

In late February the Leinster Stage Society were back in the Abbey with a programme that featured plays by painter and mystic Æ, James Cousins, and Willie's nephew Alf as well as a Dickens adaptation by Mary Brigid. Posters were hung all over the city and the production attracted a large attendance. Willie, Mary Brigid and Alf all acted, while Marcella Dowling, Alf's future wife, was also involved. Marcella's sister Charlotte, herself a playwright, helped to sell tickets. The Dowlings were radical nationalists with Fenian connections, and Marcella's brothers (including Frank, who had once played Cúchulainn) were in St Enda's. Willie played a Presbyterian minister in the Cousins play. While most reviews were moderately favourable, focusing on the Society's potential to improve with experience, in his private diary Holloway was scathing about Willie's performance in Æ's *Deirdre*, stating that Willie, playing the hero, Naoise, looked like an 'Indian chief' and spoke 'with a sort of inanimate monotone that never suggests manliness'.[32]

Willie was particularly successful in his next dramatic role, that of Pontius Pilate in the Passion Play in Irish, which was adapted from the Gospels and folk tradition by Patrick and staged on 7 and 8 April 1911 in the Abbey Theatre. The play's young cast was made up from pupils at both St Enda's and St Ita's, joined by teachers and friends. Tomás Mac Domhnaill played the part of Christ and also composed the music, while Willie played Pilate to much acclaim, impressing Mary Bulfin, who played Christ's mother, with the 'astonishing variety of his frowns'.[33] Patrick and Thomas MacDonagh acted the roles of the thieves, and even the gardener at St Enda's, storyteller Micheál Mac Ruaidhrí, was involved, playing the part of Barabbas. Mary Bulfin and Willie featured in the photographic publicity material. Máire Nic Shiubhlaigh recalled of the Passion Play that in its own way it 'created somewhat of a minor sensation in Dublin'[34] and stated that reports of it travelled to America and the Continent. Joseph Holloway's description of the play's opening performance also gives a flavour of its impact:

> It was all most impressive and very beautiful to behold …
> As the people pray on the hillside, the ominous sound of
> hammering is heard and soon after our Lord's voice and

those of the thieves who hang on either side of him are heard away in the distance until at last all is still and the stage darkens and the thunder rolls and the lightning flash and in awe we feel all is over and the greatest tragedy of the world consummated and all who had followed the incidents were deeply and wonderfully moved ... Never had I seen a more profoundly impressive and beautiful picture than that I had beheld during the Crucifixion. William Pearse was excellent as Pilate ...[35]

In his review, the *Irish Times* critic also praised the lighting and the 'pictures of solemn beauty'.[36] Willie, who with Alf and Thomas MacDonagh was responsible for the choreography and costuming of St Enda's productions, must surely have been pleased. The Passion Play was intended to be a triennial event but it was never repeated as the actors, among them Willie, soon found themselves on a very different path.

Chapter Six

• • • • • •

1911–1913

'That Terrible Beautiful Voice'

The theatrical circles that Willie was involved in were strongly nationalist, and the Abbey Theatre had itself refused to close as a mark of respect following the death of King Edward VII in 1910, as other Dublin theatres did. When a visit to Ireland by the newly crowned King George V was announced for July 1911, several leading nationalist organisations formed a coalition called the United National Societies to express their opposition. Some radical nationalists known to Willie, including Jack Morrow and Countess Markievicz, were involved in a clever propaganda stunt instigated by Seán MacDiarmada and Michael O'Rahilly against the impending visit. A banner bearing the motto 'Thou art not conquered yet, dear land', which advertised a forthcoming nationalist demonstration, was hung at the bottom of Grafton Street. The police removed the banner, but since permission to hang it had been obtained from the relevant section of Dublin Corporation, much publicity ensued and a crowd variously estimated at between ten and thirty thousand people attended the subsequent demonstration in Beresford Place.[1] Nonetheless, and notwithstanding the refusal of Dublin Corporation to offer a formal welcome to the British monarch, thousands of ordinary Dubliners lined the streets to see King George during his five-day visit in July.

While his half-brother James Vincent lived in a tenement, Willie continued to enjoy the beautiful surroundings of St Enda's at the Hermitage and to mix in the art world. He had shown two pieces at the 1911 RHA exhibition, opened in early March by the Lord Lieutenant. Willie's 'Memories' had already been exhibited elsewhere and was obviously highly thought of by the artist, as it was priced at £15; the second work, 'Wild Flowers', was more modestly priced. In early August of 1911 Willie exhibited his 'Mater Dolorosa' in the Rink Building beside the Rotunda at the Oireachtas exhibition, where the Irish Art Companions also exhibited. In another example of the overlap between the Gaelic League and the wider cultural scene in Dublin, many of the same artists exhibited at the annual RHA exhibitions and the Oireachtas Arts and Crafts exhibitions. Dermod O'Brien, an artist and close relative of the famous nationalist leader William Smith O'Brien, was president of the RHA from 1910 while also sitting on the Oireachtas Art Committee. As arguments about Home Rule rumbled on, divergence grew in the general contexts for the two exhibitions. The Oireachtas literary and performance competitions, held concurrently with the art exhibitions, emphasised radical Irish nationalist history: newspaper accounts of the more prestigious RHA exhibitions still featured detailed descriptions of ladies' dresses. Even young girls, it seems, were caught between two worlds. On 10 August 1911 Mabel asked Willie in a letter, 'Did you see the King?'[2] Unfortunately, we do not have Willie's answer. That same day the House of Lords, under pressure from King George, passed the Parliament Act – which removed their own veto – by a narrow majority. From then on, they could only delay bills for up to two years. With the removal of this major obstacle, Home Rule, it seemed, was just around the corner. For the unionists in northeast Ireland, this meant crisis. Following an invitation from leading northern unionist James Craig, Edward Carson addressed a huge anti-Home Rule rally at Craig's estate outside Belfast in September 1911. Carson now became a major figure in mobilising Ulster resistance to Home Rule.

Although Willie was well liked by pupils at St Enda's and St Ita's, it seems that discipline was sometimes an issue – even with Mabel. A group of pupils, including Mabel, wrote a letter on 14 November 1911 apologising for their conduct in his combined history and geography class and promising not to cause any more trouble. The day after the letter of apology, Mabel wrote to Willie saying she couldn't meet him after school as 'Muriel [a fellow pupil] would wonder'.[3] It seems that Mabel was still modelling for Willie, as the letter then alludes to meeting him in the studio. Though the existing correspondence from Mabel suggests that the friendship between the young girl and the artist was an important one, these later letters show a certain lack of interest in modelling on Mabel's part. But without Willie's letters, it is hard to evaluate the reasons for the sustained friendship or what appears to be its gradual fading.

Speaking at the opening of the newly expanded gallery of the Irish Art Companions on Clare Street on 18 November 1911, Douglas Hyde, President of the Gaelic League, noted that 'a great change was coming over Ireland'.[4] As the Home Rule Bill was debated, and perhaps as a natural result of the Sinn Féin Aonach's interest in economic development, the political aspect to the emphasis on Irish goods became more prominent. In 1910 Alderman Thomas Kelly, secretary of the Aonach committee, had lamented in an opening speech that 'because Sinn Féin inaugurated these Aonaigh, certain people would not support them, believing erroneously that Sinn Féin was a political movement, which it never was and never would be'.[5] Alderman Kelly was a little naïve in his understanding of what could be perceived as being 'political'. The Emmet Choir, the most prominent of the musical acts which provided entertainment at the Aonaigh, would end up practising in the same building that hosted radical labour activist James Larkin's union as well as various Fianna meetings (Liberty Hall, home of the union from 1912). Most of the choir's singers were advanced nationalists, with many in the IRB, and this radicalism surfaced in some of the repertoire performed at the Aonaigh.[6] Meanwhile, in a nod to contemporary politics, an exhibitor at the 1911 Aonach, Boland's, named one of their flours 'Home Rule'. Ex-IPP MP Charles Dolan, now aligned with Sinn Féin, cited the development of Irish industries in the specific context of Home Rule in a speech discussing economic development at that same event. Many artists were now displaying an increased interest in national affairs. Among Willie's fellow exhibitors at one particular Aonach (the catalogue is undated) were Jack Morrow, Sadhbh Trinseach and Grace Gifford, all of whom were confirmed nationalists, and Jack B Yeats, who showed, among other items, a picture of Sarsfield. And while members of Inghinidhe na hÉireann might have been selling crochet at the 1911 Aonach, they were known radicals, as were the Fianna, who also attended. The Rotunda was also the venue for the Oireachtas, and from 1911 those attending both Aonach and Oireachtas had to pass by the Saint-Gaudens statue of Parnell. The statue had been unveiled by John Redmond at the beginning of October, and a motto underneath reproduced Parnell's famous claim that 'No man has a right to fix the boundary to the march of a nation' (although Redmond himself had pulled back somewhat from such sentiments and his vision for Home Rule was one of federation, rather than separation).

The Leinster Stage Society was still active and Willie, Mary Brigid and Alf had a busy Christmas in 1911. Unlike the Emmet Choir, the Stage Society's repertoire always leaned more towards entertainment than politics. On St Stephen's Day 1911, the Society performed four plays in the Abbey Theatre, including two light-hearted pieces by Mary Brigid and Alf. According to the *Irish Independent* critic, Willie 'displayed considerable ability'.[7] The staging of the first play in particular, James Cousins's short tragedy *The Racing Lug*, was judged 'highly creditable'. Frank Walker and Willie were among the actors, with Willie reprising his role as a kindly young Presbyterian minister. These December productions were a relative success, and a gratifying review in *The Irish Times* hailed the Leinster Stage Society as a 'valuable adjunct of the modern Irish dramatic movement'.[8]

On 5 February 1912, to celebrate the centenary of Charles Dickens's birthday, the Society staged plays adapted from his works, including 'The Baron of Grogzwig', adapted from *Nicholas Nickleby,* and 'The Cricket on the Hearth'. Along with Shakespeare, Dickens was a particular love of Willie's. Desmond Ryan recalled that 'nothing delighted him so much in all the volumes of that writer than David Copperfield slapping Uriah Heep in the face'.[9] Despite his modest school results, Willie seems to have possessed a genuine love of literature, and he shared with Patrick an interest in modern playwrights such as Ibsen and the works of Russian novelists.

Willie was still involved with the Irish Art Companions, who sold a nude figure on his behalf to a client in February 1912.[10] The following month his sculptural work 'Eileen, a study' was displayed at the RHA exhibition. The sculpture section in general was slated by *The Irish Times* as being 'very poor indeed'.[11] Among the paintings shown by the president of the Academy, Dermod O'Brien, at that same exhibition was a portrait of the Lord Lieutenant with 'his right arm resting on the jewelled hilt of his state sword'.[12] While Willie's energies were increasingly drawn towards teaching, his old friend Albert Power was continuing to gain recognition as an important artist and had become an associate of the RHA in 1911. Willie, it seems, was not the jealous type, and during 1912 he helped Power to build a studio behind his new home at Number 18 Geraldine Street in Phibsboro, Power having supported Willie with St Enda's productions in the previous years.

In early March, Willie finalised the Leinster Stage Society's arrangements for a touring production in Cork. This time Willie was accompanied by Mary Brigid, Desmond Ryan, Máire Hughes, and Patricia 'Gypsy' Walker, Máire Nic Shiubhlaigh's younger sister. Mrs Pearse also travelled, as did James Crawford Neil, a Presbyterian poet and later the fiancé of Gypsy. But the society's programme of plays attracted only small audiences. The venue chosen, the Opera House, proved very costly, and the people of Cork were hard to please. Ryan recalled the doorkeeper's chiding: 'It's all over the town that your show is a rotten show. The whole town knows it's a rotten show, man. You have to be very careful what you bring down here from Dublin or anywhere else.'[13] One newspaper reported that the prompter's voice was louder than those of the players and that a vendor for the *Evening Echo* had refused a free pass. However, sympathetic local activists and literati turned up to support the performances, including Con O'Leary, Terence MacSwiney, and Daniel Corkery, whose play *The Hermit and the King* had recently been performed in Dublin by the Society. These three had founded the Cork Dramatic Society in 1908, and they showed the visiting Dublin players some of the local sights and social diversions. The Society and their Corkonion hosts had much in common, as the Gaelic League loomed large in the lives of both Leesiders and Dubliners; MacSwiney was heavily involved in the Celtic Literary Society and both he and Corkery were playwrights. There was also a political edge to the company: MacSwiney had been an early contributor to *Irish Freedom* and was attending meetings of old Fenians, while Corkery was also a confirmed nationalist. But notwithstanding the amenable company, the tour was unprofitable and ended in some ignominy as Patrick had to be contacted to send money to pay the Society's bills and their way home. A message sent to Margaret by a distraught Mrs Pearse attests to the financial pressure the family was under at this time, as well as the extent of Willie's disappointment:

> Poor Willy is to be pitied. I feel for him and he doing everything for the best and after all his hard work ... Poor poor Pat how I feel for him and he so good to us Willy is in a state about him ...[14]

This is not to imply, however, that Willie was financially dependent on Patrick. Even after the dissolving of the family business, his studentship at the School of Art, which he held from 1910 to 1912, would have given him an allowance of 21 shillings a week during term time, and he had his own bank account. But none of the Pearses pursued money for its own sake, and it has been stated that Willie, like his brother and mother, drew only a partial amount of the salary due to him at St Enda's.[15]

That spring the merits of the planned Home Rule Bill were debated in the House of Commons, in the newspapers and in the many political clubs and gatherings now operating across Ireland and among the diaspora. On 12 April Prime Minister Asquith introduced the Third Home Rule Bill in the House of Commons. Patrick's belief that the proposed bill did not encompass a sufficient measure of independence was articulated in various articles in *An Barr Buadh*, a radical newspaper that he published from March until May. In a series of spoof letters printed in the paper, he suggested that nationalist leaders like John Redmond and John Dillon had lost their nerve and that the attainment of meaningful freedom lay in the hands of a younger generation. But while the Home Rule bill was being debated by the House of Commons in 1912, Unionists in Ulster were determined to show that they meant business, and in September nearly half a million loyalists signed a covenant pledging to resist Home Rule by any means, including force, if necessary. Small militias had been springing up across the northeast in this time, and these would be subsumed into the Ulster Volunteer Force in early 1913. Although the Government of Ireland bill was passed by the Commons in late 1912, it was rejected by the Lords, which meant that Home Rule would become a reality in late 1914. In ascertaining Willie's evolving views on Home Rule, it is worth noting that Desmond Ryan and Máire Nic Shiubhlaigh both assert that Willie and Patrick agreed about everything. The most salient difference between the brothers lay in the nature of Willie's involvement in art and theatre. Patrick's commitment first to the Gaelic Revival, then to education, and to the advancement of the nationalist cause, meant that he had less time for the enjoyment of art and culture – and other people's company – for its own sake.

Undaunted, though maybe a little chastened, by the Leinster Stage Society's ill-fated solo venture, Willie made overtures to the Ulster Literary Society on 30 May 1912, suggesting that they come to Dublin to share the Abbey for a week. He already had connections with the Ulster dramatists through Bulmer Hobson, James Cousins and the Morrows. His modesty and circumspection were evident in a surviving draft letter, but there was also a palpable sense of his pride in the Leinster Stage Society: 'We have done fairly good things here and we hope to do better. But we are a bit afraid just yet.'[16] It seems nothing came of the invite. Despite the various positive notices Willie's acting received in the press, Máire Nic Shiubhlaigh believed he 'was never terribly successful as a actor'.[17] Not everyone agreed with her opinion, however. At one stage, it appears that Willie had been asked to join the Bensons' repertory group. Frank Benson was a famous Shakespearean actor, and it is possible that it was performances in Dublin by the group during their childhood that had first ignited Patrick and Willie's interest in Shakespeare. David Sears stated that Willie knew Frank Benson well and greatly admired him.[18]

During these years, Willie was always well dressed, sporting a pocket watch in some photographs, personable and yet unpresumptuous, an artist and an actor who appears to have been unsure of his own talent. His gentle nature was later frequently remarked upon, as was his shyness; some even went so far as to say he was withdrawn. For St Enda's student Kenneth Reddin, Willie had 'the utter gentleness of a St Francis'.[19]

According to Nic Shiubhlaigh, Willie was 'a slight figure in
the fitted suits and poets' cravats he favoured' but he had 'high
cheeks and dark gentle eyes' and 'was rather better looking
than the other [Patrick], not so powerfully built but with a
little more height which his slimness accentuated'.[20] Geraldine Plunkett, the sister of Joseph, used to see Willie in the
National Library and loved to 'watch his quiet face and beautiful hands'.[21] Though Willie's shyness was often remarked
upon, it seems that closer acquaintance revealed a multifac-
eted personality, a man who was sociable and engaging:

> In conversation William Pearse had an interesting and con-
> fidential manner. He spoke generally of books, very often
> of politics, while his criticisms of bumptious and snobbish
> persons were a joy to hear. He had a great reverence for
> women, and trusted them more than men. His religious
> convictions were very deep and earnest.[22]

In late May 1912, a notice in *Irish Freedom* showed that
Willie was on the All Purposes subcommittee of the Wolfe
Tone and United Irishmen Memorial Committee. He was
presumably chosen and certainly approved by Tom Clarke
and Seán MacDiarmada, who were using the organisation
as a front for the IRB. Clarke, president of the executive
committee, stated in the notice that 'the standing and ability
of every member of the subcommittee is a guarantee that
the work entrusted to them will be effectively attended to',

a considerable public declaration of faith in Willie and his fellow subcommittee members.[23] Willie's colleagues also formed a 'who's who' of militant nationalism, including Seán MacDiarmada, Bulmer Hobson, Patrick McCartan and Major John MacBride. His fellow artist Jack Morrow was also on the subcommittee; Morrow and Hobson were long acquainted through the former's involvement in Hobson's Dungannon Clubs, which, as we have seen, had been absorbed into Sinn Féin. Morrow was also a close friend of Seán MacDiarmada's and indeed lived only three doors away from the *Irish Freedom* offices in D'Olier Street. Clarke's confidence was not misplaced. The Wolfe Tone and United Irishmen Memorial Committee was the driving force behind the annual 'pilgrimages' to commemorate Wolfe Tone at Bodenstown and succeeded in attracting a wide spectrum of political and civic bodies, as well as representatives from the worlds of music and culture, to the many other concerts and parades they organised. These included commemorative celebrations of republican heroes like the Manchester Martyrs and Robert Emmet.

Willie had not shown any particular politicisation in his own art or – as yet – in the theatre work he participated in outside of St Enda's, but the circles he was now associating with included many advanced nationalists. Seán Keating, famous later for his nationalist paintings, was in the School of Art, and the fact that some of the Keating family stayed at

Cullenswood suggests that he and Willie formed a bond.[24] Willie also submitted a design, which failed to win, for the competition for the Wolfe Tone monument. Perhaps Willie's proven track record in organising and publicising various events, in particular for the Students' Union, was the reason for his presence on the committee; perhaps he provided an acceptable public face for networking, as the tact and social skills attributed to Willie by David Sears and Desmond Ryan would have been valuable assets.

While Willie's co-option onto the subcommittee might appear a big step for a man hitherto not noted for his political views, it is not necessarily surprising. It is harder to ascertain Willie's political opinions at this time as, unlike his prolific brother, he did not leave written sources charting their development. But whatever the reason, Willie was now participating on a committee run by the most advanced (and militant) nationalists in Ireland at this time, and the events which this committee planned would have a profound influence on the intensification of nationalist sentiment in the years ahead. The Fianna invariably acted as stewards at the events organised under the auspices of the Wolfe Tone Memorial Committee, which meant a military aspect was now being introduced to public events that in other respects might seem innocuous or sentimental. This radicalisation extended to St Enda's; during 1912, Con Colbert of the Fianna (and the Wolfe Tone Memorial

Committee) brought some of the older students and ex-students into the newly reorganised IRB.[25]

Meanwhile, the latest St Enda's play, *An Rí,* penned once again by Patrick, considered the glory or horror of war. Though the subject matter was serious, the setting for the play's production was genteel: staged outdoors in the grounds of the Hermitage by an arch close to the banks of the river, it was the main attraction of a garden party held at St Enda's on 15 June 1912. Photographs show that costumes and props were carefully designed, as before, but the impact of the costumed warriors might have had an extra edge this time, given that many of the St Enda's boys were by now members of the Fianna (and even, in some cases, the IRB).

Willie was also, of course, busy with his teaching duties at St Enda's. Desmond Ryan, writing home to his father, the journalist WP Ryan, mentioned an 'éirí amach beag' (a small uprising) in which the boys had a 'grievance' against Willie and caused a scene on the evening that Patrick gave his lecture on 'Some Aspects of Gaelic Literature' in December 1912. Despite such occasional episodes, the students were very fond of Willie and their familiarity with him is evident from a humorous piece of doggerel published in *An Scoláire,* a pupils' magazine, in the spring of 1913:

> William Pearse's locks are long,
> His trousers short and lanky,
> When in the study hall he stands

He does look very cranky.

… he claps his hands and lets a cry

But all the claps and all the crys

Have no effect on the bad boys.[26]

While describing Willie's positive outlook, David Sears also detailed what he saw as Willie's relative naivety:

[He had] a tolerably keen insight into the characters of the boys, except that he was inclined to see only their good points. In fact the small-mindedness of the world escaped him. A noble mind cannot understand a knave. This fact led to our feeling for him a kind of protective interest. We fancied that we understood the seamy side of life much better than he. Possibly we did.[27]

Despite his membership of the IRB-controlled Wolfe Tone subcommittee, Willie still had connections to the artistic scene which enjoyed the patronage of Countess Aberdeen and her husband, the Lord Lieutenant. However, in the charged atmosphere of the time, the broad alliance of political opinion that had supported the development of Irish art was splintering. Countess Aberdeen, who had long supported indigenous crafts to the extent of signing her name in Irish on a visit to the Cuala Industries, was now accused of bringing in imported labour to build a sanitorium she championed in Peamount. Her defence, which cited her long interest in Irish industries, was dismissed as a 'nonsensical rhapsody' by

Irish Freedom.[28] Shortly before the publication of the piece mocking Lady Aberdeen, the annual exhibition of the RHA, opened by the Lord Lieutenant, began. Willie, who according to the satirical poem quoted above maintained a studio in the gymnasium at St Enda's even after the closure of the family business, exhibited 'An Old Sinner'. A few days after the opening, the Emmet Anniversary Concert, organised under the auspices of the Wolfe Tone Committee, was held in the Mansion House. As one event acknowledged and affirmed the position of British government in Ireland, and the other was run by and celebrated an organisation bent on ending British governance of Ireland by military action, it was clear that Willie would eventually have to take sides.

Patrick, distracted by his immersion in the short-lived *An Barr Buadh* and radical politics, had allowed the financial situation at the school to get out of hand. St Ita's had to be closed and Patrick's allegorical political drama, *An Rí*, was staged at the Abbey as a fundraiser for St Enda's. Rehearsals were soon underway for the reprisal of the play, which was very well received when it was staged in the Abbey on 17 May 1913 along with the Indian writer Rabindranath Tagore's *The Post Office*. This fundraising production was facilitated by WB Yeats. Willie played the wise old abbot and spoke lines that would soon find echoes in his real life:

Fanann gach seanóir leis an mbás agus téann gach orgánach
ina choinne ... An dóigh leat dá labhródh an glór álainn

uafásach úd lena mbíonn na hógánaigh ag síorfhanúint agus cluas le héisteacht orthu, é do labhairt anois san ionad úd mar a bhfuil an lucht cathaithe agus na heachraí agus an ceol, go gcoinneoinn sibh dá n-éireodh sibh chum a fhreagartha?

['The old wait for death but the young go to meet it … Do you think if that terrible beautiful voice for which young men strain their ears were to speak from yon place where the fighters are, and the horses and the music, that I would stay did ye rise to obey it?']²⁹

In late May of 1913 Patrick wrote a series of articles for *Irish Freedom* 'with the deliberate intention, by argument, invective, and satire, of goading those who shared my political views to commit themselves definitely to an armed movement'.³⁰ Desmond Ryan's correspondence to his father during these years features anecdotes whose tone and thrust are in marked contrast to the hagiographical slant evident in his later pen pictures of Patrick and Willie. Though he admired both Pearse brothers, Ryan saw himself as a more advanced nationalist than either of them. He recounted their political progress with impatience and an almost paternalistic interest.³¹ But the radicalisation of the Pearse brothers was ongoing. Ryan also mentioned their growing sympathies with the labour leader Jim Larkin, whose sons were now among Willie's pupils. It was unsurprising that the Pearse brothers would feel a natural empathy for Larkin, although neither they, nor their father, were socialists. As the sons of an artisan, Willie and Patrick would have had a natural affinity with workers. After all, the Pearse firm family stationery had carried the motto chosen by father James: *Labor Omnia Vincit* (Labour Conquers All).

The threads binding theatre and politics were becoming increasingly interwoven. A week-long festival at Jones's Road (Croke Park) was planned for the week of 9–14 June 1913 in order to raise funds for St Enda's. In April, Bulmer Hobson had presided over a meeting of the organising committee for the fête, while Jack Morrow reported on lighting and choreography. Jim Larkin printed twenty thousand handbills at his own cost, while Sean O'Casey, himself involved with Larkin and the labour movement as well as the IRB, wrote a letter to *The Irish Worker* urging readers to attend. The festival was publicised on the front page of *Irish Freedom*. On 26 May, Willie wrote to Éamonn Ceannt to check that he had organised pipers. Ceannt did not disappoint: three piping bands were listed on the programme.[32]

Three pageants were performed during the week's programme. The most important of these, *The Defence of the Ford*, was performed late in the evening on Monday, Wednesday and Saturday, alternating with another pageant entitled *The Fianna of Fionn*, and *An Rí*. The festival programme credited Patrick with the arrangement and Willie with the production of the pageants. *The Defence of the Ford* was based, like *Macghníomhartha*, on an episode from the Ulster Cycle, and its topical theme was the re-invigoration of the fighting spirit of the men of the North. Interestingly, the programme credited 'Captain Colbert, of the Fianna Éireann' with the 'military movements' in that same pageant.[33] This was one of the first public displays by the Fianna. The melding of the imaginative realms of cultural nationalism and the real world of militant nationalism was gaining momentum: outside of Abbey performances, this was also the first time that the general public, as opposed to invitees, had attended St Enda's pageants. Advanced nationalist ideas, whether cloaked as literature, song or drama, blurred the lines between sentiment and reality also in *The Fianna of Fionn*, the second new pageant of the week, performed on Tuesday and Thursday evenings at 10pm, presumably to ensure the dramatic effect of its centrepiece, a torch-lit parade. The programme description reveals the painterly and ritualistic nature of the production. The final tableau, depicting 'the triumph of the sword drawn at the bidding of the poets' is of particular note:[34]

> This pageant does not tell any story but is in the nature of a rhythmical march symbolising the activities of the ancient Fianna. Fianna parade armed with sword and spear. A Hunter enters bearing a slain deer, and a tableau is formed symbolic of the chase. A Smith enters and a sword is forged, the Fianna singing the Song of the Sword. A Warrior enters and a tableau is formed, symbolic of an ancient battle. A

Harper enters, and the pageant concludes with a tableau representing the triumph of the sword drawn at the bidding of the poets.[35]

While the programme summary of the tableau's meaning was probably written by Patrick, Willie, as producer, had creative input. The marshalling of costumed youth in militaristic movements and the playing of 'gay and stirring tunes'[36] was clearly designed to mobilise as well as entertain. A powerful dynamic which had been developing for several years was now crystallising, and through his organisational role on the Wolfe Tone subcommittee and as choreographer of the St Enda's plays, Willie was just as much part of this process as his brother Patrick. Where Patrick explained and composed, Willie organised and showed. The artistic merit to Willie's choreography was again noted; though inclement weather affected attendance on some evenings, the Jones's Road pageants were visually memorable. Joseph Holloway heard that 'by all accounts' the pageants made 'a delightful spectacle as the shades of night close in and the torches of the marching armies flare ...'[37]

The ambitious scale of the week-long fête tells us much about the co-operative nature and evolving politics of the cultural-nationalist milieu in Dublin at this time. *The Defence of the Ford* involved over 150 performers and crew members, including fifty St Enda's students. The programme lists twenty-nine different groups and individuals who had 'offered their services' for the concerts that took place alongside the pageants. The volunteers included members of numerous bands, piping groups, choirs and dancing groups, from the National Foresters Band to the Father Mathew Choir, from traditional singers to Gaelic Glee singers and tenors and baritones. Willie would have built up valuable contacts through his work with the Wolfe Tone Committee. Indeed there was some crossover between those who volunteered to perform at the June fête and several groups that were mentioned in that same month's issue of *Irish Freedom* as being involved in collections for the Memorial Fund for the Wolfe Tone Committee: the Foresters Band and the O'Toole Pipers (who often frequented the same events as the Fianna) were listed for both, as were the republican-leaning Emmet Choir.[38] On 22 June Patrick gave the oration at the Wolfe Tone commemoration at Bodenstown. The fundraising for St Enda's continued beyond the festival, and at the end of June a programme of plays performed for three days in the Hardwicke Street Theatre included one performance in aid of the school, which Joseph Holloway's diary entry notes Willie as having attended.

Willie's continued input into the work of the Wolfe Tone Committee seems to have been appreciated. In July 1913 he was again noted in an article in *Irish Freedom* as being on the subcommittee, now renamed the 'General Purposes Committee', along with Thomas Clarke, Patrick McCartan, Arthur Griffith, James Deakin, Seán MacDiarmada and others.[39]

Albert Power now joined the committee. Another of Willie's network involved with the Wolfe Tone Committee in these years was Kitty Gibbons, the sister of his old friend Fr Gibbons. Given Willie's long acquaintance with Morrow, Patrick's now overtly stated support for an armed nationalist movement, and subsequent events, it seems unlikely that Willie was unaware of the purpose of those who held the power on the committee. Later that summer he attended the 1913 Oireachtas of the Gaelic League, which was held in Galway from 27 July to 2 August. The Oireachtas attracted many prominent members of Irish cultural and nationalist groups, and Douglas Hyde's attempts to keep the League apolitical were not reflected in the attendance. A group photograph taken during the proceedings shows Patrick and Willie alongside Éamonn Ceannt, Seán MacDiarmada, Bulmer Hobson, Cathal Brugha, Countess Markievicz, Seán T O'Kelly, The O'Rahilly and many others.[40]

September brought a return to teaching duties, and Willie was now a full-time member of staff at St Enda's. That same month saw the beginning of the real-life drama of the Lockout, the struggle which placed striking union members against a powerful group of employers headed by William Martin Murphy. The conflict was bitter and often violent. On 8 September, *The Irish Times* published Yeats's 'Romance in Ireland' (known later as 'September 1913'). This poem had the refusal of the city corporation to fund a municipal art gallery as its immediate context, but it also evoked the contrast that Yeats detected between the narrow monetary focus of contemporary society and the selfless sacrifice of republican heroes. Though 'Romance in Ireland' famously declared that 'Romantic Ireland is dead and gone/It's with O'Leary in the grave', the repetition of the poem's dynamic chorus suggested that the dead Fenian, along with Emmet, Wolfe Tone and Lord Edward FitzGerald, still had important witness to bear. Willie was now working closely with some of those seeking the logical conclusion of that witness: the achievement of Irish independence through military means.

Chapter Seven

1913-1914

The Irish Volunteers

The Home Rule Bill had – predictably – been rejected by the House of Lords. However, without their veto, they could only delay the inevitable, and Home Rule was set to become law in late 1914. During the hiatus, the extent of unionist opposition in Ulster slowly became clear to leading Westminster figures like British prime minister Herbert Henry Asquith and John Redmond. Adamant they would not fall under the legislature of a Dublin parliament, the Ulster unionists had formed a militia, the Ulster Volunteers, in early 1913, which led some to believe that the time was ripe for organising a force that would defend the interests of nationalism. The impatient parties included some of Willie's associates in the Wolfe Tone and United Irishmen Memorial Committee, in particular the IRB men Clarke, MacDiarmada and Hobson. A few astute commentators, including Standish O'Grady and Willie's brother Patrick, had long before predicted the emergence of a military movement from the cultural one.[1] Following a meeting in July 1913 of the Dublin Centres Board, which represented the individuals who ran the local units of the IRB, drilling of IRB members in Dublin began, with members of the Fianna operating as drill instructors. But the real impetus was an article by Gaelic League co-founder, Antrim-born Eoin MacNeill. 'The North Began' was published on the front page of *An Claidheamh Soluis* on 1 November; it noted the momentum created by the arming of the Ulster Volunteers in April and advocated an armed force for nationalists. Observing that a precedent had been set, MacNeill wrote:

> It appears that the British Army cannot now be used to prevent the enrolment, drilling, and reviewing of Volunteers in Ireland. There is nothing to prevent the other twenty-eight counties [outside Ulster] from calling into existence citizen forces to hold Ireland 'for the Empire'.[2]

The advanced nationalists sensed an opportunity. Wary as ever of creating a movement which would be labelled extremist and therefore suppressed, they now sought to involve MacNeill as the head (or, in their view, figurehead) of a new Volunteer force, ostensibly created to defend Home Rule but in reality controlled by the IRB. MacNeill, an esteemed scholar, was a trusted public figure, and he was approached by Bulmer Hobson and *An Claidheamh Soluis*'s editor, Michael ('The') O'Rahilly (the latter also a contributor to *Irish Freedom*). Though not yet a member of the IRB, Patrick Pearse was one of those invited to a meeting chaired by MacNeill in Wynn's Hotel that same November, to plan for this new Volunteer force. Writing in *Irish Freedom*, Patrick stated that 'the Orangeman with a rifle [was] a much less ridiculous figure than the Nationalist without a rifle'.[3] After further meetings, membership of a Provisional Committee was finalised and included Patrick, Bulmer Hobson, The O'Rahilly, Eoin MacNeill, Seán MacDiarmada, Éamonn Ceannt, Thomas MacDonagh, Joseph Plunkett and Roger Casement, as well as representatives from the Fianna and from the Ancient Order of Hibernians, a Catholic nationalist organisation that had strong connections to the IPP. While the committee sought to portray itself as widely representative, in reality it was under the control of physical-force advocates. MacNeill, though not aligned to any party, was a friend of many of those on the committee, as nearly all of them were active in the Gaelic League. A giant public meeting was organised for the Rotunda on 25 November to launch what would be called the Irish Volunteers, with MacNeill and Patrick among the speakers. Interest was such that the Rotunda could not contain the crowds. Thousands signed up for membership of the new body, which enjoyed broad support from a wide cross-section of nationalists. Unlike Willie, many of those who joined would have been unaware of the more advanced views of its committee members (especially as few at this time knew of the IRB's involvement). Meanwhile, Carson and the Unionists were now insisting that Ulster – or a part of it yet to be defined – would be excluded from the jurisdiction of a Home Rule parliament in Dublin. The idea of a temporary or partial exclusion of Ulster was also being mooted by a minority element within Asquith's cabinet.

Two days before the huge gathering at the Rotunda, the Wolfe Tone Committee had organised a Manchester Martyrs anniversary procession to Glasnevin. As a member of the sub-committee, Willie can reasonably be presumed to have been involved. The new impetus behind nationalist agitation was evident as 'the celebration was the largest and most representative in the city for many years past'.[4] As a scene-setting exercise for the dramatic Rotunda meeting, the timing of the procession was well chosen, and, of course, members of the IRB were masterminding both events. A report in *Irish Freedom* gives an impressive roll-call of participants, including James Larkin's Irish Transport and General Workers' Union, the GAA, Sinn Féin, the Inghinidhe, Na Fianna Éireann, the Irish Women's Franchise League and 'members of public bodies'.[5] The procession, like all those organised by the Wolfe Tone Committee, had a powerful performative and symbolic impact as the various nationalist organisations took ownership of the streets. An estimated twelve to fifteen thousand marched, while the Fianna carried swords and pulled an ammunition wagon. The procession provided a striking visual and aural display of independent local civic governance for the thousands of spectators: numerous bands played stirring national airs, flags and banners proclaimed the identity and aims of the various participating organisations, and the Lord Mayor took part, attended by a costumed guard of honour. The marshalling of the procession was left to the Wolfe Tone Committee, as the police were reduced to the role of passive spectators.[6] The coalition of cultural, sporting and political bodies represented was indicative of the committee's aim – and ability – to attract wide support. The dramatic impact of such demonstrations reflected the input of the many artists and theatre practitioners involved in nationalism at this time: the General Purposes Committee itself included, of course, Willie, Jack Morrow and Albert Power. The committee's awareness of the power of propaganda even extended to the procession being filmed for cinema presentation.

The emotional draw of the procession, followed by the meeting at the Rotunda, helped to ensure the Irish Volunteers were soon a mass movement. Willie Pearse was among the scores of thousands who joined, and this 'brought a new purpose and enthusiasm into his life'.[7] Given that he was an esteemed member of the organisation that had used a carefully choreographed procession to stoke nationalist feeling two days before the enlistment meeting, it would be incorrect to suggest that Willie was drawn to the Volunteers under any undue influence from Patrick, or that he was somehow an *ingénue* caught up in the general excitement. Through his connections with the Wolfe Tone Committee, Willie had found his own path to the Volunteers, one which, in tandem with the work of his fellow subcommittee members, had an equal (if not greater) impact at the time than the speeches and articles now being written by Patrick and others. Driven as it was by theatrics and performance, this new departure in the militarisation of Irish nationalism would have been familiar to Willie and his circle. In his work on the St Enda's plays and pageants, he was long used to creating rousing atmospheres through the use of image, movement and music, especially with pipers. At the huge enlistment gathering at the Rotunda (itself the scene of many Oireachtas exhibitions), the throngs listened to speeches from various stages. Cecil Salkeld, the young son of Willie's fellow actor Blánaid Salkeld, recalled it as a festive occasion in which a serious political message was imparted alongside amusements for children in 'an atmosphere of great hilarity'.[8]

But despite the theatrics, the Volunteers were a serious organisation. Willie was initially part of E Company of the 4th Battalion of the Dublin Brigade, to which many ex-pupils of St Enda's were attached, and he 'attended manoeuvres, route marches and parades religiously, and became, from frequent practice, an accurate marksman'.[9] While Patrick was at this point part of a leadership circle of the Volunteer movement, it should not be forgotten that Willie, while also participating as an 'ordinary'Volunteer, was close to the same prominent leadership figures; he knew leading republicans like Tom Clarke, Seán MacDiarmada, and Seán McGarry independently of Patrick. It is not clear when exactly Willie joined the IRB, or whether his enrolment involved bringing an element of formality to an already established role, given his close connections to many of those in the IRB's inner circle. According to one source, Willie and Patrick were in the [James] Fintan Lalor circle of the IRB, as was Seán O'Casey, with Bulmer Hobson as 'secretary'. Another source corroborates the (Patrick) Pearse connection with the Fintan Lalor circle and has Seán MacDiarmada as 'centre'. What is certain is that the circle associated with Patrick and Willie met at 41 Rutland Square, the epicentre of Volunteer activities – and the home of the Wolfe Tone Memorial Committee.[10]

While all this was happening, life at St Enda's continued as normal for Willie, although his work as a sculptor was increasingly sidelined. After showing 'An Old Sinner' at the RHA in early 1913, there is no record of Willie exhibiting in public again. He still had his workshop at St Enda's and, in an interesting aside, David Sears, who lived there as a pupil and later as a university student, recalls Willie destroying a bust of Patrick that he had been working on as he was displeased with his efforts (though Sears thought the bust very good).[11]

The growing emphasis on the republican heroes of the past could also be seen in the subject matter of the St Enda's plays. Patrick's next play, *Owen*, was short and simple, a propaganda piece centred on the 1867 Fenian uprising that had more in common with the polemics of *Irish Freedom* than the artistic *tableaux* of the Inghinidhe and the Gaelic League. It was performed, presumably with the usual assistance of Willie, at a *céilí* held by the Five Provinces Branch of the Gaelic League in the Mansion House on 1 December, and also at a *céilí* in the Hall of the Colmcille Branch of the Gaelic League. The Five Provinces Branch, fondly known as the Branch of the Five Protestants, included some deeply politicised artists, such as Willie's School of Art acquaintance Cesca Trench and Neilí Ní Bhriain (a relative of Young Irelander William Smith O'Brien).

The Wolfe Tone Memorial Committee did not just organise processions; there were also lectures, concerts and constant fundraising activity at various nationalist, sporting and cultural events. The concerts often featured mainstream performers, with music ranging from sentimental ballads to rousing piping tunes, and such events were enticing to supporters with moderate political views. Many of these would have seen only the 'public' Willie, the long-haired creative type who moved in artistic social circles; nothing about his modest personality and circumspect behaviour suggested advanced nationalist views. Indeed it is not possible to state categorically how advanced Willie's views were, or if he advocated physical force as a means to achieving Home

Rule or a republic at this stage. Desmond Ryan believed that Willie was deeply interested in politics, however, and both he and Máire Nic Shiubhlaigh asserted that Willie's views were those of his brother Patrick. Patrick was now openly advocating fanning the flame of the 'Fenian spirit' in his 'From a Hermitage' column in January 1914's edition of *Irish Freedom*; Willie's presence on the Wolfe Tone Committee was a *de facto* espousal of the same sentiments.

During all the political excitement, the financial situation at St Enda's was becoming critical. The school's creditors were losing patience, and after Christmas, Patrick took action. In early February 1914 he embarked on a fundraising tour of America while Willie remained as acting headmaster. On the whole, it seems that Willie coped well during Patrick's absence, though Desmond Ryan, writing to his father, thought that Willie was getting thin while Patrick was away. Patrick wrote home to Willie regarding the pupils' progress and with detailed instructions on the school finances. Willie's letters to Patrick are upbeat and encouraging, his resilience under pressure evident in his sense of humour. In her biography of Patrick, Ruth Dudley Edwards has rightly noted the contrast between Willie's effusive letters and 'Patrick's barren messages home'. Quoting from one of Willie's letters to his brother in America ('I read your letter for Mother. She was delighted, nearly broke her neck running when she heard it came') she describes how 'in one artless sentence' Willie 'could conjure up the family's devotion to Patrick'.[12] While Willie was not a wordsmith, his letters show his innate good manners and generosity of spirit. In addition to the financial pressures and his many responsibilities, Willie's former child model, Mabel Gorman, of whom he was very fond, was dying of consumption (although it is unclear what contact, if any, Willie had with Mabel at this stage). Despite his workload, however, Willie did manage to have a few short days' break in Warrenpoint in County Down with his mother over Easter. They were obviously close, to the extent that one young boy who delivered milk to Willie in the Great Brunswick Street period formed the opinion that the long-haired young man who greeted him politely was a 'Mammy's boy'.[13]

During Patrick's absence there were some key political developments as matters reached a head for Ulster unionists. They wanted permanent exclusion from Home Rule; Redmond and the IPP would only concede a temporary opt-out. As rumours of possible civil war circulated, a group of British army officers based at the Curragh army base got wind of contingency plans to deploy British troops in a possible confrontation with unionists. Twenty resigned, citing their unwillingness to be deployed against a political group with whom they were in broad agreement. The UVF now made a bold move: on 24–25 April, they landed 25,000 rifles at Larne in County Antrim. The authorities, according to a breathless report in *The Belfast Telegraph* on 25 April, 'might as well have been in Timbuctoo'.[14] The audacious gun-running had gone unchallenged, and despite Redmond's opposition to any part of Ireland being left out of a Home Rule settlement, he was now keenly aware that the long-anticipated enactment of the Home Rule Bill might involve facing up to an armed unionist militia – or compromise.

On 10 May, Captain Frank Fahy, one of the founders of the Volunteers, came to St Enda's along with Countess Markievicz, and a new group of the Fianna was organised among the students (the earlier Fianna groups had apparently faded). By now various *sluaite* or companies of the Fianna were a familiar sight at the Hermitage, calling in during their regular marches in the area and bathing in the river or camping in the grounds. While Eamon Bulfin and Desmond Ryan may have spearheaded the Fianna revival, Willie was acting headmaster and there is no reason to believe he was not of one mind with his activist students: he had, after all, served on a subcommittee of the Wolfe Tone Memorial Committee with Con Colbert, a leading member of both the Fianna and the IRB. By now Colbert was a familiar presence at St Enda's, where he drilled students. A week after Captain Fahy's visit, on 18 May 1914, Mabel Gorman died at the age of sixteen, but there was little time for Willie to grieve as his brother returned on 25 May. Patrick received a tumultuous welcome from the students, some of whom were standing on the roof as Willie ceded leadership once more to his charismatic brother.

Less than three weeks after Patrick's return, on Saturday 13 June, yet another pageant, *Fionn: A Dramatic Spectacle,* was performed at St Enda's. Another outdoor production featuring heroes from Gaelic literature, it told the tale of how Fionn came to be leader of the Fianna, the mythical band of warriors that gave Na Fianna Éireann their name. The pageant was the main event in a programme designed to showcase the school's activities and achievements. Photographs and accounts of social events at St Enda's show that occasions like this served various purposes: ladies attired in long dresses and fashionable hats sipped tea while key figures in politics and culture networked. There were displays by the Fianna and, later on, the Volunteers; the genteel refreshments and varied entertainments served to take the edge off the military aspect. Douglas Hyde, still an ally despite reservations about the politicisation of the Gaelic League, presented the school prizes. *The Irish Times* recorded the day's events and gives a sense of the atmosphere preceding the performance of the pageant, including the playing of 'pathetic' and 'tragic' Irish airs by the school pipers as afternoon tea was served on the lawn.[15] The official programme has Willie Pearse playing Goll Mac Morna in the pageant, though *The Irish Times* has him playing Conn of the Hundred Battles, with David Sears as Fionn. A photograph shows Willie resplendent in feathered head-dress and warrior's costume but looking rather sombre.[16] He may have been in character.

Some of the former students who had returned for the June 1914 gathering were now established members of the Fianna and the IRB. This was not primarily due to the Pearse brothers' influence, as many came from radical backgrounds: David Sears's father, William, was the editor of *The Irish Volunteer*, the official newspaper of the movement, and had been the subject of British surveillance as early as 1910, as had William Bulfin, the father of ex-pupil Eamon. Among students and alumni of St Enda's who took part were Eunan McGinley, Joseph Sweeney and David Sears, all of whom would be involved in the Rising. In June 1914, however, *The Irish Times* reported the day solely as a social event and did not interest itself either in the radical aspect of the gathering or the impact the 'pathetic' and 'tragic' piping tunes might be having on some of those gathered. One week later the annual Wolfe Tone commemoration took place and, for the first time, the Irish Citizen Army attended. This workers' army (in reality more of a militia) had been instigated by labour leader James Connolly.

The Irish Volunteer movement had become a leading element in the campaign for national self-determination and was too big for John Redmond and the IPP to ignore. In the same month as the St Enda's pageant, Redmond, perhaps under pressure from Asquith, wrested control of the Volunteers by pressurising the existing committee to accept twenty-five of his own nominees, who would form a majority and, of course, vote as Redmond instructed them.

As the school term drew to a close, Willie's mind was again on drama, and on another kind of politics. On 27 June 1914 he attended a staging of Æ's *Deirdre* in the garden of Number 64 Upper Leeson Street, an open-air performance featuring elaborate Celtic costumes. Members of the Reddin family, whose sons were St Enda's boys, 'Mrs Stopford' (presumably Alice Stopford Green, the nationalist historian who would later play a central role in smuggling arms for the Volunteers) and writers Ella Young and Susan Mitchell were also in the audience. This time the beneficiary of the gathering – and the reason for the preponderance of women in the audience – was the Irish Women's Reform League, founded by well-to-do Protestant Dubliner Louie Bennett. Feminist politics, like nationalist politics, often asserted itself in genteel surroundings with a diverse audience: on this occasion the *Irish Times* noted that the Quaker Bewley sisters, as well as Lady Stokes and Lady Cowan, were present.

Willie's social contacts, based in the arts, theatre, and radical politics, brought him into contact with many capable and charismatic women and, though less confident than Patrick, he seems to have been at ease in female company. There is, however, no record of his having a romantic relationship with any particular woman, even though his social life afforded him plenty of eligible company. Mabel Gorman asks after a Miss Cotter in some of her letters, but the lady in question, Mary Cotter, would have been known in any case to both

Mabel and Willie as she was a teacher at St Ita's.[17] In a fascinating throwaway comment, Máire Nic Shiubhlaigh later recalled 'how careful Mary B [Mary Brigid] was of always playing leading parts herself, afraid of anyone making love to [i.e., flirting with] her brother. Dear knows they were very amusing, a peculiar family.'[18] One could speculate that the first part of Nic Shiubhlaigh's comment suggests that Mary Brigid, at the very least, thought Willie could attract female interest. But was Nic Shiubhlaigh amused by Mary Brigid's overprotectiveness or by the notion that his sister considered Willie the target of female attention in the first place? David Sears states that Willie lacked 'the virility of his brother's character' but also, perhaps tellingly, asserts that there was nothing 'weak or unmanly' about his gentleness.[19] Some contemporaries attest to Willie presenting as being relatively innocent in the ways of the world. Willie's sister Margaret felt that Willie shied away from anything suggestive of sin, so the bohemian mores he embraced (working from nude models, for example) may not have extended to a relaxed attitude to sexual relationships. The fact that there is no record of Willie having a romantic relationship does not preclude the possibility that he had one, or that he experienced sexual attractions. What we do know is that Willie was much loved by a wide circle of friends, male and female. Desmond Ryan remembered Willie, like Patrick, as being deeply human and alive to the beauty of the world around him, with an openness to life and people:

In [Patrick's] writings passages frequently occur breathing a tenderness and compassion towards all the outcasts and oppressed of mankind, an austere joy in simple things, in the shapeliness or variety of animals, in the shade vivid or subdued of any plant or flower, a love of beauty and the suggestion of a great sadness. The only thing you will not find is melodrama or sensationalism. In such passages you will discover and know William Pearse.[20]

Chapter Eight

• • • • • • •

1914–1916

'Difficult Things'

On 28 June 1914, Archduke Franz Ferdinand of Austria was shot dead in Sarajevo, triggering a diplomatic crisis that led to the major powers being drawn inexorably towards war by late summer. Against this backdrop, guns were landed for use by the Irish Volunteers at Howth on 26 July. Given that the Larne gun-running was undertaken to defend unionism from a perceived threat to Protestant (and loyalist) identity, it was perhaps ironic that the nationalist gun-running was masterminded mainly by a group of well-off Protestant nationalists, some of whom moved in the circles in which Willie socialised. Among these were Alice Stopford Green and Bulmer Hobson, as well as Mary Spring Rice, a leading Gaelic Leaguer and a cousin of Dermod O'Brien, the artist who exhibited a portrait of the Lord Lieutenant at the RHA exhibition two years previously. Willie's fellow artist Cesca Trench was present as an observer in Howth, but it seems the Pearse brothers were in the West at the time, though Patrick received updates on the event. Attempts by the police to seize the arms were mostly unsuccessful, and that evening, tensions escalated when shots were fired by the military following a confrontation between a hostile crowd of Volunteer sympathisers and the King's Own Scottish Borderers at Bachelors Walk. Three deaths ensued and soldiers were confined to barracks.

From the outset there was anger among nationalists at the differing treatment meted out to them. The Larne gun-running had not been the subject of police or army inter-vention, and armed Ulster Volunteers had been marching openly in Belfast on the day of the Howth gun-running. A few days later, tens of thousands of Dubliners took part in the funeral procession of the Bachelors Walk victims, with many sobbing openly at the scene of the shootings. Crowds cheered the armed Volunteers who marched along-side numerous other groups, including the Lord Mayor, the Fianna, marching bands, trade union representatives, forty priests and sixty Christian brothers.

On Saturday 1 August and in the early hours of Sunday 2 August more arms were landed at Kilcoole, County Wicklow. This time Willie was fully privy to the plans, as members of the Fianna and others were on standby at St Enda's overnight. During the long evening and early hours of the morning, Willie and Patrick gave the Fianna present a talk concern-ing the Hermitage and its former resident, the famous lawyer

and one-time defender of the United Irishmen John Phil-
pot Curran. There was also a semaphore demonstration.[1] As
they waited for news from Kilcoole, Willie took part in an
animated round-table discussion with Patrick and 'barristers,
solicitors, carpenters, doctors, labourers, unemployed etc. etc.
discussing revolution'.[2] When a charabanc (a large open-
topped vehicle) carrying arms broke down on the way from
Kilcoole, cars were sent out and the guns were brought to
St Enda's, from where they were later distributed to those
Volunteers known to be sympathetic to the more militant
nationalists who opposed John Redmond. The Irish Volunteers were now, like their Ulster counterparts, an armed par-
amilitary organisation, and while the IPP leader might have
had a controlling majority on the committee, the IRB had
its own plans for the guns.

Over the course of that same dramatic summer, yet another
theatre group, the Irish Theatre, was founded by playwright
and critic Edward Martyn, playwright and ex-St Enda's
teacher Thomas MacDonagh, and poet Joseph Plunkett (an
important new figure in the IRB at this stage). Given the
Pearses' close connections with all three, it is not surprising
that Willie was soon drawn in. Joseph Carré, a leading sculptor with the Irish Art Companions, was also involved in these
initial stages. After opening performances on Sackville Street,
the Irish Theatre soon made its home in a hall in Hardwicke
Street. The Hardwicke Hall had a history which blurred the

lines between performance and real life (like 41 Rutland Square, a Volunteer drilling hall which was also a concert hall and even a cinema). It had recently been used by the Theatre of Ireland, and members from three Fianna *sluaite* had assembled there on the morning of the Howth gun-running. Though the surroundings were modest, the three directors had an ambitious vision for their new enterprise: they aimed to take the focus of the Irish theatrical movement away from peasant plays and towards works of psychological import, seeing themselves as an alternative to the prestigious Abbey Theatre. In addition to all his other activities, Willie would soon be treading the boards in Hardwicke Street.

In the summer of 1914 the Pearse brothers paid their usual visit to the west of Ireland, but even during their sojourn away from Dublin they continued to engage with the Volunteers. Willie accompanied Patrick to the Irish College in Spiddal, where a company of Volunteers had been started by Mícheál Ó Droighneáin. The visit by the Pearse brothers went along familiar lines. Patrick drilled the company through Irish, and a photograph, which was subsequently lost, of the Volunteers drilling included Willie among the ranks.[3]

In August Britain declared war on Germany, the day after the latter had declared war on France. In early September, Patrick was among a small group of advanced nationalists and physical-force advocates who met secretly in the office of Seán T O'Kelly at the Gaelic League headquarters in Dublin. The group included the seven future signatories to the 1916 Proclamation of the Irish Republic as well as Arthur Griffith and Major John MacBride. Connolly was now aligned with the IRB men, at least in his commitment to an armed rebellion in certain circumstances. As O'Kelly recalled:

> At that meeting it was decided that a Rising should take place in Ireland, if the German army invaded Ireland; secondly if England attempted to enforce conscription on Ireland; and thirdly if the war were coming to an end and the Rising had not already taken place, we should rise in revolt, declare war on England and when the conference was held to settle the terms of peace, we should claim to be represented as a belligerent nation.[4]

It is noteworthy that even at this early stage the proposed rebellion was mooted in terms of taking a stand to make a political point, and not as a venture with prospects of military success. Meanwhile, Home Rule was on the statute books at Westminster, but its enactment was suspended for the duration of the war under an emergency bill. On 20 September John Redmond gave his now-famous speech in Woodenbridge, County Wicklow, where he urged the Volunteers to support the allied war effort (in effect the British war effort). Redmond had not consulted the Provisional Committee of the Volunteers, and a manifesto was released, signed by MacNeill and the non-Redmondite members of the committee, denouncing his unilateral commitment of Irish Volunteers to the British war effort 'while no National Government which could speak and act for the people of Ireland is allowed to exist' and furthermore repudiated the 'proposed legislative dismemberment of Ulster'.[5] A split in the Volunteers ensued, with the vast majority of the 180,000-strong force declaring for Redmond, while only a small group of about 11,000 dissented. Unlike the Redmondite Volunteers (now called the 'National' Volunteers), most, though not all, of the anti-Redmondites (now the 'Irish' Volunteers) were committed nationalists with a more radical outlook. Many of them were also members of the IRB.

Around this time, a small pocket notebook used by Willie, mainly for recording small loans and charges to pupils, reminds us of the practical impact his connection with the Irish Volunteers was having. There is an allusion in late 1914 to a Lee-Enfield Mark 2 (a standard rifle). Among the references to blotting paper and schoolbooks there is also mention of 'musketry at range' and a list of names, suggesting, perhaps, that Willie had a role in organising rifle practice. Though he was not among the leadership of the small group who now contemplated rebellion, Willie showed, according to David Sears, a keen understanding of the necessity for military strategy should that rebellion take place:

In the last two years of his life he took a keen interest in all

military matters, and used to study the plans of various battles, especially in Irish history or where irregular troops were
engaged. He could explain these with wonderful clearness.
I remember going over the plan of the siege of Dublin
in the seventeenth century with him. He pointed out the
mistakes made and how they could have been avoided or
rectified and the siege successful.[6]

In March 1915, Patrick was part of a small group that made
tentative plans for a rebellion, which was initially due to take
place in September of that year. A military committee within
the IRB contained Patrick, Plunkett and Ceannt; Clarke
and MacDiarmada soon joined them. Patrick was Director
of Military Organisation for the Volunteers, and MacDonagh and Plunkett also had special responsibilities. Although
Eoin MacNeill was still the *de facto* head of the now much-
reduced Irish Volunteers, he was not a member of the IRB,
and he believed that military action should only be used as a
last resort in the event of a direct threat to Home Rule or the
Volunteers. While he knew that many of his men were in the
IRB, he was not aware of any plans for a Rising. Though the
mooted September rebellion did not happen, the Volunteers
were becoming bolder, openly parading in public with arms.
Meanwhile, with the Great War continuing despite the belief
of many at the outset that it would be over by Christmas of
1914, the British government was distracted from the threat
posed by the Irish Volunteers.

With the increasing radicalisation of Irish political life, Willie's social circle began to fracture. Not all of his friends from the School of Art connected their interest in Irish culture with political radicalism. Joseph Carré, initially involved with the Irish Theatre, soon turned his attention to acting in benefits for the British Red Cross and Irish army units serving in the Great War. In March 1915, students from the School of Art presented Mr Tilly, the registrar at the time of Willie's signing-their-names-in-Irish controversy in 1903, with an antique silver coffee pot and cake basket on his being made a lieutenant in the Army Service Corps. Willie's fellow artist Kathleen Fox deemed the atmosphere in the School of Art in the years before the Rising very 'anti-Irish' and 'Protestant', and, incidentally, credited Willie with being in the know about political developments: 'Only if you got into private conversation with people like Willy Pearse did you hear one or two things.'[7] A similar fragmentation was happening in the Gaelic League. Douglas Hyde had been unhappy for some time with the idea that the Gaelic League be used in the cause of advanced nationalism, and had spoken in Cork in 1914 about the need for 'moderate men' to ensure that the organisation remained representative of diverse identities.[8] But there was a fracturing in loyalties even closer to home for the Pearse brothers: while Willie's nephew Alf joined the Irish Volunteers, his other nephew James Pearse, the son of James Vincent, joined a cavalry regiment of the British Army;

and in late 1915, James Vincent's daughter Florence married William Scarlett, an Enniskillen-born soldier in the British Army who had already seen action on the battlefields of Europe. Willie's sister Margaret was a witness at this much-loved niece's marriage to a soldier in the British Army in their family church of St Andrew's.

Though Patrick played a central role in the inner circle now plotting a rebellion, Willie was not one of the leaders, at least not in any official capacity. He was, however, again mixing with many of the same advanced nationalists through his involvement in the Irish Theatre. Along with Joseph Plunkett and Thomas MacDonagh, one of the more prominent of these was Stonyhurst-educated playwright Eimar O'Duffy, who was also involved with *The Irish Volunteer* newspaper and would later take part in the Rising. For the week commencing 19 April 1915 Willie played Theramenes in O'Duffy's play *The Walls of Athens*, a political allegory set against a backdrop of war which was staged by the Irish Theatre on a double bill with Thomas MacDonagh's *Pagans*. The military backdrop to *The Walls of Athens* was echoed by the real-life experience of some of the actors: as Volunteers, Willie and the Reddin brothers (who also played roles in the drama) had received military training together from Charles O'Grady of the Fianna (and later of the Volunteers).[9] Another of Willie's fellow actors, MW O'Reilly, had been drawn into the IRB several years earlier through his involvement with the Thomas Davis Amateur Dramatic Society in Blackrock. Republican Jack Morrow designed the set and the Dún Emer Guild, who were also based at the Hardwicke Hall, provided the costumes. Reviews of *The Walls of Athens* were generally favourable; the *Freeman's Journal* critic reported that the play was 'warmly received'[10] and the reviewer in the *Irish Citizen*, the organ of the suffrage movement, gave Willie and his fellow actor Kerry Reddin modest praise.[11]

On 23 April 1915 the pupils from St Enda's performed *tableaux* depicting incidents from the life of Brian Boru for a Brian Boru celebration held in the Mansion House, reported as being arranged by 'Mr Pearse', helped by James Crawford Neil of the Leinster Stage Society. This Mr Pearse is almost certainly Willie. JJ O'Kelly, a leading Gaelic Leaguer, gave the opening lecture. Like Willie, he had Fenian antecedents. Another leading Gaelic Leaguer, Piaras Béaslaí, also contributed to the programme. Béaslaí was on the editorial board of *Irish Freedom* and a member of the IRB. Willie's friend Máire Nic Shiubhlaigh also took part. In fact the concert bore all the hallmarks of the brilliant propaganda machine that was the Wolfe Tone and United Irishmen Memorial Committee.[12]

The following month Patrick's *Íosagán* and his new play *The Master* were performed at the Irish Theatre from Thursday 20 May to Saturday 22 May. The opening night drew a 'considerable audience' and was 'much applauded'.[13] In *The*

Master Willie played Ciarán, a medieval Christian school master who is set against Daire, a pagan king more interested in worldly things. *The Master*, like *The Walls of Athens*, could be seen as reflecting the political questions of the time. The prayerful Ciarán is warned of the coming of Daire but stands his ground, stating that 'he is a sorry champion who forsakes his place of battle'.[14] Patrick wrote all his plays with specific actors in mind, and certainly elements of Ciarán's character echo Willie's own life, down to Willie, like Ciarán, being 'first in manly games' while Daire was first in 'learning.'[15] (Unlike Willie, Patrick never participated in team sports.) If Willie was the inspiration for aspects of Ciarán's character, then his statements about Daire offer a striking insight into possible tensions between the Pearse brothers. 'I said I would be his master and he said he would be my master. And we strove against each other,'[16] says Ciarán before describing his own efforts at self-assertion:

> I sought out difficult things that I might become a better man than he: I went into far countries and won reknown among strange peoples, but very little wealth and no happiness … and when I came back to my own country I found Daire was its king and that all men loved him. Me they had forgotten.[17]

The thoughtful Ciarán states that he had decided to do 'this hard thing, though I would fain have stayed in my father's house'.[18] But he is no pushover: when Daire offers to place Ciarán at his right hand, Ciarán retorts: 'You would bribe me with this petty honour.'[19] At other times, it seems that Ciarán echoes Patrick's own thoughts and fears about the morality of war and that Willie, as actor, is citing lines that spell out Patrick's own spiritual questioning. Whatever about the politics of the play and the provenance of the characters, it seems the performance had considerable merit as an artistic production. Joseph Holloway attended on Saturday and was impressed by the 'stillness of the whole production' which 'had the air of a dream'. Holloway noted that the audience were very still and attentive and 'never made a move during the entire enacting of the play'.[20] He thought Willie excellent as Ciarán. Most of the cast – Willie Pearse, Eamon Bulfin, Eunan McGinley, David Sears, Joseph Sweeney, Desmond Ryan, and John Kilgallon – were already active in militant politics. Kilgallon was a teacher at St Enda's, while the others were a group of former pupils fondly known as the 'Dogs', who lived at St Enda's and enjoyed family status there while attending university. Known by various nicknames, they often dropped in unannounced to the room off the basement kitchen where Patrick and Willie drank tea, made plans and discussed pupils, plays, politics and finances. Like Willie, the 'Dogs' were part of E Company in the 4th Battalion of the Irish Volunteers.

Patrick was now speculating publicly about the possible scenarios that the delay in enacting Home Rule might bring about: 'What if a Unionist or a Coalition British Ministry repudiate the Home Rule Act? What if it be determined to dismember Ireland?' he wondered in May 1915.[21] The day after the last performance of *The Master*, on Whit Sunday, Willie accompanied his brother and Thomas Clarke on a Volunteer march in Limerick. This time the stage was the streets of Limerick City, the costumes were Volunteer uniforms, and some of the audience were less than appreciative. Over a thousand Volunteers and Fianna members from Dublin, Cork and Charleville converged on Limerick for the march, where they were joined by about a hundred and fifty locals, including Edward 'Ned' Daly. Two future Cork mayors, Tomás MacCurtain and Terence MacSwiney (the latter had supported the Leinster Stage Society during their ill-fated trip to Cork in 1912), were among those present. Armed and uniformed, the Volunteers and Fianna assembled at Pery Square in the city and, headed by a band, marched without major incident until they reached the Mungret Street area, where they were booed and stones were thrown. As the situation became threatening, the Volunteers fired a number of blank shots before continuing on. They were set upon again in the Broad Street area, and as the march passed through Irishtown, an older, poorer part of the city, cheers were raised for the Munster Fusiliers and other regiments by relatives of soldiers serving with the British Army. Later, at the railway station, the Cork Volunteers were greeted with boos and jeers on the way to their train home, and had to struggle to gain entrance. Amid the melee, blank shots were fired again and when the Dublin Volunteers arrived the violence escalated. A number of rifles were seized by the hostile crowd, and as the local Limerick Volunteers prepared to offer assistance, Patrick intervened, sensing the damage any violence would do to the movement's reputation. A group of local clergy finally succeeded in calming down the crowd and order was restored late that evening. The hostile crowds had come from the poorer areas of the city: for many, 'John Bull' – the income from British army service – was paying the bills. Later that week, Limerick Corporation thanked the clergy who had calmed the crowd, and paid tribute to the Volunteers who 'showed great restraint in not retaliating under the provocation they received'.[22]

From 28 June to 4 July 1915 Willie was back in action in the Irish Theatre, playing Professor Serebryakov in Chekhov's *Uncle Vanya*. Many of the cast had also acted together in *The Walls of Athens*, and included Maire Nic Shiubhlaigh, artist Katherine McCormack from Dún Emer, Thomas MacDonagh's brother John, Blánaid Salkeld, the witty young student James Anthony Meagher, Gaelic Leaguer Seán Mac Caoilte and Kerry Reddin. Cesca Trench came to see the play and sketched some of the actors. Willie forgot his lines during one performance; he found it hilarious when one audience member took his hesitation to be deliberate and told Willie that his pauses were 'sublime'.[23] Willie had a real interest in Chekhov, admiring the writer for his 'deep spirit of sincerity and compassion towards all the weak and broken-spirited men and women of the world'.[24] However, notwithstanding the desire of MacDonagh, Plunkett and Martyn to provide cutting-edge foreign drama for Dublin audiences, the Dublin public – and many critics – didn't appreciate the Chekhov production. Indeed the ultimate ignominy visited the idealistic young cast when Percy French produced a pastiche of the Hardwicke Street production called *Gloom as Done at the Irish Theatre* in January 1916, though by then it is likely that the attention of some of the actors was elsewhere.[25]

Less than a fortnight after the production of *Uncle Vanya*, Willie, Patrick, Mrs Pearse and one or both of the Pearse sisters travelled west to Ros Muc with Desmond Ryan, who recalled a memorable holiday. The weeks spent in the holiday cottage owned by Patrick were leisurely, though Willie was less than impressed that he had no bed for the first few days.[26] Patrick, in expansive mood, spoke nightly to Willie and Desmond Ryan of his ideas about language and nationalism, and they also discussed the collection of short stories he was completing. On one occasion Patrick, a poor swimmer, swam in the nearby lake while protected by a rope held by Willie. Towards the end of the holiday there was a sixteen-mile walk to Caiseal and back, and an encounter with a religious proselytiser. Patrick laughed about the proselytiser's use of the word 'peasantry' and lamented that he had not given him a seditious leaflet in return. The ever-sensible Willie noted that 'it was just as well' as they would have 'ended in jail and with the police on to them'.[27] On one particular rainy day in Connemara, Patrick busied himself by drafting the speech he would give at the grave of Jeremiah O'Donovan Rossa, the legendary Fenian who had recently died in New York and was due to be buried in Glasnevin in Dublin. Willie laughingly recalled an oath he had taken as a young child at Pat's command – 'to live for Ireland and die for Ireland' – and they repeated the anecdote to their mother when she returned to the cottage. Ryan also recalled a fifty-six-mile round cycle through Recess, Gleninagh, Kylemore, Leenane and Maam Cross. Willie and Patrick were obviously fit and physically strong.

On the trip home, there was more drama in Galway, where Patrick was followed by plainclothes detectives. Willie found amusement in a drunken passenger who shared their journey, and Patrick's reaction to him. The passenger insisted on smoking in the non-smoking carriage and became abusive when Patrick confronted him. Patrick seethed while Willie 'laughed quietly, warning his brother with looks to say no more to the combination of "clay pipe, wild hat and whiskey bottle at his elbow"'.[28] As usual, Patrick, though irate, listened to his even-tempered brother. Amid the interruptions, Patrick was still working on his soon-to-be-famous O'Donovan

Rossa speech on the train, and the Pearse brothers arrived in Dublin to an electric atmosphere on the eve of his funeral.

The O'Donovan Rossa funeral is often seen as a watershed moment in Irish history. Thomas MacDonagh, on the request of Clarke, took a leading role in organising the event, reminding us of the emphasis placed on the performative aspect of public commemoration by the IRB through the Wolfe Tone Committee. Another figure familiar to Willie from the Irish Theatre, Joseph Plunkett, was responsible for organising the various delegations that took part. Many of those who had previously co-operated in supporting the Pearse brothers' warrior-themed pageants were now pulling together again towards very different ends; *The Irish Times* noted that this was the first time the Citizen Army and both bodies of Volunteers (National and Irish) had marched together. Reflecting the theatrical aspect to the proceedings, the newspaper even described the procession as a 'pageant'.[29] It was, according to the *Freeman's Journal*, 'one of the most memorable incidents which has marked the history of the Irish capital … There has certainly never been in our own generation a more remarkable demonstration of feeling.'[30] The procession, estimated at twenty thousand, 'comprehended every section of nationalist thought and patriotic activity'. In a deliberate move, bands played national airs in 'quick march' as the procession was envisaged as 'at once a funeral and a triumphal march'.[31] *The Irish Times*, noting the lack of trouble, described the role of the DMP (Dublin Metropolitan Police) as 'spectators'.[32] The tendency of police to stand aside from shows of Volunteer force was now becoming a pattern. The *Freeman's Journal* noted the conspicuous presence of Volunteers who occupied the city streets, while *The Irish Times* estimated that at least five thousand rifles were carried in the procession, and that at least seven thousand young men of military age took part. The personal experience in drama that many advanced nationalists had came into play yet again in the careful choreography which evoked the 'demonstration of feeling' mentioned by the *Freeman's Journal* and which built to a crescendo at Glasnevin Cemetery. Solemn music was played as the procession neared the graveyard and the assembled crowds – or audience – maintained a dignified silence. Among those closest to the grave were Fr Albert and Fr Aloysius of the Capuchin Friars, whom the Pearses knew well. After Patrick's electrifying graveside oration, a volley was fired over the grave; a dramatic innovation which made a powerful impression.

On 4 August 1915, a few days after the funeral, Willie Pearse was promoted to captain on the staff of the Director of Operations of the Volunteers, who was, of course, his brother. He was now Patrick's official right-hand man. Writing in 1917, David Sears surmised that Willie was unsuited to a position of authority:

Lacking the virility of his brother's character, he had little control over men. He would have made a bad captain, for, though courageous to a fault, he lacked the personality that makes men face certain death at the word of command. He was not born to occupy a prominent place or to take a leading part, but to fulfil to perfection the part allotted to him – that of chief of staff to his brother.[33]

At the end of that month, Willie was involved in organising Volunteer sports that were to be held at St Enda's as part of the Aeraíocht (an outdoor social and cultural gathering) on 5 September. Several thousand attended and the extensive programme was testament to the diversity of Willie's activities and interests at this time. Beginning at 1pm with Volunteer drills and finishing at 10.30pm with dancing, Willie's influence was particularly noticeable in the theatrical aspects of the programme, which included a two-part outdoor concert and a production of Seumus MacManus's amusing farce *The Lad from Largymore*, which was attributed to members of the Irish Theatre. The Aeraíocht had familiar ambitions: to raise funds for the school and showcase the Volunteers. But such events, while notable for the loyal network of dynamic and committed nationalists who frequented them, were still representative of a minority group. The vast majority of Irish citizens at this point supported Home Rule, many either supported or had relatives fighting in the Great War, and most would have been shocked to learn of the IRB's plans for revolution.

For the school year 1915–1916, Willie was part of a skeleton staff of five full-time teachers who taught at St Enda's. Numbers had fallen after the move to Rathfarnham and there was an ongoing funding crisis, with Willie even being chased by a creditor over a bill for a bicycle.[34] Pat and Willie were joined by Frank Burke, Peter Slattery and 'PÓC' (perhaps ex-pupil Pádraic Óg Ó Conaire), while also being assisted by Margaret Pearse, who taught some Christian doctrine. Burke and Slattery, like the Pearse brothers, were involved in the Volunteers, while Ó Conaire too was sympathetic to militant nationalism. A timetable shows the classes themselves were now called *cathanna* or battalions, and Willie had a full schedule, usually beginning at 9.30am and ending at 3.30pm. He taught history and geography as well as English and drawing. There was a half-day on Wednesdays to allow the boys to play football and hurling, but this short break was made up for with study and classes on Saturday mornings.[35] The dwindling student body was augmented by some ex-pupils (and teachers) who boarded at the school while pursuing their university courses. Many of these Willie knew particularly well, not just through his teaching but also through his involvement in school sports, pageants and plays. By January 1916, residents in St Enda's would include Conor McGinley, Eamon Bulfin, Desmond Ryan, John J Kilgallon, Joe Sweeney, Bryan Joyce, Frank Burke, Fintan Murphy and Eunan McGinley.

Willie's role as Patrick's right-hand man had him sometimes signing orders as 'Acting Chief of Staff'. One such
order, to 'Comd. The [i.e., Michael] O'Rahilly' was signed
by 'W Pearse, Captain' at Irish Volunteer HQ at 2 Dawson
Street on 17 September. O'Rahilly was to provide himself
with a bicycle, a map of South County Dublin, a field message book and a day's rations, then report to Willie at Rathfarnham to act on the 'staff of Commandant P.H. Pearse,
GOC Dublin Brigade'.[36]

Despite Willie's heavy workload, he still found time for
theatre. He was cast as Nikita Ivanitch in a revival of Chekhov's short play *Swan Song*, one of the four pieces that made
up the Christmas programme at the Irish Theatre. When an
actor with parts in the three other plays on the programme
became ill, Willie took on these additional roles. He played
the hapless Knight, one of the main characters, in John
MacDonagh's satirical comedy *Author Author!*, and his 'study
of drunken imbecility' in this role was praised in a review
in the *Irish Citizen*.[37] The play was a satire on the Abbey's
peasant plays and offered, among other things, a pastiche
of Synge's dialogue. Joseph Derham, who acted alongside
Willie in this light-hearted comedy, would take part in the
Rising, as would John MacDonagh, Máire Nic Shiubhlaigh
and Pádraig Ó Seachain. Ironically enough, Willie's other
stand-in role that Christmas was that of a policeman, Constable Higgins, in Eimar O'Duffy's *The Phoenix on the Roof*.[38]

While Willie acted his various roles in the company of his radical friends, Patrick was formulating his thoughts on the nature of freedom and the morality of rebellion in a series of pamphlets, *Tracts for the Times*. He finished the first of these, 'Ghosts', just before Christmas. In it, Patrick outlined the heritage of radical separatism which he deemed Redmond and his associates to have betrayed by their acceptance of a compromise Home Rule settlement. The 'ghosts' who had died for Ireland included Wolfe Tone, Emmet and even Parnell. The message in 'Ghosts' was clear: Patrick was endorsing the tradition of armed separatism, claiming that the arguments of the leaders of nationalism who advocated a peaceful achievement of devolution were like 'the gibberings of lost souls'.[39]

It is clear that by now both brothers were of one mind about the need to prepare for an armed rebellion. Known across Dublin and elsewhere for his influential organisational role in the Volunteers and as a member of the inner circle that was planning a Rising, Patrick was also concentrating on theory, morality and propaganda. Though Willie was treading the boards of the Irish Theatre while his brother was writing 'Ghosts', he would soon be focusing on a practical element of revolution: bomb–making.

Chapter Nine
• • • • • •

January to April 1916

'He Was No Pacifist'

By early 1916 Eoin MacNeill and others within the Volunteer leadership sensed that unilateral military action was being planned by a faction within the movement, and he wrote a letter to Patrick expressing his unease. A small group, including Bulmer Hobson, wanted MacNeill to go further, and in mid-February 1916 the latter read out a memorandum to the Volunteer leadership at a meeting in his brother's house in Rathfarnham. In it he explicitly expressed his opposition to an insurrection taking place unless there was a reasonable prospect of military success, not, as he stated, 'some future moral or political advantage'.[1] MacNeill was, however, in favour of further arming and strengthening the Volunteers. Patrick rejected the suggestion that there were any plans for insurrection. This was not the truth: the military council of which Patrick was a member were now making definite preparations for a rebellion at Easter. Willie, as Patrick's *aide de camp*, was one of the few who knew about this. Sir Roger Casement – a former British consular representative, now a human-rights activist and Irish nationalist – and Joseph Plunkett had arranged for arms to be imported from Germany, and the IRB were in positions of control in the Dublin battalions and 'to a significant extent throughout the country'.[2] The IRB military committee (now termed council) planning the insurrection operated with a high level of secrecy, and not all members of the Supreme Council of the IRB were privy to the details of the insurrection being planned. Meanwhile James Connolly, whose very small Citizen Army had been contemplating military action of their own, had been convinced by Pearse and Clarke that joining with their insurrection would be far more effective than going it alone (an action which might provoke the British authorities into a clampdown on every advanced nationalist group in Ireland).

A former student at St Enda's later recalled that in these years 'during intervals between the classes the Pearse brothers devoted every spare moment to arranging on a large map details of the activities in which they were both so deeply engaged'.[3] In early spring of 1916 Willie and Patrick, along with chemistry teacher Peter Slattery, who was Chief Engineering and Explosives Officer for the Rathfarnham Volunteer company, tested bombs that had been prepared by Francis Daly, an IRB member with knowledge of explosives. Under the Pearse brothers' direction, a considerable amount of ammunition was prepared and stored by the 'Dogs', the former pupils lodging at the school. The preparation of munitions brought Willie even closer to this group: David Sears recalled that it was only in the last six months that he really got to know Willie, 'to really appreciate him and call him by the sacred name of "friend"'.[4] Sears noted that the younger Pearse brother's artistic skill 'made him invaluable in drawing up plans and diagrams'.[5] Definite action was scheduled for Easter Sunday, 23 April, and in the weeks before the planned insurrection Willie made plaster moulds for the shotgun ammunition being prepared by the 'Dogs'.[6] Fintan Murphy later recalled that, 'The whole crew of St Enda's ... were engaged in making buckshot. There was a great quantity made there. We were continuously at it for several weeks before the Rising took place.'[7]

Meanwhile, the Volunteer displays and drilling continued. This presence of a rival (and illegally) armed force was an affront to the police and military, and the authorities sensed the threat implicit in the growing boldness of the Volunteers. Rumours spread that there was to be a clampdown on the leadership. In Dublin, a show of force took place on St Patrick's Day when Eoin MacNeill reviewed over a thousand Irish Volunteers at the historically significant location of College Green, the seat of the Irish parliament which had been dissolved by the 1800 Act of Union. Patrick addressed the Volunteers later that day, with Willie presumably taking his place among the ranks. It was a sign of the mounting tension that the two brothers arranged for Volunteers to guard St Enda's during the course of the day's events.[8] Dublin Castle files show that the number of Volunteers parading around the country on St Patrick's Day was noted, as was the number of Volunteers deemed to be opposed to Redmond. Another document notes the number of British soldiers in Dublin, which was surprisingly small, even given the deployment of extra troops to the Great War. While the motivation and aims of the Irish Volunteers were acknowledged, the British authorities' dismissive attitude is evident in a report from the Inspector General of the Royal Irish Constabulary:

> There can be no doubt that the Irish Volunteer Leaders are a pack of rebels who would proclaim their independence in the event of any favourable opportunity but with their present resources and without substantial reinforcements it is difficult to imagine they will make even a brief stand against a small body of troops. These observations however are made with reference to the provinces and not to the Dublin Metropolitan Area, which is the centre of the movement.[9]

After 'violent speeches' were observed at public meetings on 7 April, the Chief Commissioner sent a report to the Under Secretary, which was forwarded in turn to the Chief Secretary and to the Lord Lieutenant, who both noted the difficulties a policy of disarming would involve. Again, nothing was done.

In the months preceding the Rising, Willie was involved in organising social gatherings which provided a front for Volunteer meetings. On 21 March 1916 there was a *céilí* in St Enda's attended by Volunteers, guest singers, friends and students. Patrick reportedly made an unguarded speech in which he stated that it had taken the blood of the Son of God to redeem the world and that it would take the blood of the sons of Ireland to redeem Ireland. As news reached the *céilí* of an affray in Tullamore Volunteer Hall that morning – a shot had been fired – the atmosphere became even more charged. A messenger from Tullamore was brought on the stage during an interval and Willie noted that nationalist songs were performed with increased fervour: 'Strange the effectiveness sincerity lends to a song. For years we have listened to these songs. Only today have we fully realised their meaning.'[10] Willie's comment (as recalled by Desmond Ryan) shows his ability to step back from a situation in order to observe it dispassionately; and, no doubt, his experience in the theatre would have sharpened his ability to assess the emotional impact of performance. Patrick also had this capacity but was likely to react with less circumspection when his emotions were aroused. Willie was not, however, beyond rising to moments of indignation himself, and around this time he wrote an outraged letter of complaint to the Lord Mayor when Patrick was refused permission to use the Mansion House for an unnamed event.

Perhaps Willie's observations at the *céilí* were the result of a dawning realisation of the implications of a planned revolt. St Enda's teacher Frank Burke, also present at the *céilí,* thought that 'poor Willie Pearse looked sad and lonely as if he had a premonition of the fate that was in store for him and his beloved brother'. Patrick — though not unconflicted himself — may have been motivated partly by ideas of sacrifice whose expression had apparently already caused alarm to Eoin MacNeill; the latter's February memorandum had specifically rejected 'some future moral ... or political advantage' as constituting grounds for an uprising. Willie, it seems, may not have fully shared his brother's enthusiasm.

Real-life events were now encroaching on the theatrical world so beloved to Willie. Patrick had written one final drama, *The Singer,* which focuses on Colm and Macdara Ó Fiannachta, two brothers caught up in the preparations for an insurrection in the west of Ireland while their mother (based on Mrs Pearse) resignedly awaits developments.[11] As usual, the play reflected the personalities of the actors Patrick had in mind. Gypsy Walker, Willie's old comrade from the Leinster Stage Society, was to play the young girl, Sighle, who is both appalled and entranced by the idea of a rebellion. Mrs Pearse later claimed that Willie was Colm, and Patrick was Macdara.[12] In this regard it is interesting that, as in *The Master,* there is a palpable tension between the aspirations and motivations ascribed to the two: Macdara believes that one man can redeem a people, while Colm, impatient with the constant wait for the right opportunity, goes out to fight with 'ten or fifteen of the young lads'.[13] While on one level the impatient Colm might seem an unlikely version of 'gentle' Willie Pearse, the fact is that Willie was a member of an armed force and was making bullets and bombs in the basement of St Enda's with a group of impatient young men. Desmond Ryan was quite sure of Willie's viewpoint on military action, stating that 'he was no pacifist'.[14] In the end it was apparently decided by Patrick, Willie and Thomas MacDonagh not to proceed with a public performance of *The Singer*, as it would have attracted unwanted attention, although it may have been performed privately at St Enda's.[15] At Liberty Hall, meanwhile, the ongoing theatrics on and off stage – the raising of a flag over the building, marches, a performance of James Connolly's own rebel play *Under Which Flag* at the end of March, and spoof notices about planned attacks on Dublin Castle – meant that when Easter Monday came, the authorities would, initially at least, be somewhat indifferent to the sudden eruption of costumed drama on the streets.

Anecdotes about Patrick and Willie often portray Willie as playing a supportive role to his brother. One such snapshot of the brothers' relationship has Patrick as the chief speaker at a lecture in No 2 Dawson Street, the final one of a series of talks organised in the run-up to the Rising, attended by all officers of the Dublin Brigade. Willie accompanied Patrick to the event and is recalled only as helping his brother remove his great coat and slouch hat.[16] But, even when it comes to the preparations for the rebellion so synonymous with Patrick, this idea of Willie as a deferential assistant to his brother is overly simplistic. We know, for example, that a fortnight or so before the Rising, Willie, seemingly without Patrick, travelled to a gathering of officers of the 4th Battalion in Old Bawn in Dublin. Arriving with others under the guise of having been invited to afternoon tea, Willie proceeded to an inner room where he took part in prolonged discussions with Cathal Brugha and Éamonn Ceannt while the other officers chatted in the main room. Willie, whether there as an officer or on his brother's behalf, was in the inner circle.[17]

As plans for the Rising were being finalised, the preparation of munitions intensified at St Enda's. The tense atmosphere meant that Willie and Patrick slept at the top of the house with a rope ladder and a bicycle on standby in case of a raid.[18] Willie had to call upon his acting skills as, despite the many comings and goings at the school, most of the pupils had no idea that a rebellion was being plotted. In fact, they were allowed home for the Easter holidays slightly earlier than usual in order to let those involved in planning the Rising go about their work without distraction. On Wednesday 19 April, at a meeting of Dublin Corporation, Alderman Thomas Kelly, now an unwitting accomplice in the schemings of the inner circle of the IRB, circulated copies of a document purporting to be from Dublin Castle that suggested that the authorities were planning the mass arrest of the leaders of Sinn Féin, the Volunteers and the Gaelic League as well as the military occupation of buildings associated with the same organisations and others. The document, whose message was partially fabricated, added impetus to the ongoing discussion of what the Volunteers should do in the case of a provocative attempt at disarmament. Even the moderate Eoin MacNeill had expressed belief that the Volunteers would have no choice but to mount an armed response in such a scenario. Nonetheless many within the movement were sceptical, with fellow teacher Peter Slattery apparently asking Willie Pearse jocosely, 'Whoever forged that?'[19]

In the week before the date set for the Rising, Sunday 23 April, the grenades, bullets, rifles and bombs which had been prepared at St Enda's were removed as young men took turn on guard. On Monday of Holy Week, Éamonn Ceannt, his wife Áine, and their young son Rónán visited the school, now closed for the holidays. It was a 'glorious morning, sun shining, birds singing, fruit trees in full blossom'.[20] Mrs Pearse, Margaret, Patrick, Willie, the Ceannts, and Fianna organiser Liam Mellows (who, dressed as a priest, was on the run and hiding out in St Enda's) had lunch together and, at least while Áine was present, the conversation moved 'from books to music, with no word of the impending fight'.[21] Despite the frantic clandestine planning, the brothers took time out a few days before the intended insurrection and 'visited every place and scene of their happy childhood'.[22] Seldom out of each other's sight during these busy last days and weeks, Patrick and Willie travelled mainly by bicycle as they attended meetings and ran messages.

On Holy Thursday, the brothers dropped in to their usual barbershop in Rathmines for haircuts. The man who cut their hair, John Doran, later recalled that 'they did not speak much as they waited their turn in the chair ... but then again, they seldom did'.[23] Patrick and Willie were definitely in St Enda's very late on Thursday night when Eoin MacNeill arrived with Bulmer Hobson and JJ O'Connell to confront Patrick about his plans for military action. At this stage the plans for a Rising involved a country-wide insurrection that would begin on Sunday under the pretext of the usual Volunteer manoeuvres. MacNeill had been tipped off by O'Connell and Eimar O'Duffy, who had got wind of the scheme, and was determined to prevent it. Following the showdown with Patrick, MacNeill gave counter-orders for Hobson and O'Connell to distribute to prevent the Rising, which he, as head of the Volunteers, had not authorised. The anti-insurrectionists went into rapidly organised conclaves, and heated conversations and confrontations followed. Messages were relayed between those for and against the insurrection, with MacNeill determined to stop it and the pro-insurrection leaders equally determined that it should go ahead. Fintan Murphy recalled that the young men based in St Enda's were working on munitions until three or three-thirty in the early hours of Good Friday when Patrick and Willie 'arrived in, presumably from the city and had a conversation with – probably – Eamon Bulfin, as the senior'[24]. Murphy and McGinley then set off to bring messages to Clarke, MacDiarmada, MacDonagh and Ceannt. A demonstration of the confusion prevalent at this time can be seen in the fact that Murphy only realised that plans were afoot for more than manouevres when he overheard some Cumann na mBan members at Volunteer Headquarters saying 'oh you will see in time' when questioned about the bandages and first aid kits they were preparing.[25]

However, for Patrick and Willie on Good Friday, after a sleepless night and the round of meetings, plans seemed to be back on track. Patrick, along with MacDonagh and Plunkett, visited MacNeill again that morning. When MacNeill was informed of the extent of the preparations – the *Aud*, a ship carrying German arms, was expected at any time – he was briefly convinced of the inevitability of proceeding with the insurrection.

At 5pm that day, Willie signed a mobilisation order for 'Commandant "The O'Rahilly" (Michael O'Rahilly)'. The letter specifically ordered O'Rahilly to 'report yourself to me' (i.e., to Willie) at 4pm on Sunday 23 and to 'hold yourself in readiness to act on the staff of Commandant P.H. Pearse'. As with Willie's 1915 mobilisation order to O'Rahilly, the phrase 'Acting Chief of Staff' is in type immediately underneath his signature (of 'William Pearse, Captain'). The authority implicit in this order, and in other later orders signed by Willie, shows that, even if he was signing orders emanating from Patrick, he clearly had a certain status as the Commandant's *aide de camp*.

That evening Patrick and Willie travelled to Mount Argus Church during the ceremony of the 'Seven Last Words' (phrases attributed to Jesus on the cross in the various Gospels, which offer an exemplar to those who might also embark on a path of suffering). The panel of St Paul of the Cross at Mount Argus had been carved by their father, while Willie himself had carved the statue of Mary in the Sanctuary.[26] The brothers had gone to Mount Argus looking for their good friend Fr Eugene Nevin (yet another nationalist cleric) but he was away preaching in the city and they had no time to wait for his return. In his absence, one of the student clerics brought the Pearse brothers into the monastery by the door at the altar of Saint Mary Magdalene and found a priest who heard their confession in the duty room near the church. Since childhood Willie had an overactive conscience, and he would be back at confession within a few days.[27] The brothers' deep faith meant that they had also planned to receive communion with their mother the next morning, on Holy Saturday, but at around 5am Patrick was called away for an emergency meeting.

As the date for the Rising drew closer, it was felt that it was no longer safe for the main protagonists to stay in their own homes. Willie and Patrick arranged to stay in Seán T O'Kelly's family home on the corner of Rutland Street and Charles Street on the north side of the city, arriving by bicycle in full uniform and carrying heavy loads of equipment, which they covered with their raincoats. Seán T's sons Michael and Matthew were St Enda's boys, now with F Company of the Volunteers. His sister Máiréad Ní Cheallaigh recalled that on the arrival of the 'distinguished visitors', her mother directed the Pearse brothers into the drawing room where she had set up two beds for them.[28] She also recalled the equipment the brothers had brought, which included wirecutters as well as ammunition for revolvers, carried on bracelets that they wore on their wrists.[29] Mrs O'Kelly and Seán T stated that both Pearse brothers had Sam Browne belts and recalled Patrick in particular as carrying ammunition.[30] A Sam Browne belt (a belt with an additional vertical strap) was usually a signal of higher rank; it was often used to carry a pistol. Máiread did not see the Pearse brothers again until the Sunday morning, though they had slept, albeit for short periods, in the house.[31]

Throughout Easter Weekend the Volunteers were busy ordering uniforms and making arrangements, though few outside of the leadership spoke directly of the intended insurrection. By that Saturday evening most of the ammunition stored in St Enda's had been taken away, but the Pearse brothers delayed as one final load awaited collection. Just as it was decided that Patrick would leave alone and Willie would remain until the ammunition had been loaded, Dr Kathleen Lynn of the Citizen Army arrived. She and Willie loaded up a car with ammunition, disguising their load by covering it with theatrical materials, and brought it to Liberty Hall. The brothers parted from their mother and their sister Margaret at the main gate of St Enda's in some haste due to their fear of attracting the suspicion of the police. At this stage, to the best of the Pearse brothers' knowledge, the planned military action was still scheduled to begin the following evening, and Mrs Pearse and Margaret believed that this hasty farewell at the gate at dusk was their final goodbye. Blessing her sons, Mrs Pearse told them that if they did not meet again they would 'meet in heaven'.[32] The farewell to the two Margarets would prove premature.

The Pearse brothers called again to the O'Kellys on Saturday evening, hoping to meet Seán T. They departed after quick refreshments, with Willie apparently making a brief return alone around ten o'clock to collect equipment. However, news of the loss of the German arms (the *Aud* was scuttled after being intercepted by the British authorities), had reached Dublin during the course of Saturday. After hearing this, Mac-Neill decided that the Rising had no chance of success, and on Saturday afternoon he sent out orders to Volunteer companies around Ireland cancelling any action the following day. Later that evening, messengers sent for by MacNeill gathered in the house of Dr Seamus O'Kelly in Rathgar, where they were issued with more countermanding orders. The house became

William Pearse in typical artistic attire. Geraldine Plunkett loved to watch his 'quiet face and beautiful hands'.

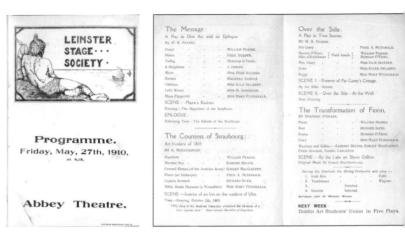

The playbill for a programme of plays performed by the Leinster Stage Society in the Abbey Theatre in February 1910.

The Pearse family on holiday in Killarney.

Willie Pearse as Pilate in the Passion Play, 1911.

Willie's half-brother, James Vincent Pearse, who was also a sculptor and carver. He died in 1912.

Above: The cast of *Fionn*, performed at St Enda's, Rathfarnham, in 1914. Willie is in the centre.

Below: A playbill for *The Master* and *Íosagán*, both by Patrick Pearse, which were performed in the Irish Theatre in 1915.

THE IRISH THEATRE

HARDWICKE STREET

PLAY-BILL

THURSDAY, FRIDAY, AND SATURDAY, MAY
20TH, 21ST, AND 22ND, 1915. THREE NIGHTS AT
8.15 P.M., AND SATURDAY MATINEE AT 2.30 P.M.

THE STUDENTS OF ST. ENDA'S COLLEGE WILL PERFORM

IOSAGAN

A Miracle Play

BY P. H. PEARSE

Maitias, an Old Man	- FRANK CONNOLLY
Darach	JOSEPH HUCKLEY
Padraic	BERNARD SWEENEY
Coilin } Boys	BRIAN MacGINLEY
Briocan	EDWARD FINUCANE
Eoghan	DONAL SWEENEY
Cuimin	OWEN CRONIN
Iosagan - - -	DIARMAID MacGINLEY
A Priest - - -	FRANK BURKE

Place, the seashore near a village in Iar-Connacht.

The lowering of the curtain for half-a-minute towards the end of the play represents the lapse of eight hours.

The name *Iosagan* is a loving diminutive of *Iosa* and may be translated *Jesukin*. "In bringing the Child Jesus into the midst of a group of boys disputing about their games, or to the knee of an old man who sings nursery rhymes to children, I am imagining nothing improbable, nothing outside the bounds of the everyday experience of innocent little children and reverent-minded old men and women. I know a priest who believes that he was summoned to the deathbed of a parishioner by our Lord in person."

The play was originally produced at St. Enda's College in February, 1910.

THE MASTER

A Miracle Play

BY P. H. PEARSE

(Translated by the Author from his Original Irish)

Art	EUNAN MacGINLEY
Breasal	JOSEPH SWEENEY
Maine } Pupils of Ciaran	DESMOND MURPHY
Ronan	AUGUSTINE GEARY
Ceallach	DAVID SEARS
Ciaran, a Teacher - -	WILLIAM PEARSE
Iollann Beag, a little Pupil of Ciaran's - -	OWEN CLARKE
A King's Messenger	DESMOND RYAN
Daire, a King - -	EAMONN BULFIN
Michael - - -	JOHN KILGALLON

Place, a cloister in a wood.

The play is now produced for the first time.

The persons in both plays are named in the order of their entry.

The airs sung are by Thomas MacDonnell.

During the interval Mr. Pearse will deliver a short address on the Irish Style of Dramatic Speaking. The address will be illustrated by the performance of the only surviving fragment of an Irish drama prior to the language revival. The fragment was taken down in Co. Kerry in 1898, and is part of a play that was enacted among the people up to sixty or seventy years ago. The subject is the hero Dunlaing and his Fairy Lover, and the action takes place just before the Battle of Clontarf.

Dunlaing Og - - MICHAEL O'SULLIVAN
An Leannan Sidhe - MARY BULFIN

Right: Patrick and Willie Pearse deep in conversation at an event in St Enda's.

Above: Walter Paget's iconic image of an imagined scene from inside the GPO during the rebellion.

Above: General Sir John Grenfell Maxwell and his entourage inspecting troops in the aftermath of the Rising.

Below: A view of Sackville Street [now O'Connell Street] from O'Connell Bridge in the days after the Rising.

Above: The yard in Kilmainham (pictured before the restoration of the Gaol) where Willie, Patrick and other 1916 leaders were executed.

IRISH REBELLION, MAY, 1916.

WILLIAM PEARSE
(Younger Brother of P. H. Pearse, also Executed),
Executed at Kilmainham Prison, 4th May, 1916.

Left: Willie Pearse in memoriam.

Above: Margaret Pearse, mother of Willie and Patrick, pictured in later years with Hanna Sheehy-Skeffington (wife of Francis).

Below: The Pearse Museum, located in the former St Enda's School in Rathfarnham, holds many of Willie's artworks.

a hive of activity, with vehicles drawing up outside, bicycles piling up, and people coming and going. As plans changed by the hour, many were conflicted: The O'Rahilly, for example, initially sided with MacNeill before later joining the rebellion. At 1am MacNeill travelled to the offices of the *Irish Independent* to place a notice cancelling all Volunteer activity in their Sunday edition.

No number of orders, however, could alter the fact that the endgame was now underway. On Easter Sunday, Fr Aloysius of the Capuchin Friars in Church Street was on his way to say Mass in Gloucester Street Convent at 8.30am when he saw Patrick Pearse and a man later identified to him as Willie ride past on bicycles.[33] They had come into Gloucester Street from Rutland Square (presumably from the O'Kelly household). Willie and Patrick attended Mass in Gardiner Street Church that morning, while Fr Columbus of the Capuchin Friars, noting the huge number of Volunteers seeking the sacraments over the weekend, had begun to wonder if something was afoot. At some stage during the morning, Seán T O'Kelly came home with further news for Patrick and Willie: the order signed by MacNeill cancelling manouevres had been published in the newspaper. Patrick was much angered and joined Seán T and Willie in the O'Kelly drawing room to discuss events.[34]

At a meeting in Liberty Hall that same Sunday morning, a decision was taken by the Military Council to proceed with the

planned action but to postpone events by one day. That afternoon the Pearse brothers, with Thomas MacDonagh, travelled
to Cullenswood House. MacDonagh confirmed to the Volunteers from E Company, 3rd Battalion, who had gathered there
that the mobilisation was cancelled. Willie and Patrick had
time for one final visit home and returned to Rathfarnham
that afternoon. Both were very upset at the countermanding
order and hardly able to speak. Willie was recalled as remark-
ing sadly that the countermanding order was a dangerous hint
to the military that something was in the wind.[35] Recalling
the sense of crisis at St Enda's that afternoon, Desmond Ryan
wrote: 'We felt that at any moment a spring, the spring of
the whole Irish-Ireland movement, might snap and nothing
would ever in our lifetimes mend it again', adding that it was
'the beginning of a curious feeling that we were in a dream'.[36]
The Pearse brothers had a light meal of cold chicken and tea,
and spoke with their family for about an hour before leaving
quietly. This time the farewell took place at the bottom of the
steps leading to the hall door – the final time the brothers saw
their mother and older sister before the Rising. The brothers
did not say goodbye to their sister Mary Brigid, who did not
live at the Hermitage; nor did they speak to their sister-in-law
Mary Pearse, whose son James and son-in-law William were
fighting for the British Army. Willie's nephew and close friend
Alf McGloughlin was ill with pneumonia.

Following another meeting in Liberty Hall, Willie, Patrick,

and Seán MacDiarmada were among a group which met later that evening in an office over a shop in North Frederick Street that was used by the Keating Branch of the Gaelic League. Here they were to prepare for the rescheduled Rising, organising messages and oiling guns. Arrangements were made for couriers to be dispatched around the country with messages. The atmosphere was tense and Ned Daly guarded the door with a rifle. Maria Perolz, one of the messengers, recalled that the group struck her as 'men going out into a losing cause'.[37] Willie and Patrick also spent at least part of Sunday night in the O'Kelly household; they arrived very late and slept in their uniforms, outside of the bedcovers.

Monday morning brought bright sunshine. Before heading out to Mass, Mrs O'Kelly prepared a very substantial breakfast of bacon, eggs and mutton chops for the two brothers. Máiréad Ní Cheallaigh was alone in the dining room when they came downstairs and 'they stood shyly outside' until she called them in.[38] To the satisfaction of Mrs O'Kelly, who had been concerned at their lack of sleeping and eating, they ate every last scrap of food, including an entire loaf of bread. The two brothers then gathered their belongings and equipment and asked for Mrs O'Kelly in order to thank her. Finding her gone, they said goodbye to Máiréad, took their bicycles from the hall and cycled along Upper Rutland Street towards Liberty Hall. Years later, Máiréad wrote: 'I can see them still.'[39]

Chapter Ten

24 April to 1 May 1916

'We Are Still Here'

By mid-morning on Easter Monday, Willie and Patrick had arrived at Liberty Hall on the Dublin quays, where members of the Citizen Army, the Volunteers and some others were gathering. Fianna member Seán McLoughlin recalled the Pearses arriving together 'with broad-brimmed hats pinned up at one side and the Volunteer badge'.[1] McLoughlin saw the two brothers go into a committee room with Volunteer captain Seán Heuston, where others, including James Connolly, had gathered. A demonstration of Willie's personal authority was shown when Michael O'Flanagan arrived with Seán MacEntee: Willie led MacEntee away to a room before telling O'Flanagan to go home and await further instructions. Another example of this authority was that the counterfoil for one of the mobilising orders issued by Willie earlier in the week indicated that the mobilised officers should report to 'you' (at a temporary headquarters which were not indicated); the 'you' being 'Capt Willie Pearse'. The officer should then hold himself 'in readiness to act on the staff of P.H. Pearse, Commandant of the Easter Manoeuvres'.[2] A captain on Patrick's staff who held the same rank as Willie, Seán T O'Kelly, was among those who received mobilisation orders from him. Shortly before noon, those gathered at Liberty Hall set off, with James Connolly, the two Pearse brothers, Seán McGarry and Joseph Plunkett at the front. Tom Clarke and Seán MacDiarmada left separately and not in uniform (neither were Volunteers; in addition, Clarke was elderly and MacDiarmada was lame). The route of the main body took them from Liberty Hall to Sackville Street via Abbey Street. It was recalled that during this short journey Willie expressed hope that, come what might, the railway bridge over the Liffey (which obscured the fine vista of the Custom House downriver) would disappear.[3] The story reminds us that Willie, even as he marched to war, retained his aesthetic sensibility. It also shows that he was aware of the scale of destruction that might ensue following the Volunteers' occupation of Dublin; others seem not to have anticipated the extent (and the indiscriminate nature) of the shelling the British forces would use on property. As the Angelus bells pealed for twelve noon, the rebels entered the General Post Office, better known as the GPO, and ordered customers and staff to leave. Willie welcomed his old friends from St Enda's in the E Company of the 4th Battalion when they eventually arrived, their mobilisation having been delayed. Though the details of who raised the two flags over the GPO (a tricolour and a green flag with 'Irish Republic' written on it) are often disputed, Willie is generally recalled as having been present alongside his second lieutenant, Eamon Bulfin. Willie's knowledge of performance would have given him a deep insight into the importance, and the impact, of these symbolic images of the soon-to-be-declared Republic.[4]

Meanwhile, other companies occupied strategic positions around the city while select specialist units attempted to cut off various communication channels and gas supplies. Occupied positions included the Four Courts, the South Dublin Union, Stephen's Green, Boland's Mills and Jacob's Biscuit Factory, and street barricades were set up to offer cover and block movement of troops. Snipers occupied houses and took up positions on the roofs. For a time it was believed (erroneously) that Dublin Castle had been taken by the Volunteers. Rumours were rife: Willie believed for a while that Thomas MacDonagh had taken the lower Dublin Castle yard before being driven out by machine-gun fire. At this stage, and notwithstanding the failure to capture the Castle, the rebels had succeeded in a stunning takeover and brought the city to a standstill with, in Desmond Ryan's slightly understated description, 'little more noise and excitement than many a public meeting'.[5] The pre-emptive strike favoured by the Military Council had resulted in the desired element of surprise. Many soldiers were at the Fairyhouse races and in any case, the Volunteers had established their right to march with arms in the previous two years.

As the sunny Bank Holiday Monday afternoon wore on, the atmosphere outside the GPO was festive, even surreal. Desmond Ryan recalled the holiday crowd staring and even waving at the insurgents. Former St Enda's pupil Dick Humphries recalled that he had to struggle to get through the crowds of onlookers to enter the GPO. Inside the building, windows were smashed and barricaded with furniture, boxes of sand, and any other materials at hand. The central area of the post office was used as headquarters, and all accounts show Willie to have been constantly by Patrick's side, or standing a little way away while Patrick wrote various dispatches and propaganda accounts of progress. Humphries recalled seeing Tom Clarke conversing with the two Pearse brothers.[6] Seán T O'Kelly also had a (presumably very interesting) conversation with the brothers. Desmond Ryan recalled Patrick as 'quiet and businesslike', Willie 'likewise, but a trifle sad and pale'.[7]

A short time after the occupation of the GPO, Patrick, as President of the Provisional Government, went outside and read the Proclamation of the Irish Republic. Though many in the crowd were nonplussed, the Proclamation expressed ideals that would have been unsurprising to Willie. The idea that the Rising was part of an insurrectionary tradition ('the dead generations from which she receives her old tradition of nationhood') had been the *raison d'être* of the Wolfe Tone Memorial Committee and was well known to Willie's maternal relatives. The Proclamation's declaration of 'religious and civil liberty, equal rights and equal opportunities to all its citizens' and its intention to bring in place a government elected through the 'suffrage of all its citizens, men and women' would also have been familiar to Willie, who had a Fenian grandfather, and a father who rejected religious absolutism. Willie himself supported events espousing equal rights for women. About half an hour after the reading of the Proclamation a group of Lancers who entered Sackville Street to investigate the disturbances were shot at: four were killed. Later on in the day there was looting outside, but the streets were empty by 2am.

On Tuesday, further preparation for battle took place in the GPO, including the preparation of a field hospital. A sortie by The O'Rahilly, who had joined his old friends in the GPO despite having initially opposed going ahead with military action, ensured that there were ample food supplies to withstand a prolonged siege. Willie and Patrick made frequent visits to the roof, where many of the men on duty had St Enda's connections. Some of Willie's other friends were scattered across the city: Máire Nic Shiubhlaigh was in Jacob's Biscuit Factory with her Cumann na mBan comrades under the command of Thomas MacDonagh, while her brother Charles and her father, Matthew Walker, were

involved in printing the *Irish War News*, the short-lived newspaper put out by the rebels, and various bulletins. Meanwhile,
operating from her own home, Kitty O'Doherty, the sister of
Willie's old friend Fr Gibbons, had played an important role
in organising the distribution of arms to individual Volunteers. Visits by friends, relations and supporters bearing food,
messages and even ammunition, were a feature of the early
days of the Rising. Cesca Trench, a familiar face for Willie,
called to the GPO with first aid supplies and brought a note
to St Enda's – and a report to Eoin MacNeill. Unknown to
Willie, one of the early civilian casualties of the rebellion was
someone who had worked closely with him in theatre: James
Crawford Neil, Gypsy Walker's fiancé, was (seemingly acci-
dently) shot that same day as he made his way back home to
his mother on the northside, having visited Gypsy.[8] Almost a
year to the day before, Crawford Neil had helped Willie with
the Brian Boru *tableaux* and also accompanied Willie on the
Leinster Stage Society's ill-fated visit to Cork.

Until now, there had been little military activity outside of
the attack on the Lancers, sniping, and occasional skirmishes
with soldiers and the police. The Volunteers were in effective control of the city. But the British Army was mobilising,
and reinforcements were en route. The military authorities,
having been taken by surprise, were planning a combination
of heavy shelling and attacks on individual outposts to crush
the rebellion. On Wednesday, those in the GPO garrison

could hear artillery fire in the distance. Willie accompanied Patrick on a tour of the Sackville Street positions, where both men narrowly avoided being hit by gunfire. They then passed along the roof of the GPO, from where they could view Volunteers on guard in neighbouring buildings and snipers further afield. According to Desmond Ryan, Willie was both objective and somewhat sad:

> 'A curious business,' comments Willie Pearse in his slow lisping voice as he looks in passing at the fires and chaos in view, 'I wonder how it will all end? I know a lot of good work has been done but there is a great deal more to do.' There is a melancholy and patient look in his sensitive dark brown eyes ... [9]

Desmond Ryan's several allusions to Willie looking sad in the weeks prior to this and during the Rising itself could appear to suggest that Willie was an unwilling revolutionary. But Ryan himself refutes this possibility. For him, the 'suggestion of a great sadness' which was imparted by Willie was a part of his character, but only one part, and one that did not preclude him from embracing militant politics wholeheartedly:

> 'The beauty of the world had made him sad,' and he had gone too upon his way sorrowful. But you must remember that the sadness of the world neither soured him nor robbed him of a keen sense of humour. Nor did it indispose him

for action as his enthusiastic participation in the Irish Volunteers goes far to prove.[10]

That evening Patrick sent a letter to their mother, and Willie added a short postscript that would be almost comically taciturn were it not for the seriousness of the situation.

Have really nothing to say. We are still here. Don't worry. I saw a priest again (confession) and was talking to Father Bowden also.[11]

Willie was present, along with Plunkett, MacDiarmada, and Clarke, when Patrick made a formal address to the GPO garrison and attempted to boost morale with (false) assurances about a countrywide uprising. At night no one got much sleep; there were shots, explosions, and odd bursts of patriotic song. Some distance away, buildings on Tyler's Corner were on fire. As Willie gazed at the flames, Desmond Ryan, bedding down behind the counters in the GPO, heard him state that 'nothing will stop that fire from spreading down the whole block'.[12]

On Thursday the GPO, where nerves were now on edge, sustained serious shelling from 3pm onwards. During a lull in the firing Patrick spoke to the men and raised their spirits. But the shelling had set even more buildings on fire, and that evening areas of the GPO were as bright as day because of the lurid flames. When an oil works near Abbey Street was hit, a terrifying sheet of flame slid onto the street, followed by a thunderous explosion. Dick Humphries provides a dramatic description of the experience of the men in the GPO:

> The intense light compels one to close the eyes. Even here the light is so terrible that it strikes one like a solid thing as blasts of scorching air come through the glassless windows ... The whole thing seems too terrible to be real. Crimson tinged men moved around dazedly. Above it all the sharp crackle of rifle fire predominates, while the deadly rattle of the machine gun sounds like the coughing laughter of jeering spirits.[13]

Among the buildings to be destroyed in the conflagration in Abbey Street was a place familiar to Willie – the Royal Hibernian Academy, scene of the annual exhibitions in which his work was shown. The fine three-storey building, along with the hundreds of valuable artworks being displayed in that year's exhibition, was completely destroyed. Though Willie could not know yet about the loss of the RHA, the terrifying scenes now surrounding those in the GPO must have impacted on his artistic sensibility. Nonetheless he remained calm and organised. Humphries recalled that at 12.30 the two Pearses, The O'Rahilly and some other officers made a tour of the defences and seemed satisfied with progress.

Men from nearby outposts had already retreated to the GPO, but the complex was now under serious threat from the fires which were beginning to surround it. On Friday, fire had taken hold of the GPO itself and pressure increased on the leaders. Humphries recalled Patrick and Joseph Plunkett speaking excitedly.[14] Willie went after some men, including MW O'Reilly, who were evacuating a wounded comrade to Jervis Street Hospital through a path tunnelled through various buildings. Willie ordered the men to return to the GPO. When O'Reilly demurred, another man, Patrick Caldwell, intervened, stating that Willie was a 'senior captain' and that his orders must be heeded.[15] This important detail tells us that Willie's rank was greater than that of O'Reilly, who was an officer. The incident could also suggest that Willie's problems with discipline at St Enda's had followed him to the GPO, or perhaps the familiarity of old acquaintance may have prompted O'Reilly's protest in the heat of battle: he had played alongside Willie in *The Walls of Athens*. On the men's return to the GPO, Willie led them to an exit door facing Henry Place where Patrick was waiting, the building having been evacuated. At one stage Willie was part of a group of about a dozen men headed by his brother which included George Plunkett and Frank Henderson. They gathered by the door to Henry Street across from Henry Place. The firing from nearby barricades was intense. These attacks, along with the fire, the thunderous din of the guns and the sound of collapsing buildings, must have made for a terrifying experience. Patrick, Willie and MW O'Reilly were among the last to leave. The O'Rahilly and others had been shot by the British during an earlier attempt to make a break for the Williams & Woods factory nearby. As confusion reigned, MacDiarmada, having spoken to the injured Connolly, asked Seán McLoughlin, who knew the area and had kept his cool, to give orders. McLoughlin arranged for a motor van to be used as a screen for the Volunteers' movements. During the evacuation, Willie and (it seems) Patrick may have helped to carry Connolly on a stretcher across Henry Place (though accounts differ greatly).

Headquarters was set up in a provision shop on the corner of Moore Street. Barriers were built, sentries posted, and some men were told to break through the walls of the houses in order to move as far down Moore Street as possible. McLoughlin recalled:

> After that, a meeting was held of the Headquarters Command. Those in the kitchen at the time were P.H. Pearse, Willie Pearse, James Connolly, Sean McDermott, Tom Clarke, Joe Plunkett, Harry Boland, Winnie Carney, Frank Scollan, the man who had guided the Swords men into the Mendicity a few days before, and two wounded prisoners.[16]

It was proposed that McLoughlin be given command. The Pearse brothers slept upstairs as there wasn't enough room downstairs. They spread blankets on a wide table and McLoughlin slept under it. The next day the burrowing continued and headquarters was moved halfway up Moore

Street to Number 16. The critical nature of the situation was clear, and an initial decision was made for a detachment of twenty men to attack the nearby British barricade at the end of Moore Street. When a man called Michael Cremin identified a window in a storehouse as an ideal location for the delivery of covering fire during the proposed attack, Willie and Eamon Bulfin were sent to assess their chances. Patrick asked how many lives would be lost in the initial attack: McLoughlin guessed twenty or thirty. The survivors were also to be charged with contacting the group holding out in the Four Courts. Just as the twenty men were assembled, a message came that the attacks were to be postponed for an hour. Some of the Volunteers had by now witnessed harrowing scenes of civilians, including some with white flags, being gunned down by indiscriminate fire. The rebels themselves had been the cause of one particularly traumatic incident in which a young girl was accidentally shot dead as they attempted to seek shelter in a house in Henry Place. Patrick questioned McLoughlin further about the likelihood of civilian casualties and whether the route envisaged would involve going through populous areas. McLoughlin agreed 'that this was so' and Patrick asked him to give notice of a ceasefire order that would last an hour.

Willie was part of a group which gathered around Connolly in their improvised headquarters in 16 Moore Street to discuss seeking terms for surrender. Having stepped out to ask for a safety razor for his brother, Willie told Desmond Ryan that the decision to surrender was made 'to save the men from slaughter, for slaughter it is'.[17] The leadership's concern for the lives of both combatants and civilians stands in sharp contrast to the prevailing attitude of military and political leadership on both sides of the Great War. Patrick shook hands in silence with those in the room and left with Nurse Elizabeth O'Farrell to seek the terms of surrender. Julia Grennan recalled that all present were in tears, except for MacDiarmada and Willie.[18] As Patrick left, Desmond Ryan entered and recalled that Willie 'shook his head sadly, and then sighed with relief at the thought the men might be saved … "But say nothing yet as it may not come to anything" [he said].'[19] Willie would never see Patrick again.

Patrick's offer of a conditional surrender was refused by General Lowe and he was forced to surrender unconditionally, though on his request this was only for the men under his own command. He was taken away to Arbour Hill and Nurse Elizabeth O'Farrell was sent back to Moore Street to bring news of the surrender before conveying messages to the outposts. One by one, the other leaders accepted the surrender; some reluctantly, as they had not been under the same pressure as those who had occupied the GPO. Exhausted and dishevelled, the rebels now faced the end of a dream that had been years in planning. After a short speech by MacDiarmada, Willie was one of those who took a prominent part in organising the formal surrender of the garrison, chosen perhaps because he was well-known. He was not in overall command, however, and acted under the instructions of Seán McLoughlin. Fintan Murphy recalled that it was Willie who conveyed the message to him and his group that surrender was imminent. Willie, in Murphy's recollection, seems to have spoken with authority and, given the circumstances, much dignity:

> Presently we saw Willie Pearse ... approaching with some other officers. He stood before us and, calling us to attention, told us how hopeless our position was and how Pearse and the general staff had decided we must surrender. He praised the gallant stand that had been made against such overwhelming odds and then gave us our instructions. We were to march down Moore Street, through Henry Street and into Upper O'Connell Street [Sackville Street] where we would be met by the British and where we would make our surrender and lay down our arms. There were protesting murmurs from the ranks, and mutterings that we would never lay down our arms, when Willie Pearse called us to order and told us to uphold our honour with dignity, not to flinch at our final humiliation, but to realise we had fought bravely for the Irish Republic and only overwhelming force had defeated us.[20]

At around 3pm Willie shouted the message of surrender to

a group hiding out in a stable near Moore Street, which included Seán MacEntee. On hearing voices up the street calling out 'any Volunteers here?', MacEntee recalled running up to Willie and a Captain Breen who accompanied him. MacEntee asked if the reports of surrender were true.

> 'What', I cried out to Pearse, 'has it come to this?' 'It has', he replied sorrowfully, 'but we have got terms, the best possible terms – we are all to march out with arms in our hands and no one will be detained but the leaders.' 'What then, are we to do?' 'Bring along all the men and all the arms you have, and fall in behind Mr Breen here.' 'We have some badly wounded. What shall we do with them?' 'Let some person stay with those who are not able to walk but let the others fall in here. And please hurry. We have to round up all we can before night.' In a minute or two we had arranged ourselves as Willie Pearse had desired ...[21]

In most of these accounts Willie speaks with the confidence of someone with some authority. Though prominent, he was not in overall command of the actual surrender, which involved the men marching to Sackville Street to the British Army position there. Willie, Eamon Bulfin recalled, was present when the men emerged from the various buildings and yards in the Moore Street area where they had been sheltering and lined up, but did not take charge.[22] In Desmond Ryan's (perhaps somewhat romanticised) recollection, Willie and

Joseph Plunkett headed the surrender march 'waving white flags as if they were banners of victory'.[23] It was recalled that the advance party marching at the head of the main body contained Seán McLoughlin, Seán MacDiarmada, Willie and possibly Joseph Plunkett. Given the correspondence between various accounts, it is fairly certain that Willie, along with others, was at the head of the main group surrendering. Commandant James Connolly was gravely injured and Patrick had departed with General Lowe. That Willie was granted (or assumed) a special status beyond his role as *aide de camp* seems clear: others of a similar or greater status were – perhaps prudently – not to the fore in the surrender.

Eerie scenes greeted the surrendering rebels. The city was deserted except for the soldiers lining the streets and the bodies that lay here and there. One of these was The O'Rahilly, on whose body a mobilising order from Willie would later be found. On Sackville Street buildings still smouldered, the eastern side of the street devastated by fire and shelling. As the surrendering rebels made their final march, the street was lined with British troops. The Volunteers were lined up in front of the Gresham Hotel where, in a final show of pride and 'to the extreme annoyance both visible and vocal of the senior British officer present', McLoughlin gave the order to ground arms and take four paces back.[24] Names and addresses were taken and an initial sifting began. After about an hour the men were escorted to the gardens in front of the Rotunda and told to get down on the grass. Willie, along with other Volunteers and members of the Citizen Army, spent Saturday evening in discomfort in an open space near the Rotunda, the scene of so many cultural and nationalist gatherings. McLoughlin recalled being near the front railings in a group that included Willie, MacDiarmada, and Tom Clarke. Willie gave McLoughlin some money in case of need. As it grew dark the prisoners were joined by Volunteers from the Four Courts and North King Street garrisons. Amid the fear, discomfort and silence, a lone Dublin fireman came to the railings and shouted, 'God bless you boys!'[25] There were guns and even a machine gun trained on the prisoners. No food was distributed, but Willie was slipped a raw Oxo cube by MW O'Reilly.[26]

Later, a volatile officer threatened to shoot the prisoners and took a whistle from Willie 'with a sneer'. This episode seems to have taken place on the Sunday morning; another prisoner recalled the threatening officer cutting the epaulette from Willie's tunic and tearing up of a piece of paper which contained details about the sending of rations to an outpost of the GPO. The prisoner surmised that the treatment of Willie was an effort to goad others into reaction.[27] However, another story has Willie himself in a more belligerent mood. It was recalled that 'Willie Pearse began to insult a young man, a young English officer, who was very polite, very courteous altogether. So Seán McGarry brought him aside and he said "For God's sake, shut up or we'll all be shot." And Willie … said, "Listen, I cannot go home to my mother without Paddy."[28]

After their difficult night the Volunteers were marched to Richmond Barracks on Sunday. It must have been a strenuous march for the men, who had not slept properly, if at all, for several days, and who had not eaten since early the day before. On their way the prisoners were heckled by some local women in Thomas Street, though others along the route appeared to show sympathy. They were marched first of all to the main square and then through an archway before another search took place. In the barracks they were taken to a room where they were kept separate from those who had fought elsewhere. An armed soldier guarded the centre of the room and others were stationed around the sides. Food was distributed along with a chilling warning from a sergeant that this would be the prisoners' last meal. The room was dark, lit only by a lantern by the feet of the soldier in the centre of the room, his bayonet glinting in the shadows. Willie found a spot to lie down. Again he was close to the leaders, this time lying down beside Clarke, MacDiarmada, Plunkett and McGarry, who all shared a quilt that had been used by Connolly in the GPO. A prisoner called Liam Ó Briain, who was to his right, recalled that Willie, on laying his head to the ground, slept immediately, though the sleep was fitful and he spent the night tossing and turning, occasionally shouting 'The fire! The fire!' (possibly remembering the flames in the GPO). In this he was not alone: Seán McGarry also had nightmares about fire.[29] The next day, tea and food were brought to the prisoners by soldiers who showed some kindness towards their captives. The prisoners walked up and down, speaking to each other and waiting for something to happen.

That evening, the group was separated in two halves. At some stage a group of detectives from the Dublin Metropolitan Police entered and moved through the prisoners gathering information. These 'G-men' were summoned as, having followed the activities of the various radical groups for some years, they could identify the leaders and significant members of the Volunteers out of the huge numbers of prisoners. Though the G-men did not initially recognise him, Willie's uniform and the yellow staff tabs on his lapels drew attention and when he gave his name to a 'big stout red-faced G-man' he was immediately brought across the room to join others deemed of importance.[30] Willie was brought out of the room with Clarke, MacDiarmada and others. They were now among the group which had been selected for court martial.

There are numerous reasons why Willie might have been chosen but his identity as an officer – obvious from his uniform – may well have sufficed. His leading role in the formal surrendering of arms and men would also have drawn attention. The decisive factor, however, seems to have been that the G-man recognised Willie's surname: Pearse.

Chapter Eleven

• • • • • • •

May 1916

'So True a Brother'

Following his arrest by General Lowe, Patrick had been a prisoner in Arbour Hill where, on Monday 1 May, he wrote a letter to his mother. He had not seen Willie or the St Enda's boys since the previous Saturday, but believed they were well and 'not now in any danger'.[1] The note was not delivered, but details added in the margin regarding a German expedition on which Patrick had 'counted' provided damning evidence for the authorities. Indeed, given the specific reference to 'aiding the enemy' in the Defence of the Realm legislation under which the court martials were to be carried out, the reference to German aid was so glaring that it seems almost like a deliberate ploy by Patrick (a trained barrister) to take personal responsibility. Around this time Patrick also wrote a poem for Willie, which his younger brother would never see:

To My Brother

O faithful!
Moulded in one womb,
We two have stood together all the years
All the glad years and all the sorrowful years,
Own brothers through good repute and ill
In direct peril true to me
Leaving all things for me, spending yourself
In the hard service I taught to you
Of all the men that I have known on earth,
You only have been my familiar friend
Nor needed I another. [2]

In the early hours of Wednesday 3 May, Patrick, now in Kilmainham Gaol, wrote again to his mother, sisters and Willie, alluding once more to his hope and belief that 'Willie and the St Enda's boys will be all safe'.[3] Patrick also wrote a short note for Willie alone:

Dear old Willie, goodbye and God bless you for all your faithful work for me at St Enda's and elsewhere. No one can ever have had so true a brother as you.[4]

It was probably written in haste as Patrick, aware that he was to be executed, knew Willie had been called for and was on his way.[5] However, Willie would not reach Patrick in time for a final farewell, and never saw the note.

Later that same Wednesday, Willie ('William Pearse') was tried by Field General Court Martial alongside 'John Dougherty' (the false name given by Glasgow-born John McGallogly), John [Seán] McGarry and Corkman JJ Walsh. The order convening the court was dated 2 May. Three officers presided: Colonel EWSK Maconchy, Lieutenant Colonel MA Bent and Major FW Woodward. The charge was that the prisoners 'did an act to wit did take part in an armed rebellion and in the waging of war against his Majesty the King, such act being of such a nature as to be calculated to be prejudicial to the Defence of the Realm and being done with the intention and for the purpose of assisting the enemy.' Willie may have been subject to a brief initial charge: John McGallogly later recalled being charged, along with Tom Clarke and Eamonn Duggan, on an earlier occasion when the wording (on a torn piece of foolscap) was the same as that of the court martial.

The entire court martial took only fifteen minutes, the prisoners had no legal representation and the records show only the barest details.[6] Only Willie pleaded guilty. The first witness, Lieutenant LS King of the Inniskilling Fusiliers, stated: 'I know William Pearse was an officer but I do not know his rank.' He saw 'Pearse, McGarry and Walsh wearing equipment, belts and pouches'. Of course, Willie would have been easily identified as a member of the group stationed in the GPO, where Lieutenant King had been kept after being taken

prisoner on the Tuesday of the Rising. Captured British soldiers ate with rebellion leaders and staff in the canteen in the
GPO.[7] Willie is recorded by the court martial as having stated:
'I had no authority or say in the arrangement of the rebellion.
I was throughout only a personal attaché to my brother P.H.
Pearse. I had no direct command.' A handwritten note shows
that, for some reason, Willie's age was later checked. His name
is underlined in red with an 'x' alongside; an 'x' in the same
red ink is beside the single word at the bottom of the page:
'Death.' All four prisoners tried in Kilmainham on 3 May
were found guilty and condemned to death, but the sentence
was only confirmed and carried out in the case of Willie.

The reasons for Willie's guilty plea remain unclear.
McGarry later recalled Tom Clarke passing word around
that the clause involving 'assisting the enemy' provided a
reason for those court-martialled to plead not guilty. Given
that Willie was court-martialled with McGarry and had
spent hours on end in the company of Clarke after the surrender, it seems unlikely that word of this strategy had not
reached him. Though Desmond Ryan is quoted as having
heard from an eyewitness that Willie Pearse 'practically condemned himself to death by the exultant attitude he adopted
at the court martial', the brief statement noted in the court-
martial records shows only that Willie identified himself as
having a minor supporting role.[8] The witness statement of
McGallogly alludes, like the court-martial records, to Willie

saying he was merely an attaché to his brother.[9] This suggests that Willie may indeed have heeded Tom Clarke's advice. However, and rather strangely, the account of JJ Walsh gives information not found in either McGallogly's memoir or the court-martial record:

> Willie Pearse, Sean McGarry and myself formed a trio. The word had been passed round that we were merely to say we had answered a mobilisation order and had carried out the instructions of our superior officers. McGarry and I followed instructions, but Pearse volunteered the information that he was aware of all the steps leading to the Rising, and that all his brother Patrick knew was known to him also. There was no cross examination.[10]

In his unpublished memoirs, Colonel EWSK Maconchy (by then a Brigadier General) specifically stated that when called on for their defence, many of the accused in the court martials 'generally only convicted themselves out of their own mouths ... In many cases I refused to put down what they said as it only made their case worse.'[11] This may explain the brevity of Willie Pearse's recorded defence and the discrepancy between it and the recollections of JJ Walsh. Maconchy's decision not to record evidence which might '[make] their case worse' is another strong hint that, although he was in charge of the court martial, the final decision for executing prisoners was not his to make. In fact, it is largely accepted that the decision was made by military commander General John Maxwell and approved by Prime Minster Asquith and the British cabinet. An Irishman who did not relish his role, Maconchy was 'much relieved' when eventually released from his duties.[12]

We may never know why Willie pleaded guilty. It may have been that a man so sensitive about sin was led to his guilty plea by his Catholic misgivings about lying. Perhaps he was traumatised and exhausted; perhaps he was broken by grief and shock; perhaps he was indeed uncaring and exultant, and beneath his 'gentle' exterior was a long-repressed temper that manifested itself in a final show of defiance. Perhaps his convictions were so strongly felt that he could not envisage a prudent denial of the extent of his immersion in the plans for the rebellion. The Defence of the Realm Act was not mentioned in General Maxwell's summary of Willie's details in his 'Short history of rebels on whom it has been necessary to inflict the supreme penalty', the title of the report he sent to Prime Minister Asquith on 11 May 1916. General Maxwell, summarising the rationale for the execution of William Pearse, mentioned only Willie's relationship to Patrick, the fact that he was associated with the 'Sinn Féin movement from its inception', that he was present in the GPO during the fighting and was 'acting as an officer and surrendered with the rebels in Sackville Street'. Maxwell also stated that Willie held the rank of 'Commandant in the rebel army.'[13] Yet the witness who identified Willie at the court martial clearly stated that he did not know Willie's rank.

Maxwell's allusion to Willie's involvement in the 'Sinn Féin movement' in the context of justifying his execution showed his ignorance of the finer details of the Irish political and cultural scene: Sinn Féin did not plan the rebellion and the organisation had been in decline for some years. Maxwell was not alone in confusing Sinn Féin with the Irish-Ireland cultural movement: the press was already referring to the Rising as the Sinn Féin rebellion, as were English MPs in the House of Commons. This may have arisen due to the fact that even within Irish nationalism the term had been used for several years as shorthand for activists connected with the wider Gaelic nationalist scene. Maxwell's allusion to Willie being associated with Sinn Féin is also an indictment of his own careless attitude, where a vaguely described association with a moderate political and cultural movement was deemed a relevant point in his (very brief) synopsis of the context for ordering Willie's execution.

As with the previous day's executions of Clarke, MacDonagh and Patrick, it seems there was a gap between the convening of Willie's court martial (when the court martial was arranged and its personnel summoned) on 2 May, the court martial itself (3 May) and the executions in the early hours of 4 May. Fr Columbus of the Capuchin Friars, who attended to some of the prisoners before their executions, was convinced that this gap was to allow for time to refer the matter to the British Cabinet. Statements made later in the House of Commons by Asquith confirm Cabinet knowledge – and approval – of the executions.[14] John McGallogly recalled that after the court martial, the prisoners were removed to Kilmainham where they received news of their sentence in their individual cells. McGallogly, McGarry and JJ Walsh were told that they were to be executed before being informed the sentences were being commuted. No one, it seems, really believed that Willie would be shot. Young Seán McLoughlin expected the signatories to be executed, as did at least some of the signatories themselves:

> But Seán Heuston! And Con Colbert! I had known them both so well ... And Ned Daly and Willie Pearse! For these I felt the keenest sorrow – deaths so terribly unnecessary.[15]

On Wednesday morning, 3 May, Fr Aloysius of the Capuchins in Church Street had brought news of the earlier executions to Thomas MacDonagh's wife and Mrs Pearse. He recalled:

> I told Mrs Pearse that I believed Willie would be spared; that I could not conceive of them executing her second son. 'No,' she said, 'I believe they will put him to death too. I can't imagine Willie living without Pat. They were insepa-rable. It was lovely to see the way they bade goodnight to each other every night. Willie would never be happy to live without Pat.'[16]

Towards midnight on that same day, Margaret and Mrs Pearse were awoken by the arrival of a military lorry. According to her own account, Margaret went to the hall door and was given a note saying that the prisoner William Pearse wanted to see them. Margaret realised at once what the message meant and told her mother, 'More bad news. Willie wants to see us as he is going too.'[17] Mary Brigid, who lived elsewhere, is not mentioned in Margaret's account. The two Margarets dressed quickly and accompanied the soldiers. It was a stressful journey as the lorry broke down in Terenure and had to be repaired. In the early hours of the morning they arrived at Kilmainham, where there was another long delay. The prison, which had not been in use for some time, appeared even more grim as the interruption of gas supplies during the fighting meant that there was no light. Finally the two Margarets were brought to Willie, whose cell was in the more modern wing of the prison:

> When our turn came we entered the cell and found Willie standing, ready to receive us. There were three military officers with him, each holding a candle, the only available light. We talked quietly, calmly and chiefly about personal matters – some letters and books about which Willie was anxious. We told him how proud we were of him, and of Pat and that we were satisfied they had done right.[18]

Willie was calm, despite the death of his brother. Margaret

recalled his description of the shocking way he learned of his beloved Pat's death:

'Last night', he said, 'I had a terrible experience. I was in prison over there (indicating across the road) when a guard of soldiers came and brought me here. About half way over we heard shots. The men looked at each other and one said "Too late". I think they were bringing me here to see Pat, but we heard only the volley of shots which took him.'[19]

In Margaret Pearse Snr's version, which betrays her tendency to romanticise, Willie tells her: 'I was brought across a yard. When we got to a gate, the man with me knocked. The answer we got was "You are too late". On the minute the spirit in me grew strong.'[20] Willie told his sister that he had asked for a priest but none had come so far (it later transpired that the prison authorities had sent a message to the James's Street Presbytery but it was misunderstood). Mrs Pearse and Margaret bade Willie a last goodbye 'and left him gazing after us, one longing, sad look, till the cell door closed'.[21] Margaret recalled a feeling of terrible resignation. They returned home and prayed.

After hearing his request for a priest, Willie's sister had insisted on one being called. His final visitor was the Pearses' old supporter Fr Augustine, who had been summoned urgently with three of his fellow friars from the nearby monastery in Church Street to attend to those who were to be executed. After a fraught journey Fr Augustine and the others reached Kilmainham, where the four prisoners were about to be led out of their cells with their hands bound behind their backs. The governor of the prison was 'all excitement'; the four men, Joseph Plunkett, William Pearse, Michael O'Hanrahan and Edward Daly, were due to be shot at 3.25am.[22] Fr Augustine was extremely distressed, writing later that 'horror struck [his] soul' on seeing the prisoners. For now he remained calm and decided that each priest would attend a prisoner. He himself attended Willie, as the executions were delayed for a quarter of an hour.[23] Another priest present, Fr Columbus, recorded his impressions of those about to be executed:

> How did they conduct themselves? As brave, courageous and dauntless as could be. It was we rather who appeared pale, pallid and timorous as if we were to be the victims. What to say? To encourage them, there was no necessity.[24]

Like Margaret, Fr Augustine repeatedly remarked on Willie's calm demeanour:

> He was beautifully calm, made his confession, as if he were doing it on an ordinary occasion, and received Holy Communion with great devotion.

> I remember – at the time I didn't quite understand the situation – he knelt down beside the table and tried to balance

himself on one knee because his hands were tied behind his back, but there was no fear in his face and no fear in his heart.[25]

Before Willie's confession was finished, a knock came on the cell door and an officer apologised that the time was up. Fr Augustine then walked over to where Joseph Plunkett and Michael O'Hanrahan were and recalled that when he turned around 'poor Willie Pearse was gone'.[26] Willie was the second prisoner to be shot that night. Fr Columbus recalled the 'callously informal' atmosphere at this second round of executions in Kilmainham:

Here they stood chatting with one another; with us; with the soldiers. There was none of that solemnity one associates with an affair of the kind. Merely the Governor appears; mentions a name; gives the signal – ready. The prisoner shakes hands all around; then his hands are tied behind his back; a bandage is placed across his eyes; soldiers take up their place, one at either side to guide him and the priest goes in front. As he reaches the outer door another soldier awaits to put a piece of white paper over his heart. The procession goes along one yard, then through a gate leading into the next. Here the firing squadron of twelve are waiting, rifles loaded. An officer stands out to the left, a little in advance, on the right are the Governor and Doctor. The two soldiers quickly withdraw to one side; a silent signal from the officer, a deafening volley, he falls in a heap on the ground – dead.[27]

The rushed atmosphere and the proximity of the prisoners and priests to the executions added to the horror of the situation. Inside the prison, the other priests, prisoners and soldiers heard the crash of bullets and then Michael O'Hanrahan, who had been clasping Fr Augustine's hand and asking him to console his mother and sisters, was led out. Like Fr Augustine, Fr Columbus felt the whole experience to be 'horrible, ghastly, disgusting, sickening. And then the butchery goes on till all four are dead.'[28] After the executions the friars were driven back to Church Street, where they said Mass for the souls of the prisoners. Fr Columbus felt 'sick with the callousness and horror of it all'.[29] Later that night they began to react to the confused and disturbing events they had witnessed:

> Why the summons only at the last moment? Why was not decent time given for the sacraments? Why the extra cruelty of depriving the men of the help and comfort of a priest to get sympathy and company during those long dreary hours of the night awaiting death?[30]

The friars, respected and articulate, would prove powerful advocates for nationalism in the years ahead, and their horrified reaction to the hasty executions would be echoed across broad sections of Irish nationalist society. There were scores of priests in positions of leadership in the Gaelic League, and the Pearses in particular had many connections with nationalist clergy through the family firm. A Loreto nun called Mother

Columba, another sister of Willie's friend Fr Gibbons, was among the first to react, penning the ballad 'Who Fears to Speak of Easter Week' almost as soon as word came of the executions. In May 1916 Fr Tomás de Bhál, a County Limerick priest who had commissioned a Statue of Mary from Willie Pearse and invited Patrick to speak to local Volunteers, was one of two priests defended by Dr O'Dwyer, the Bishop of Limerick, after General Maxwell had complained of their public displays of sympathy for the nationalist cause.[31]

Speaking in the Commons on 4 May, Prime Minister Asquith stated that it was 'not desirable to say more at the moment than that all appropriate measures have been taken, and are being taken, to deal with the rebellion and those responsible for it'.[32] His observations reflected the secrecy and haste that were a feature of the court martials being conducted under the Defence of the Realm Act. On that same day, Harold Tennant, the Under Secretary of State for War, was questioned in the House of Commons about the case of a young boy who had been sentenced to death by court martial a month after his release from hospital, where he had been treated for a nervous breakdown. Mr Tennant's answer revealed that the boy had already been shot. The 'unnerving unpredictability' which has been detected in relation to the death sentences handed out during the Dublin court martials of May 1916 was not unusual for the times.[33] Political and military expediency meant that it was not just in Dublin that the fine details of innocence, guilt and due procedure were dispensed with in the name of providing an example.

Like the other executed prisoners, Willie Pearse was buried in quicklime in a mass grave at Arbour Hill. In an Ireland which was known, then as now, for the care and time taken for wakes and funerals, this lack of respect for the dead would have been particularly upsetting. Artist Cesca Trench, who knew all the prisoners executed on 4 May, often waxed long and lyrical in her diaries, but the entry concerning the execution of Willie and his three comrades contains only the bare facts, almost as if they rendered her speechless. Many of those who knew Willie through the art world and the theatre were particularly shocked at his execution, and from the moment that news of his death emerged his case was the focus of particular discussion. Not everyone would have been privy to Willie's position on the subcommittee of the Wolfe Tone and United Irishmen Memorial Committee, and his personality was so gentle and unassuming that many people were shocked at his role in the rebellion, never mind his execution. The IPP MP and deputy party leader John Dillon was reportedly never so 'downhearted' as when he heard of the younger Pearse brother's death.[34]

While many Dubliners were unsympathetic to the rebels' fate, even as the early executions were announced, the widespread shock caused by the continuing and seemingly relentless and arbitrary executions soon led to further radicalisation among those with a broad sympathy for the rebels' aims, if not their methods. The imprisonment of thousands of nationalists, many of whom had not been involved in the Rising, was soon another focal point for activism as the rebels from various outposts exchanged stories and ideas. Furthermore, the secret nature of the trials and executions, as well as news of the murder by British soldiers of pacifist Francis Sheehy-Skeffington and of a number of unarmed civilians in North King Street was already radicalising moderate nationalists in Ireland. On 11 May John Dillon told the House of Commons that

> Thousands of people in Dublin, who ten days ago were bitterly opposed to the whole of the Sinn Fein movement and to the rebellion, are now becoming infuriated against the Government on account of these executions [and] that feeling is spreading throughout the country in a most dangerous degree.[35]

On 15 May questions specific to Patrick and Willie Pearse were raised in the House of Commons. After some questions specific to Patrick, IPP MP Laurence Ginnell mentioned the case of Willie who, for some reason, he believed to be a minor:

> Mr Ginnell: Can the right hon. Gentleman say why his young brother, a minor in every respect, condition, and age, and not a signatory of the republican proclamation, has been shot?

Mr Tennant: He was convicted by a court martial.

Mr Ginnell: Was he convicted of any offence but that of being a brother of P.H. Pearse?[36]

He received no satisfactory answer. On 25 May, Ginnell returned once more to the subject of Willie's execution and asked the Prime Minister 'whether, in the case of William Pearse, summarily executed in Dublin, not being either a leader or a signatory of the republican proclamation, any evidence was produced differentiating him from those not executed other than his relationship to his executed brother P.H. Pearse?'

The Prime Minister: Yes, Sir, ample evidence of this man's guilt was, of course, produced before the court martial. Mr Ginnell: Can the right hon. Gentleman state any evidence but the fact of his relationship to his brother?[37]

The Irish Times reported Mr Asquith's answer as being: 'There was ample evidence.'[38] There may well have been, but neither the Prime Minister nor the court martial appear to have been in a position to provide it. Always independent in his political convictions and actions, and deeply angry at the deaths of men who were personally close to him, Ginnell resigned his IPP seat and joined a newly invigorated Sinn Féin the following year.

Outside of the technical issue of his guilt or innocence under the Defence of the Realm legislation, how involved was

Willie in the preparations for the Rising? Geraldine Plunkett's statement that Willie 'was not a leader'[39] is correct both in regard to his personality and to his official role in planning the Rising. Nonetheless, Willie was present with the leaders at vital meetings in the run-up to the Rising, at meetings in Liberty Hall and at the crucial gathering in the Gaelic League office on the Sunday night after it was decided to go ahead with the Rising. He was also in the leading group as the insurgents marched from Liberty Hall to the GPO. In the GPO itself, he was constantly present by his brother's side; he played a prominent role at the evacuation of the GPO, was at the front of the main group of insurgents as they marched towards the Gresham Hotel in order to surrender and, when in custody, was always in the company of the Rising's leaders. But neither his known political background nor the mere fact of his proximity to the signatories and to prominent IRB members was sufficient evidence for his being sentenced to death under the Defence of the Realm legislation, which specifically pertained to 'aiding the enemy'. Years later, the legal advisor to General Maxwell, Alfred Bucknill, said that 'beyond the Proclamation for the Irish Republic which contained the names of seven signatories, we knew very little of the prime movers in the rebellion in Dublin'. Bucknill described a document signed by James Connolly which mentioned various commandants: unsurprisingly, Willie was not among them. In addition Bucknill mentions a small number of other documents containing orders which he recalled being used at the trials. He stated, 'The only thing to do was to get the names of officers who could identify prisoners as having taken part in the fighting and having surrendered with arms in their hands.'[40] Lieutenant LS King did identify Willie as having carried equipment but this was not in itself an offence under the Defence of the Realm legislation.

There are several reasons to believe that Willie was executed in a situation where events were moving fast, mistakes were made, and little thought was given to due legal procedure or care. General Maxwell would later claim in his 'Short History of Rebels' – though this was not mentioned in the original paperwork from the court martials – that Willie was a commandant. A letter written years later to the Army Pension Board of the Irish Free State on behalf of Margaret Pearse describes Willie as a commandant, a description echoed in a letter written in support of the application by Norman Reddin. There was, however, a particular system in place for pension applications that meant, for example, that anyone who was wounded in the Rising was immediately classed as an officer. Captain Henry Murray did not mention Willie in a list he provided of those in command of the various companies in the 4th Battalion, though two lieutenants are named as being immediately under Patrick's rank. Furthermore he recalled Willie only in the role of accompanying his brother in the latter's visits to A Company: Willie made 'no particular impression'.[41] Willie is recalled as having the rank of second lieutenant before he joined headquarters staff and is specifically termed a 'captain' (and a 'senior captain') in various accounts of the fighting at and around the GPO.[42] The mobilisation order signed by Willie for The O'Rahilly, found on the latter's body, would have provided further damning evidence, but there is no record of it being used. In reality, it seems that Willie's status as Patrick's 'personal attaché' was similar to that of Seán McGarry's relationship to Tom Clarke, or Michael Collins's to Joseph Plunkett. But McGarry's death sentence was commuted. Significantly, General Maxwell – who had been in overall command of British forces since April 28 – now noted that Willie was Patrick's brother, though many sets of brothers took part in the Rising. Thomas MacDonagh's brothers were not executed, nor were the Plunkett brothers, though the connections were known in some cases at least. Willie's surname drew attention to him, but his 'guilty' plea in the charged atmosphere of what was only the second day of court martials may have been the deciding factor in his execution.

Chapter Twelve

'Rich In Ordinary Plenty'

After the Rising, Mrs Pearse was traumatised. The family campaigned without success for the return of the bodies of Patrick and Willie, and in late May, John Dillon wrote to Asquith on their behalf, describing Willie as 'a most inoffensive creature, by no means a leader among the rebels' with whom he had a 'slight acquaintance'.[1] Desmond Ryan recalled Mrs Pearse's pain in the weeks and years after Easter 1916:

> Sometimes, Margaret Pearse told me then, the long sorrow came upon her with a terrible intensity as she walked the Dublin streets by herself. She would look round and see people looking at her for she had called out 'Pat and Willie! ... Pat and Willie!'[2]

Anniversary masses provided some consolation, and in all of the commemorative events Mrs Pearse was careful to include Willie. She was also consoled by her understanding that Willie and Patrick were together in death, as in life.

In a letter to a cousin, Geraldine, she wrote, 'although my trial has been greater by my two darlings going I am more resigned at both being united in death as they were united in life'.[3] She even went as far as amending a transcription of Patrick's poem 'The Mother' to include Willie: 'Receive my first born son into thy arms' became 'Receive my two dear sons into thy arms'. Mrs Pearse told her that 'Willie was a grand fellow too, with a brave brave spirit, like unto Pat'.[4] Later, when contributing to Mary Brigid's reminiscences about Patrick, Mrs Pearse wrote that it was difficult for her 'to write about Patrick without mentioning Willie more frequently. Both were lovable and they were inseparable. Since their deaths I have never spoken of one without speaking of the other also.'[5]

In December 1917 Patrick's play *The Singer* was given its official premiere by actors associated with St Enda's in the Foresters' Hall at 41 Parnell Square, where the IRB had drilled and where many fundraising concerts had been held for the Volunteers. Having taken part in the Rising, many of the original cast reprised their aborted roles: Willie's old acting comrades, the Nic Shiubhlaigh/Walker sisters, took on the female roles, while Eunan McGinley played Colm; other actors included Eunan's brother Conor, David Sears, Eamon Bulfin and Fintan Murphy. The play about a revolution to be was now a play about a revolution that was, and many among the actors and audience would subsequently renew their military activities. When St Enda's was occupied by British military a short time after the Rising, the two Margarets moved to Cullenswood House, which became an important rendezvous point for militant nationalists during the War of Independence. Eamon Bulfin stayed there, as did Richard Mulcahy, who had an apartment. Michael Collins also had an office there for a time where, unknown to Margaret Pearse, guns and explosives were hidden.[6] On the departure of the military from the Hermitage, it was discovered that Willie's plaster casts had been broken and mutilated.[7] While this wanton destruction was a severe emotional blow for the family, it also curtailed the opportunity to assess Willie's artistic work on any substantive scale.

Despite the serene countenance that Mrs Pearse usually managed to present in public, her grief at the death of her sons was almost constant: 'The wound remained and sometimes it opened with sharp pangs of loss.'[8] It was bearing that sense of loss that Mrs Pearse made her foray into public life as a TD in the first Dáil. During the Treaty debate that followed the War of Independence, she stirred pity on both sides when, during a contribution to an already emotional discussion, she broke down and sobbed quietly, saying, 'I feel in my heart the ghosts of my sons...'[9] Later, she was able to see the humour in the role allotted to her as keeper of her sons' ideals: 'I went to the meeting and made a Pat and Willie speech. It's all I'm good for at such affairs.'[10]

Willie's sister Margaret, who was briefly a TD and then a Senator, was also deeply affected by the executions. For Nina Jaglom, a relative of the Pearses who saw Margaret frequently in the 1960s, her abiding memory of Willie's older sister was her sadness. Nina felt that the Pearse women never really recovered from their loss.[11] Patrick and Willie were forever young, forever synonymous with the Rising: Mrs Pearse and Margaret preserved the room where the two brothers had their last meal in St Enda's exactly as it had been the day they left, even keeping the two cups from which the brothers had drunk their final cups of tea.[12] Mrs Pearse slept in the room her sons had occupied until ill-health meant she had to move to a lower floor. When Arbour Hill was opened to the public in 1932 she decided against visiting their grave, as it would be too poignant, and she died later that same year.

Willie and Patrick's younger sister, Mary Brigid, must have been particularly shocked at her brothers' deaths, especially as she had not been aware of preparations for the Rising. For James Vincent's daughter Florence, Willie's half-niece, her 'whole world exploded' when she learned of the Rising.[13] Her husband had already been wounded in the Great War, and her politics were 'not republican, rather the opposite'.[14] Her brother James (Willie's godson) also joined the British Army. But notwithstanding the political differences within the wider family, the deaths of Patrick and Willie had a deep emotional impact. Noel Scarlett said that neither his mother

Florence, nor Margaret or Mary Brigid, whom he knew well, spoke often about Patrick and Willie, but he retained the sense of trauma that the executions had caused his family: 'Two from the same family, it was a terrible thing.'[15] James Vincent's widow Mary lived out her days in a tenement; her husband's early death meant her life was not easy, and she sometimes turned to drink. Mrs Pearse and her daughters stayed in close contact with the various members of James Vincent's family, though, and the Scarletts often holidayed at St Enda's, retaining fond memories of Margaret and Mary Brigid.

Willie's half-sister Mary Emily came to live in a small lodge at St Enda's in the 1920s. Her son Alf, who had worked so closely with Willie in the worlds of art and theatre, died while still a young man, from privations suffered while imprisoned during the brief but vicious Civil War which followed the War of Independence.

Some of Willie's relatives in Birmingham felt an acute sense of betrayal following their Dublin cousins' participation in the Rising. Harry Pearse, the son of Willie's first cousin Arthur, died on the Western Front that same year. Arthur believed that the British had had to divert efforts from the war to Ireland, leaving his son more vulnerable in France, and his shame about Patrick and Willie lasted his whole life.[16] When a BBC programme about the Pearses was mooted in the 1960s, family member Millicent Clayton, acting on behalf of the ninety-six-year-old Arthur,

instructed that family papers and photographs with connections to Patrick and Willie be destroyed.

Mary Kate 'May' Kelly, the cousin who had been brought up
alongside Willie, described the Rising and executions as 'a terrible business'.[17] Her English-born son, Patrick Shovelton, who
was married to a Dame of the British Empire, was nonetheless
immensely proud of both Patrick and Willie, whom he deemed
'Irish patriots'. He believed the Rising to be 'a gallant show of
what strength could be mustered against overwhelming odds'.[18]

Friends grieved and remembered too. David Sears last saw
Willie from a distance in Richmond Barracks, in a group being
photographed by a British officer. Sears recalled that Willie
had 'a calm determined expression on his face. As he stood
there with his arms folded on his chest, absolutely indifferent
to what was going on, I at last fully appreciated his greatness.' For Sears, this 'greatness' was to do with Willie's character and not his influence: Willie, 'if not among the greatest,
was certainly one of the most lovable of those who gave their
lives in the cause of Irish nationhood'.[19] He said Willie's death
'removed one of the most ennobling influences of my life
and left me only memories and regrets'.[20] For others, Willie
seemed an unlikely revolutionary. Young Larry Fleming, the
boy who delivered milk to Willie at the Pearse business in
Great Brunswick Street, was shocked when he heard that the
young man with his 'hair in his eyes' was one of those involved
in the rebellion. For decades later Larry would mimic Willie's

voice and way of talking for his grandchildren, and Willie's involvement in the rebellion remained a lifelong mystery to him.[21] TK Moylan, who knew Willie from the School of Art, wrote that it was with 'considerable surprise' he and others learned that Willie was part of the Rising:

> He was such a quiet, plodding, inoffensive, unaggressive individual, one could not associate him with bloodshed. I doubt if he ever fired a gun, even in Easter week, and I can imagine no-one less likely to try to take the life of a fellow man.[22]

We do not know if Willie fired a gun during the Rising; many of the rebels didn't. But his preparations suggest someone fully committed to military action. Willie helped make explosives and carried ammunition for a revolver on his Sam Browne belt. Sears remembered discussing the possibility of a revolution with Willie and being amazed and deeply impressed 'by the resolution in the few quiet words that he said. I never in my life received a greater impression of determination.'[23] Sears was particularly impressed by the fact that Willie went against his own character in pursuing revolution. Willie appears to have had both an acute awareness of his own character and considerable self-control: he also told Sears that as a young man he used to lose his temper but that he had conquered this tendency. Desmond Ryan recalled Willie as having spoken 'very often of politics ... His national faith was the same as his brother's, and quite as intense and ardent. Like

P.H. Pearse, he never blatantly expressed his beliefs; indeed preferred to listen a good while before he argued.'[24] Ryan's description of Willie's motivations refutes the theory sometimes advanced that the latter stumbled into rebellion on his brother's coat-tails:

> He thought an insurrection in the circumstances worth a trial. He believed implicitly in a successful issue to the national struggle, but, in Easter 1916 or similar contingencies, he doubtlessly believed circumstances had arisen to make a fight against overwhelming odds a point of honour … The simple explanation is that they both hoped for the best, but dared the worst.[25]

Ryan remembered Willie speaking of his probable death in an insurrection: 'I should not care. I should die for what I believed. Beyond my work in St Enda's I have no interest in life.'[26] It may seem strange at first that a sculptor, actor, and activist with a deep interest in literature, sport, and politics and a wide circle of friends should say this. The first part of the statement reminds us of the strength of Willie's convictions, while the second part is a reminder that in embracing these convictions Willie was leaving behind – or had already left behind – a rich cultural and personal life. It is also possible to read the statement in a broader way, that of Willie seeing his role at St Enda's as encapsulating his whole vision, a vision which he deemed worth fighting for, no matter what. Sears's memory of Willie supports this reading: 'Willie had a healthy regard for his life. He did not, like most men, morbidly covet it.'[27] Sears believed that 'having witnessed the failure of his hopes', Willie would not have minded dying, as 'to a man of his nobility of character, life was a mere nothing to forfeit'.[28]

In the years and decades following the executions, the letters and testimonies of the executed (or at least those documents released by the British authorities) were published or pored over in private by relatives, loved ones, historians and the general public. However, there is no recorded written final testimony from Willie, not even a note for friends. This is unusual, even allowing for the fact that he did not usually articulate his thoughts on paper and, unlike Patrick, had seen his mother and sister very shortly before his execution. Whatever the reason, it has left a void in our understanding of Willie Pearse. Naturally, this void has often been filled with conjecture, and has led to the creation of a simplistic narrative, the story of the gentle artist who blindly followed his more brilliant brother and was executed because of it. Patrick's articulation of his thoughts and aspirations has meant that Willie is often viewed through the prism of his brother's words, as if he was another character in his older sibling's plays. But Patrick himself never downplayed Willie's importance or took his fierce loyalty for granted. Willie might have taken an oath to serve Ireland while under the influence of

Patrick as a child but, crucially, as a grown man he related the story as an anecdote at the expense of his brother, 'to the latter's great amusement'.[29] While he awaited his execution, Patrick wrote a poem for his younger brother that acknowledged the extent of his support and the personal sacrifices he had made: '... leaving all things for me, spending yourself/In the hard service I taught to you.' It is true to some extent that Willie gave up his life for his brother, but in emphasising this, Patrick himself was largely responsible for the idea of Willie as the submissive devotee in thrall to his charismatic brother, a maker of stone sculptures who lives on in the reflected fame of a maker of history.[30] Patrick's own testimony ('You only have been my familiar friend/nor needed I another') freely admits his dependence on Willie, whose influence on his older brother has been detailed in these pages. When deleted sentences are re-inserted in his unfinished memoir, Patrick's emotional dependence on Willie (or perhaps Willie's ability to console Patrick) is even more manifest:

> Willy and I have been true brothers. *Willy's companionship has been the one solace of my sorrowful life.* As a boy he was my only playmate, as a man he has been my only intimate friend. *It seems to me on looking back now and this is a terrible confession for a man to make.* We have done and suffered much together and we have shared together a few deep joys. [deleted text in italics][31]

Though Willie was not a leader in the Easter rebellion of 1916, his role was more prominent than has been hitherto acknowledged. The decision by the government to allow a pension to family members of 1916 veterans and victims offered an unintentional but stark reminder of how Willie was sidelined from history. Margaret Pearse was informed that only one member of the family could be counted when application was being made for redress from the pension fund. On the other hand, those commemorative events associated with Willie's immediate circle – his old school at Westland Row, the Volunteers, and the St Enda's past pupils' union, Clann Éanna – always acknowledged both Willie and Patrick.[32] An artwork by Liam O'Neill at St Enda's, 'Brothers', commemorates both Pearses, as does the commemorative plaque at 27 Pearse Street (as Great Brunswick Street was renamed). In recent decades, however, memory of Willie has faded to the extent that street signs, and until recently the signs of the Dart Station at Pearse Street, sometimes had an Irish (mis)translation ('Sráid an Phiarsaigh') which commemorates only one Pearse.

What of Willie the artist? Though fellow rebel Liam Ó Briain met him for the first time while incarcerated in Richmond Barracks, Willie made an unforgettable impression. Like many, Ó Briain was struck mainly by Willie's aura as an artist, writing:

Since then I have often thought of that young artist. I felt for the short while that I was in his company that certain something – an open soulful bright something – that is felt when in the company of a true artist, whether they be a piano player, a composer, a painter, a sculptor or poet. We feel it is easier to spark his soul or to pain it and that nearer to him, clearer to him is the brightness and blackness of life than to us. It is a very imprecise memory now but I still have one nonetheless; and because of that memory it seems to me ever since then that it may be that Ireland lost not just a poet when Patrick died but also a great artist when Willie died.[33]

Margaret Pearse always felt that Willie's artistic work had been ignored.[34] Today Willie's surviving sculptures are scattered and, outside of his RHA and Oireachtas exhibits, largely uncatalogued.[35] In the case of his ecclesiastic work, Ryan states that 'throughout the countryside you may find his sculptures of the Dead Christ and the Immaculate Conception' and he specifically mentions Willie's sculpture as being extant in 'several Dublin churches, including Terenure', as well as in churches in Limerick and Letterkenny. Ryan also cites the examples of the O'Mulrennan Memorial in Glasnevin and a memorial to Father Murphy in Wexford.[36] Willie is recalled as making the sculpture depicting Calvary in the Church of the Immaculate Heart of Mary on Dublin's City Quay, as well as being responsible for a statue of Mary in Mount Argus.[37] Elsewhere, local tradition (in Dromcollogher and New Ross, for example) attributes work to Willie

Pearse. The account book of the family firm which pertains to Willie's time in the business provides limited guidance as it is unclear which commissions tendered for were achieved, and who completed them; in any case, the work at the family business was often collaborative and artistically unremarkable. The surviving examples of his sculptures kept at St Enda's (now the Pearse Museum) include the child studies 'Memories', 'A Skipping Rope', 'Éire' and 'Cailín na Carraige' as well as larger male nudes. When judged against the work completed by Albert Power or Oliver Sheppard, Willie's show a lesser talent. Desmond Ryan's account of Willie's sculpture in *The Man Called Pearse*, though an important initial record, is written in the hagiographical style of the rest of his book. Pádraig Ó Snodaigh, and, more recently, Brian Crowley, have provided brief but enlightening synopses of Willie's life as a sculptor, and Thomas Duffy's study of the stone-carving firms of Dublin includes a useful list of citations from *The Irish Builder* of commissions completed by Pearse & Sons. Though his identity as a sculptor has been evoked in various commemorative exhibitions, in particular in 1966 and again on the centenary of his birthday in 1981, there has never been a full-scale study of Willie's work. Regarding this question, Professor John Turpin has noted the absence of aspects of the story of Irish art and its influence not just from accounts of the Revival and the Rising, but also from Irish life in general.[38]

But regardless of the merit of Willie's oeuvre, his life as an artist is interesting for the light it throws on the social world in which the young sculptor moved, a world where grandees of Dublin Castle, moderate nationalists and radical republicans co-existed for a long time. Several of the artists most closely associated with Willie (Albert Power, Harry Clarke and Margaret Crilly, for example) achieved national fame, and the lives of prominent members of Willie's artistic circle – Oliver Sheppard, Albert Power, Jack Morrow – remind us that beyond the usual narratives of the Gaelic League and the Abbey, radical influences shaped artistic responses to questions of culture and identity during a crucial period in Irish history. The opposite is also true, as can be seen in the influence of Oliver Sheppard on Patrick via Willie. Sheppard continued to sculpt and among his commissions was a bust of Patrick unveiled in the Dáil in 1937. This, along with the adoption of Sheppard's 'Death of Cúchulainn' as a sculpture in the GPO, means that, ironically, Sheppard's work is now mentioned more often in conjunction with the story of Patrick than with that of his old friend Willie. Like Willie, Oliver Sheppard lost work in the conflict for independence: fire claimed Sheppard's works in the RHA in 1916, and other pieces were destroyed by the Black and Tans. 'They thought me too old to fight,' remarked Sheppard later, 'but I have tried to help in other ways. My politics are simple. I have always thought that this country should be a free country.'[39] It is a matter of conjecture if Willie himself directly influenced the militant nationalism of some of his contemporaries at the School of Art; it seems that he was discreet about such matters, if we observe the shock felt by many on discovering his role in the Rising. On the other hand Willie's leadership in achieving the right to sign names in Irish and his leading role in the School's Gaelic Society meant that he exerted considerable influence in the politics of identity there. As chairman of the School's dramatic society and later as a prominent personality in the Students' Union, he was instrumental in introducing his fellow students to the plays of advanced nationalist Alice Milligan, and probably to Milligan herself. But in these matters, as with his later more militant nationalism, Willie's membership of the Gaelic League and his family would have been the decisive original channel of influence. However, Willie certainly influenced some of his students in the realms of art and literature. His star pupil Patrick Tuohy – with no family background in art but with Willie's encouragement – went on to attend the School of Art, later achieving fame as a painter, while David Sears wrote plays that were staged at the Gate Theatre in the twenties and thirties.[40]

As with his sculpture, apart from the brief but revealing accounts in Máire Nic Shiubhlaigh's memoirs and William Feeney's book on the Irish Theatre, Willie's work in the theatre is also generally forgotten. Though evidently a skilled choreographer, Willie was not a particularly important actor, but he is an intriguing case study in how the dramatic arts influenced many of the main players in advanced nationalism. Through the theatre young radicals made important connections and learned the value of performance and imagery in advancing the identity of a putative independent nation. While Willie's contribution to the theatre was modest, his impact at St Enda's in its later years was considerable. For Desmond Ryan, 'The debt St Enda's owes William Pearse can scarcely be over-estimated. It cannot be too often repeated how largely his hand is writ upon it.'[41]

Willie's convictions were not vicariously acquired, as has been claimed.[42] He was the son of a deeply engaged radical. His father James died when Willie was a young man but, notwithstanding his many friends in the clergy, throughout much of his life Willie found himself among others whose profile did not reflect the received idea of the revolutionary as Catholic Gael. The artisan community around Great Brunswick Street had English roots, and many of Willie's neighbours in Rathmines and Sandymount were from unionist and Protestant backgrounds. The School of Art, where in one capacity or another he spent fifteen years, had links with the British administration in Ireland, as did the exhibitions of the Royal Hibernian Academy. His friends in the artistic and theatrical worlds were male and female, Catholic and Protestant, intellectual and cosmopolitan. On his mother's side,

Willie had a grandfather who supported the Fenians and the Young Irelanders and a great-great-grandfather and great-great-grand-uncles who fought with the rebels of 1798, but he was influenced by more than one tradition and through more than one channel.

This biography has shown that Willie Pearse was a more complex and interesting figure than has been previously acknowledged. His numerous overlapping connections with the leading personalities of both the Revival and the Rising, and also with lesser-known creative and political figures from the period, remind us of the close ties and shared ideals that bound the revolutionary generation. For Desmond Ryan, Willie's overshadowing by Patrick was partly due to their differing personalities:

> Not unnaturally his brother's fame has obscured his claim to recognition. His retiring disposition did not impress the casual observer to the extent that P.H. Pearse's more aggressive and concentrated personality did.[43]

David Sears also contrasted Willie's personality to that of Patrick: 'Willie was different; he moved always in the quiet, shaded paths of life, gentle and thoughtful for others.'[44] Although hers was a political outlook that differed greatly from that of the rest of her family, Mary Brigid provides what is perhaps the most insightful commentary on Willie's character: 'Pat was quick, vehement and dominating,

Willie slower, more placid and I think more farseeing.'[45]
Mary Brigid's judgement of Willie's farseeing nature is cor-
roborated by the many anecdotes in Ryan's writings which
portray Willie as someone who was able to control his emotions and stand back from events in order to assess their
true meaning and potential impact. Indeed the figure that
emerges after Patrick leaves 16 Moore Street to seek terms
for surrender is a particularly brave one. Willie was recalled
as one of only two people among the headquarters staff
not in tears at the decision to seek terms; he maintained
his cool and helped organise the surrender, and was among
those who led the rebels on their final lonely march. All
reports show him to have been calm and composed before
his execution. Finally, and alone among those with whom
he was to be executed, Willie pleaded guilty.

Willie Pearse was an artist, actor, lapsed vegetarian, and
teacher, a man whose friends came from different classes,
religions, ages, and political backgrounds, a man with 'the
utter gentleness of a St Francis' who loved Ireland and Paris,
Shakespeare and opera. As an actor he played a warrior, a
monk, a professor, a constable. He once stood on his head to
make a young child laugh. Willie led a life 'rich in ordinary
plenty' and seemed an unlikely rebel. TK Moylan believed
that to execute Willie:

> [as] one of the leaders of the Insurrection was to accord him
> a place to which I don't think he ever aspired and which

History has not conferred upon him. In fact I do not think anyone would have been more astonished than he at being so described.[46]

Few, then, can argue with Desmond Ryan that in the case of Willie Pearse, 'in one sense at least, the firing squad conferred, unconsciously, a service upon him: he would have been unknown otherwise to the succeeding generations'.[47] While both Willie and Patrick were driven by a creative impulse, Willie's creativity was less bound up with his politics. For Mary Brigid, 'Willie's dreams were more matter of fact, more definite and dealt with the realities of life and of the rich fulfilment of a noble ambition ... His dream was to give to the world beautiful works of art through which he expressed his soul.'[48] This was in contrast to Patrick, whose art and politics were almost inseparable. The contrast Mary Brigid drew between the motivations of her two brothers is the most telling reminder that Willie's life, as with the lives of all those who were executed, was a lot more than its untimely end. She gives a strikingly eloquent judgement that seems almost a deliberate attempt to reclaim for Willie his individual agency from a historical narrative that would always be skewed towards Patrick:

All Pat's life had been a preparation for that fateful Easter week [in] 1916: it was the completion of his life's work, but for Willie it meant a rude awakening from his long dreams, the consummation of all his cherished hopes. His sacrifice was therefore more complete and more bitter than that of his brother, his abnegation more entire, his courage even more fine.

As Mary Brigid stated:

Then again Pat wished to die for Ireland and in a sense was impatient at the tardy coming of death. He went eagerly forward to meet it with exultation in his soul. But Willie wanted to live for Ireland, to give her through his creative works the best that he had to give.[49]

Notes

INTRODUCTION

1 Desmond Ryan, *The Man Called Pearse*, Maunsel and Company, 1919, 191.

2 See for example Ruth Dudley Edwards, 'Is it unpatriotic to be honest', *The Irish Times* 1/4/1991. Though Dudley Edwards was the first to note Willie Pearse's membership of the Wolfe Tone and United Irishmen Memorial Committee in her biography of Patrick, she did not pursue this information further.

3 See especially David Sears; 'Some Impressions of Willie Pearse', *Cuimhní na bPiarsach*, Coiste Cuimhneacháin na bPiarsach, 1958, pp25-30; originally published in *The Cross*, Mount Argus, 1917; Desmond Ryan, 'The Brothers Pearse' in *The Man Called Pearse*, Maunsel and Company, 1919, pp60-76; Mary Brigid Pearse, *The Home Life of Pádraig Pearse*, Browne and Nolan, 1934, originally serialised in *Our Boys* in the 1920s; Margaret Pearse, 'St Enda's', Capuchin Annual 1942, pp227-30 and 'Patrick and Willie Pearse', Capuchin Annual 1943, pp86-88; Máire Nic Shiubhlaigh, *The Splendid Years*, as told to Edward Kenny, James Duffy and Co, 1955; Padraig Ó Snodaigh, 'Some Impressions of Willie Pearse', *Cuimhní na bPiarsach*, Coiste Cuimhneacháin na bPiarsach, 1958; Ruth Dudley Edwards, *Patrick Pearse, The Triumph of Failure*, Victor Gollancz, 1977; Turlough Breathnach, 'Willie Pearse & his world', *Ireland of the Welcomes*, xlviii, no. 4, 1999; Thomas Duffy, *Artisan Sculpture and the Stone Carving Firms of Dublin, 1859–1910*. Unpublished Thesis, National College of Art and Design Faculty of History of Art and Design, 1999; 'William Pearse', entry by William Murphy in the Cambridge Dictionary of Irish Biography, 2009; 'William Pearse' in Brian Barton, *The Secret Court Martial Records of the Easter Rising*, The History Press, 2010, pp172-181; Brian Crowley, 'William Pearse' in Paula Murphy, ed., *Sculpture, Art and Architecture of Ireland* Volume III, pp287-289; entry for 'William Mac Piarais' in 'Mapping the profession and practice of sculpture in Britain and Ireland 1851-1951', http://sculpture.gla.ac.uk/ and *in passim* Séamas Ó Buachalla (ed.), *The Letters of P.H. Pearse*, Gerrards Cross/Smythe, 1980; Brian Crowley, *Patrick Pearse, A Life in Pictures*, Mercier, Cork, 2013; John Turpin, *A School of Art in Dublin Since the Eighteenth Century, A History of the National College of Art And Design*, Gill and Macmillan, 1995 and *The Life and Work of Oliver Sheppard*, Four Courts Press, 2000; Elaine Sisson, *Pearse's Patriots: St Enda's and the Cult of Boyhood*, Cork University Press, 2004.

4 In correspondence with the author, 2013.

CHAPTER ONE

1 This quotation, and much of the information in this chapter, comes from Patrick Pearse's unfinished autobiography (courtesy of the OPW, with thanks to Brian Crowley). While some of this material is cited in Mary Brigid Pearse's reminiscences in *The Home Life of Pádraig Pearse*, there are important omissions, many with reference to James Pearse. Mary Brigid's book also contains additional material gathered from friends and family.

2-3 Patrick Pearse, unpublished autobiographical fragment, OPW.

4 See Thomas Duffy, *Artisan Sculpture and the Stone Carving Firms of Dublin, 1859–1910* (unpublished thesis, National College of Art and Design Faculty of History of Art and Design, 1999) for an account of James Pearse's life as a stone carver and sculptor, and the historical context.

5 Patrick Pearse, unpublished autobiographical fragment, OPW.

6 Photostat of letter and biography of Fr Devine provided courtesy of Archives of Passionist Community, Mount Argus.

7 Draft for a poem in notebook belonging to James Pearse, MS 42, p. 173.

8–9 Correspondence of James Pearse and Margaret Brady, afterwards Pearse, undated letter, MS 21,082.

10 Patrick Pearse, unpublished autobiographical fragment, OPW.

11 Énrí Ó Muirgheasa, *Amhráin Na Midhe*, Baile Átha Cliath, 1933, p. 9.

12 For a discussion of the Bradys' connection to the vibrant Gaelic culture of North Meath in the nineteenth century, see Róisín Ní Ghairbhí, 'A People That Did Not Exist? Some Sources and Contexts for Patrick Pearse's Militant Nationalism', in Rúan O'Donnell, ed., *The Impact of the 1916 Rising: Among the Nations,* Irish Academic Press, 2008, p. 161–186.

13 As stated by Patrick Pearse in a 'letter' to John Redmond in the spoof series 'Beart Litreacha do Chuaigh Amú' published in *An Barr Buadh,* 30 March 1912.

14 Margaret Pearse, 'Patrick and Willie Pearse', Capuchin Annual, 1943, p. 86–88.

15 Patrick Pearse, unpublished autobiographical fragment, OPW. Thomas Duffy discusses the merit and limitations of James Pearse's artistic achievements in *Artisan Sculpture and the Stone Carving Firms of Dublin, 1859–1910*.

16–17 Patrick Pearse, unpublished autobiographical fragment, OPW..

18–19 Letter from James Pearse to Margaret Pearse, undated. Ms 21,082.

20 Patrick Pearse, unpublished autobiographical fragment, OPW.

21 Letter from James Pearse to Margaret Pearse, undated. Ms 21,082.

22 Mary Brigid Pearse, *The Home Life of Pádraig Pearse, As Told by Himself, His Family and Friends,* 1934, Browne and Nolan, 30–31.

23 Patrick Pearse, unpublished autobiographical fragment, OPW.

24 The author would like to acknowledge her thanks at being allowed to view much of this collection in St Enda's/the Pearse Museum. She was also much aided by the unpublished bibliography of James's books compiled and provided by Brian Crowley of the OPW.

25 For a thorough discussion of James Pearse's radical politics, see Brian Crowley, 'I am the son of a good father: James and Patrick Pearse', in Róisín Higgins and Regina Uí Chollatáin, eds, *The Life and After-Life of P.H. Pearse,* Irish Academic Press, 2009, p. 19–32.

26 James Pearse, 'A reply to Professor Maguire's pamphlet "England's duty to Ireland" as it appears to an Englishman', Dublin, 1886.

27 Patrick Pearse, unpublished biographical fragment, OPW.

28 Rev P Arnold asserted that 'Willie attended Ballydesken national school in Fanad for about a year. He was then about eight years old.' His informant was Susan McGinley (formerly Friel) of Kerrykeel 'who brought Willie to school'. However, there is no family recollection of Willie attending school in Fánaid, though Mary Emily did live there for a long period. Note in PJ McGill, 'Patrick Pearse in Donegal', *Donegal Annual,* 1966, 88.

29 Desmond Ryan, *The Man Called Pearse;* See also Mary Brigid Pearse, *The Home Life of Pádraig Pearse,* 1934, Browne and Nolan, 72. Mary Brigid may have been Ryan's source.

CHAPTER TWO

1 For a comprehensive history of the School of Art, see John Turpin's excellent *A School of Art in Dublin Since the Eighteenth Century; A History of the National College of Art and Design,* Gill and Macmillan, 1995.

2 Desmond Ryan, *The Man Called Pearse,* 1919, 62.

3 Information from Alf Mac Lochlainn, Galway.

4 Beatrice Lady Glenavy, *Today We Will Only Gossip,* Constable, London, 1964, p. 90–91.

5 Willie's membership was proposed to the Coiste Gnó by Patrick in Autumn 1898. Ruth Dudley Edwards, *Patrick Pearse, The Triumph of Failure,* Victor Gollannz, 1977, 27.

6 'Dublin', *Fáinne an Lae,* 12/11/1898.

7 Ruth Dudley Edwards, *Patrick Pearse, The Triumph of Failure*, 22.

8 *Fáinne an Lae*, 5/3/1898. See also *Fáinne an Lae*, 19/2 and 26/2/1898. The notes in the paper would of course have been supplied by the Society.

9 Report by AE, *New Ireland Review*, September 1898, cited by John Turpin, *The Life and Work of Oliver Sheppard*, Four Courts Press, 2000, 60.

10 John Turpin, *The Life and Work of Oliver Sheppard*, Four Courts Press, 2000, 60.

11 Taped interview with Kathleen Fox and Nora Neiland, 1963, RTE Archives. Cited by John Turpin, 'Art and Society: Cúchulainn Lives On', *Circa* Art Magazine, No. 69, Autumn 1994, 26–31, 31.

12 Annual Report and Distribution of Prizes, 1899, 7–8. Henceforth information from annual reports are for dates given, and refer to academic year which finished the previous summer.

13 Ibid, 6.

14 *Irish Independent*, 8/9/1900.

15 Brian Crowley's notes from a conversation on 3 January 2005 with Ms Nina Jaglom, London. Ms Jaglom is the daughter of Patrick Shovelton and granddaughter of Mary Catherine Shovelton (née Kelly) who was Mrs Margaret Pearse's niece. With thanks to Brian Crowley and OPW.

16 David Sears, 'Some Impressions of Willie Pearse', *Cuimhní na bPiarsach, Coiste Cuimhneacháin na bPiarsach*, 1958, 25–28, 27, originally published in *The Cross*.

17 Book in collection of the Pearse Museum.

18 Initial information courtesy of Alf Mac Lochlainn, Galway. Further information from US census returns 1910, 1920.

19–20 Annual Report and Distribution of Prizes, 7.

21 Robert Elliott, 'Pulpits, Tradesmen and Artists', *Art and Ireland*, Sealy, Bryers and Walker, 1906, 188.

22 Ibid, 190.

23 Desmond Ryan, *The Man Called Pearse*, 66. The assertion is also made by Patrick McCartan in a letter in support of an application for a military pension for Mary Brigid in 1928 that 'Willie took over his father's place in Brunswick Street after the father's death and continued to provide as his father had done for Miss Mary Brigid ... He continued to provide for Mary Brigid until his death as Pádraig never made money on the school and did nothing for the family other than provide for

his mother ... Mary Brigid was entirely dependent on Willie.' Letter from Patrick McCartan, 25 June 1928 (33 ABP.27.C73)

24 'New Ross', *Irish Independent*, 14/6/1962. Information on James Vincent from conversation between author and Noel Scarlett, grandson of James Vincent Pearse and son of Florence Pearse, 2014.

25 1902 Cork International Exhibition catalogue, p. 53.

26 'Altars', *Irish Independent*, 14/6/1962.

27 John Turpin, 2000, 19. I am grateful to Professor Turpin for drawing my attention to the importance of New Sculpture as a backdrop to Willie's own work.

28 Newspaper cutting, 'Pádraig Pearse', n.d. Oliver Sheppard Papers, NIVAL, NCAD; Royal Hibernian Academy of Arts, Catalogue of the Seventy-Fifth Annual Exhibition, 1904 RHA Annual Exhibition Catalogue, 1904. For a comprehensive overview of Oliver Sheppard's life, see John Turpin, *Oliver Sheppard 1865–1941, Symbolist Sculptor of the Irish Cultural Revival*, Four Courts, 2000.

29 Desmond Ryan, *The Man Called Pearse*, Maunsel and Company, 1919, 63.

30 Metropolitan School of Art, William Pearse File, OPW.

31 TK Moylan, 'A Dubliner's Diary 1914–1918 by TKM', bound typescript diary, MS 9620, 98.

32 Letter from Willie Pearse to Father Gibbons, 31/10/1903, NLI.

33 James Gibbons, 'An Irishman's Diary', *The Irish Times*, 12/4/2012; 'Oldest Priest in Ireland Dies' *Irish Independent*, 8/7/1972.

34 'By the Way', *Weekly Freeman*, 19/8/1905; 'Social and Personal', *Irish Independent*, 20/3/1905; Desmond Ryan, *The Man Called Pearse*, Maunsel and Company, 1919, 63; Mary Colum, *Life and the Dream*, 106.

35 Two photographs were published with accompanying information in *The Irish Times*, 'Pearse Brothers Pictures', 22/11/1979.

36–37 'Scoruigheacht at the Metropolitan School of Art,' *Freeman's Journal*, 31/7/1905.

38 See 'Death of Mr RHA Willis', *The Irish Times*, 26/8/1905 and entry for Richard Strickland, Dictionary of Irish Artists, 1913.

CHAPTER THREE

1 Edward Martyn, preface, Robert Elliott, *Art and Ireland*, Dublin, Sealy, Bryers and Walker, 1906. See Thomas Duffy, *Artisan Sculpture and the Stone-Carving Firms of Dublin*

1859–1910 (1999) for a critique of the merit of the Pearse family firm's work.

2 Cited by Sighle Breathnach Lynch 'Albert Power, RHA', *Irish Arts Review Yearbook* (1990/1991), pp. 111-114, 114.

3 *An Claidheamh Soluis,* 9/9/1905. See also Pádraig Mac Piarais, *'Ar Thráigh Bhinn Éadair'* in Ciarán Ó Coigligh, eag. 'Filíocht Ghaeilge Phádraig Mhic Phiarais', *An Clóchomhar,* 1981, 11–12. The translation is by Patrick himself, manuscript in keeping of OPW.

4 Information from Alf Mac Lochlainn, Salthill, Galway.

5 As mentioned in letter from Willie Pearse to Father Gibbons 31/5/1906, OPW.

6 'Gaelic League and Irish Industries', *The Irish Times,* 9/2/1905.

7 A letter dated 15/2/1912 from a Mr Fogarty (who worked in the depot) to a client refers to a sculpture of Willie's being sold through the depot. (OPW)

8 Draft letter MS 21072 (1).

9 'The Irish Art Companions, An address given at No 6 St Stephen's Green, Dublin' in *Things Said And Done by the Irish Art Companions,* Irish Art Club, Tower Press, 1908. Gatty is named as speaker in an article publicising the forthcoming lecture and other lectures. 'National Literary Society', *Freeman's Journal,* 9/2/1906.

10 'The Art Companions, A Guild for the Improvement of Taste and the Revivifying of Irish Art', *The World's Work,* 1907.

11 Letter from Willie to Father Gibbons, 13/4/1906, OPW.

12 *An Claidheamh Soluis,* 5/5/1906.

13–14 'Our National Salon', *An Claidheamh Soluis,* 11/8/1906.

15 See John Turpin, *Oliver Sheppard 1865–1941, Symbolist Sculptor of the Irish Cultural Revival,* Four Courts Press, 2000, 68-71.

16 'Language Week', *The Freeman's Journal,* 8/6/1907.

17 Ibid.

18 Clár an Oireachtais, 1907; Desmond Ryan, *The Man Called Pearse,* Maunsel and Company, 1919, 63. Ryan incorrectly states that Willie first exhibited work at the Oireachtas exhibition.

19–20 Annual Report and Distribution of Prizes, 1908.

21 'Father Mathew Hall, Temperance Fête,' *The Irish Times,* 28/5/1907.

22 Mícheál Ó Riain, 'Queen Victoria and her Reign at Leinster House', Dublin Historical Record, Vol. 52, No. 1 (Spring, 1999), pp. 75-86.

23 Correspondence of Mabel Gorman to Mr (William) Pearse, various dates, MS 21,058.

24–26 Letter from Willie Pearse to Fr Gibbons, 24/4/1908, NLI.

27 Mary Colum, *Life and the Dream,* Doubleday and Company, New York, 1947, p.95.

CHAPTER FOUR

1 Máire Nic Shiubhlaigh, *The Splendid Years, As Told to Edward Kenny,* James Duffy and Co, 1955, 151.

2 Minutes of Cluichtheoirí na hÉireann for May 1906 to May 1907, Ms 7388.

3 Mary Colum, *Life and the Dream,* Doubleday and Company, 1947, 142.

4 Mary Brigid Pearse, *The Home Life of Pádraig Pearse,* Browne and Nolan, 1934, 121.

5 Hobson recalled having tea there with Sean Lester when James Connolly joined them. 'Old Ireland Free', *Irish Literary Portraits, W.B. Yeats, James Joyce, George Moore, George Bernard Shaw, Oliver St. John Gogarty, F.R. Higgins, AE: W. R. Rodgers's Broadcast Conversations with Those Who Knew Them,* BBC, 1972, 213.

6 Mary Colum, *Life and the Dream,* Doubleday and Company, New York, 1947, 153.

7 Military Service Pensions Collection; letter written by Dr Patrick McCartan as part application for pension on behalf of Mary Brigid Pearse, DP 1910.

8 Milo MacGarry, 'Memories of Sgoil Éanna', Capuchin Annual, 1930, 35–39, 36.

9 Desmond Ryan, *The Man Called Pearse,* Maunsell and Company, 1919, 68.

10 Milo MacGarry, 'Memories of Sgoil Éanna', Capuchin Annual, 1930, 35-39, 36.

11 The pupil was Dick Humphries, a nephew of Michael ('the') O'Rahilly. Both later turned up to fight in the GPO. See Dick Humphries, 'Easter Week in the GPO', Ms 18, 829. Reprinted as 'A Rebel's Tale' in Keith Jeffery, ed., *The GPO and the Easter Rising,* Irish Academic Press, 2006, 140–156.

12 Desmond Ryan, *The Story of a Success,* The Phoenix Publishing Company, 1917, 96.

13 Desmond Ryan, 'Pearse the Orator', *Irish Press,* 12/11/1954.

14–16 Douglas Hyde, *An Craoibhín Aoibhinn,* 'The New National University in Ireland and the Irish Language', *The Celtic Review,* April 1909, 319–326.

17 Mary Colum, *Life and the Dream,* Doubleday and Company, New York, 1947, 95.

18 David Sears, 'Some Impressions of Willie Pearse', *Cuimhní na bPiarsach, Coiste Cuimhneacháin na bPiarsach,* 1958, 25-28, 27.

19 'Pearse the Orator', *Irish Press,* 12/11/1954. The speech is mentioned also in *An Macaomh.*

20–21 Desmond Ryan, *Remembering Sion, A Chronicle of Storm and Quiet,* A Barker, 1934, 126. See also *The Man Called Pearse,* 72.

22–23 Máire Nic Shiubhlaigh, *The Splendid Years,* as told to Edward Kenny, James Duffy and Co., 1955, 15.

24–29 Joseph Holloway, diary entry, 22/3/1909, Holloway diaries, NLI.

30 'Exhibition of Painting and Sculpture by Young Irish Artists', *The Irish Times,* 17/4/1909. Joseph Holloway also describes the exhibition in his diary.

31 Letter From Mabel Gorman to Mr. (William) Pearse, 16/5/1909.

32 Stephen McKenna, 'Pageants', *An Macaomh*, Nollaig 1909, 36–38.

33 'By Way of Comment' *An Macaomh*, Nollaig, 1909, p.8.

34 Elizabeth Coxhead, *Daughters of Erin, Five Women of the Irish Renaissance*, Secker and Walberg, London, 1965, 156.

35 Desmond Ryan ed., *Patrick Pearse, The Story of a Success*, Maunsel & Co., 1920, 95.

36 Desmond Ryan, *The Man Called Pearse*, Maunsel and Co. , 1919, 63.

37 Much of the detail for the productions at St. Enda's are taken from *An Macaomh* and from original programmes. The plays are discussed in depth in Róisín Ní Ghairbhí and Eugene McNulty, eds, *Patrick Pearse, Collected Plays/Drámaí an Phiarsaigh*, Irish Academic Press, 2013. *An Macaomh* is also the source for much of the information on the day to day life of St. Enda's.

CHAPTER FIVE

1 'Aonach Art Exhibition', *Sinn Féin*, 18/12/1909.

2 Recording of Seán (John) Dowling, *Pearse's People*, radio documentary by Proinsias Ó Conluain broadcast on RTE Radio 18 April 1979. A section of Mary Brigid's own account of her apparent breakdown survives and was brought to my attention by Brian Crowley of the OPW.

3 William Feeney, *Drama in Hardwicke Street: A History of the Irish Theatre Company*, Associated University Presses, 1984, 55.

4 *The Irish Times* 3/3/1911.

5 Máire Nic Shiubhlaigh, *The Splendid Years*, as told to Edward Kenny, James Duffy and Co., 1955, 151.

6 TK Moylan, 'A Dubliner's Diary 1914-1918' by T. K. M. [Thomas King Moylan], bound typescript diary including an account of Dublin during Easter Week 1916, 98. Ms 9620.

7 'The Abbey Theatre', *The Irish Times*, 31/5/1910.

8 Programme for Metropolitan School of Art Plays at the Abbey Theatre, May 31 to June 4, Oliver Sheppard Papers, NIVAL, NCAD, 'Three Irish Plays at the Abbey', *Freeman's Journal,* 4/6/1910.

9 Milo MacGarry, 'Memories of Sgoil Éanna', Capuchin Annual 1942, 35-39.

10 Ibid.

11 *An Macaomh*, Nollaig 1910.

12 Sidney Gifford Czira, *The Years Flew By*, the recollections of Madame Sidney Gifford Czira, New ed./edited and introduced by Alan Hayes; foreword by Gifford Lewis, Arlen House, Galway, 30-31.

13 Interview with Noel Scarlett by the author, 2014.

14 Draft for letter, cited by Ruth Dudley Edwards, 'Willie Pearse, the loving shadow of his brother', *Irish Press*, 11/10/1979.

15 Desmond Ryan, *The Man Called Pearse*, 198.

16 Desmond Ryan, *The Story of a Success*, 94-95.

17 Desmond Ryan, *Remembering Sion, A Chronicle of Storm and Quiet*, 114.

18 Kenneth Reddin, 'A Man Called Pearse' Studies, Vol. 34, No. 134, June 1945, 241-251, 247-248.

19 Ibid.

20 MS 21, 072. Thanks to Brian Crowley, OPW, for making me aware of this and many other sources.

21-22 Ibid.

23 David Sears, 'Some Impression of Willie Pearse', *Cuimhní na bPiarsach*, Coiste Cuimhneacháin na bPiarsach, 1958, 25-28, 29.

24 Annála na Scoile, *An Macaomh*, Nollaig 1910.

25 The assertion about Willie's involvement was made by former band member Michael Whelan. 'Treasured Photograph', *Irish Independent*, 6/4/1966.

26–28 *Irish Freedom*, November 1910.

29 'Art', 'The Fianna', *Irish Freedom*, November 1910.

30 Photograph showing unveiling of monument in the Bullring, Wexford, Oliver Sheppard Papers, NIVAL, NCAD.

31 'St. Andrew's Church, Westland Row', *Freeman's Journal*, 1/12/1910.

32 Joseph Holloway, diary entry for 25/2/1911, Holloway Diaries, NLI.

33 Mary Bulfin in Mary Brigid Pearse (ed.), *The Home-Life of Patrick Pearse* (Dublin: Mercier Press, 1979), 120.

34 Máire Nic Shiubhlaigh, *The Splendid Years*, as told to Edward Kenny, James Duffy and Co., 1955, 145.

35 Joseph Holloway diary entry for 7 April 1911, Holloway diaries, NLI.

36 'Passion Play at the Abbey Theatre', *The Irish Times*, 8 April 1911.

CHAPTER SIX

1 Various press cuttings; O'Rahilly Papers, UCD archives; Michael Noyk (WS 707) mentions the Morrow involvement.

2–3 Letters from Mabel Gorman to William Pearse, Ms 21058.

4 'Irish Art Companions, Opening of New Gallery,' *Freeman's Journal* 20/11/1911.

5 'Aonach na Nollag', *Freeman's Journal*, 9/12/1910.

6 Geraóid Ó hUalacháin, WS 328.

7 Plays at the Abbey Theatre, *Irish Independent*, 27/12/1911.

8 Public Amusements, Abbey Theatre, *The Irish Times*, 30/12/1911.

9 Desmond Ryan, *The Man called Pearse*, 71.

10 Fogarty, Irish Art Companions to a Mr Griesson, 15/2/1912, OPW.

11 'Royal Hibernian Academy, Eighty Third Exhibition', *The Irish Times*, 4/3/1912.

12 'Royal Hibernian Academy, This Year's Exhibition', *Irish Independent*, 4/3/1912.

13 *Remembering Sion, A Chronicle of Storm and Quiet,* A Barker, 1934, 143.

14 Mrs Pearse to Margaret Pearse, OPW, cited by Ruth Dudley Edwards, *Patrick Pearse, The Triumph of Failure*, 1979.

15 Ruth Dudley Edwards, *Patrick Pearse, The Triumph of Failure,* Victor Gollancz, 1977, 166.

16 Letter dated 30th May 1912, OPW.

17 Máire Nic Shiubhlaigh, *The Splendid Years*, as told to Edward Kenny, James Duffy and Co, 1955, 151.

18 David Sears, 'Some Impression of Willie Pearse', *Cuimhní na bPiarsach*, Coiste Cuimhneacháin na bPiarsach, 1958, 25-28, 27.

19 Kenneth Reddin, 'A Man Called Pearse', Studies, June 1943, Vol 34, No 134, 1945,

241-251, 247.

20 Máire Nic Shiubhlaigh, *The Splendid Years*, as told to Edward Kenny, James Duffy and Co., 1955, 150.

21 Geraldine Plunkett Dillon, 'Irish Republican Brotherhood', *Irish University Review*, Vol 2, No 9, Spring 1962, 23-36, 24.

22 Desmond Ryan, *A Man Called Pearse*, 72.

23 'Wolfe Tone and United Irishmen Memorial Committee', letter/article with date May 30th in *Irish Freedom*, June 1912.

24 Éimear O'Connor, Seán Keating, *Art Politics and Building the Irish Nation*, Irish Academic Press, 2013, 33.

25 Desmond Ryan, Bureau of Military History, WS 725.

26 F. Fogarty, 'Satire', *An Scoláire*.

27 David Sears, 'Some Impressions of Willie Pearse', *Cuimhní na bPiarsach*, Coiste Cuimhneacháin na bPiarsach, 1958, 25-30, 29.

28 'Lady Aberdeen and Imported Labour', *Irish Freedom*, 13/3/1913.

29 An Rí, in Róisín Ní Ghairbhí and Eugene McNulty, eds, Patrick Pearse, *Drámaí an Phiarsaigh*, Irish Academic Press, 2013. 128-147, 134. Originally published in *An Macaomh*, Bealtaine 1913, 18-26. The English translation was also published in *An Macaomh*.

30 As stated by Pearse in preface to the book version of the articles, 'From a Hermitage', published by Irish Freedom Press in 1915.

31 Various letters from Desmond Ryan to his father, Papers of WP Ryan, UCD archives.

32–35 Original postcard and original programme courtesy of Allen Library.

36 The 'gay and stirring tunes' were promised by Seán O'Casey in a letter to *The Irish Worker*, 7/6/1913.

37 Joseph Holloway, diary entry for 14 June 1913.

38 Information from original programme, courtesy of Allen Library.

39 *Irish Freedom*, July 1913.

40 Tom Kenny, 'The Conradh na Gaeilge Oireachtas and Ardfheis held in the Town Hall 1913', 'Old Galway', *Galway Advertiser*, 5/12/1913. The photograph is now in the Town Hall Theatre, Galway.

CHAPTER SEVEN

1 See anecdote about Standish O'Grady's 1899 declaration, 'We have now a literary movement, it is not very important; it will be followed by a political movement, that will not be very important; then must come a military movement, that will be important indeed' in *WB Yeats, Autobiographies*, Macmillian, 1955, 421. A prediction is made of a (medium-term) future revolution in an unsigned article whose style and content indicate a definite Patrick Pearse authorship, 'In My Garden', Oireachtas Supplement, *An Claidheamh Soluis*, 4/8/1906.

2 The North Began', *An Claidheamh Soluis*, 1/11/1913.

3 Patrick Pearse, 'From a Hermitage', *Irish Freedom*, November 1913.

4 'Manchester Martyrs Dublin Celebration', *The Irish Times*, 24/13/1913.

5 *Irish Freedom*, December 1913.

6 Ibid; also *Freeman's Journal* 2/12/1913.

7 Desmond Ryan, *The Man Called Pearse*, Maunsel and Company, 1919, 73.

8 As recalled by Cecil Salkeld, in 'Old Ireland Free'. WR Rodgers, *Irish Literary Portraits ... WR Rodgers's Broadcast Conversations with Those Who Knew Them*, BBC, 1972, 206.

9 Desmond Ryan, *The Man Called Pearse*, 73, Maunsel and Company, 1919, 73.

10 Charles Donnelly, WS 824; Patrick O'Daly WS 387. Harry Nicholl's witness statement mentions Patrick's name in connection with the Teeling circle, of which he says Bulmer Hobson was centre. WS 296.

11 David Sears, 'Some Impressions of Willie Pearse', *Cuimhní na bPiarsach*, Coiste Cuimhneacháin na bPiarsach, 1958, 25-30, 298.

12 Ref Ruth Dudley Edwards, *Patrick Pearse, The Triumph of Failure*, Victor Golancz, London, 1977, 193.

13 With thanks to Lorraine Peavoy at the National Library, whose grandfather John Fleming delivered milk to the Pearses.

14 'Amazing Night at Larne, Wholesale Gun Running', *The Belfast Telegraph*, 25/7/1914.

15 'News of the Week', *The Irish Times* 20/6/1914.

16 Original programme, OPW.

17 Correspondence of Mabel Gorman to William Pearse, Ms 21058.

18 Letter from Máire Nic Shiubhlaigh to Desmond Ryan, May 1937, WP Ryan Papers, UCD archives.

19 David Sears, 'Some Impressions of Willie Pearse', *Cuimhní na bPiarsach*, Coiste Cuimh-neacháin na bPiarsach, 1958, 25-30.

20 Desmond Ryan, *The Man Called Pearse*, 71.

CHAPTER EIGHT

1 Robert Holland, WS 289.

2 Mr Thomas MacCarthy, WS 307. Seán T O'Kelly gives some further details about the people involved in his witness statement.

3 The photographer was Clement J. Leaper. Micheál Ó Droighneáin WS 374.

4 Seán T. O'Kelly speech, Wallach's Theatre, New York, 4 April 1926, published in *An Phoblacht*, 30 April 1926, in S T O'Ceallaigh papers NLI MS 27,716.

5 Manifesto of the Irish Volunteers, *The Irish Review,* Vol 4, no.42, September–November 1914, 281-286, 283.

6 David Sears, 'Some Impression of Willie Pearse', *Cuimhní na bPiarsach*, Coiste Cuimh-neacháin na bPiarsach, 1958, 25-30, 29.

7 Taped interview between Kathleen Fox and Nora Neiland, 1963, RTE Archives. Cited by John Turpin, *A School of Art in Dublin Since the Eighteenth Century, A History of the National College of Art and Design*, Gill and Macmillan, 1995, 192–193.

8 The Gaelic League and Politics, Pronouncement by Dr Douglas Hyde, (President). Pamphlet quoting speech made in Cork in 1914, published 1915.

9 Charles O'Grady, WS 282.

10 'The Irish Theatre', *Freeman's Journal*, 19/4/1915.

11 Irish Citizen, 24/4/1915, cited by William Feeney, *Drama in Hardwicke Street, A History of the Irish Theatre Company*, Associated University Presses, 1984, 89.

12 'Brian Boru Celebration', *Irish Independent,* 23/4/1914; 'Dublin and District', *Irish Independent*, 24/4/1915.

13 'The Irish Theatre', *Freeman's Journal*, 22/5/1915.

14-19 *The Master*, Patrick Pearse, in Róisín Ní Ghairbhí and Eugene McNulty eds., *Patrick Pearse, Collected Plays/Drámaí an Phiarsaigh*, Irish Academic Press, 2013, 181.

20 Joseph Holloway, diary entry for 22/5/1915.

21 'Why We Want Recruits', May 1915.

22 The account here is based closely on the article 'Volunteers were stoned in Limerick,

National 1916 Jubilee Commemoration Committee', *Limerick Leader*, 9/4/1966. A subsequent letter to the *Limerick Leader* made some minor corrections to the original article, which had stated that there had been two bands, the letter disputed this and further stated that a band had to be mustered as no band in Limerick at this time were sympathetic to the Volunteers. 'The Sinn Féin Band', Letter signed Thomas Glynn, Castle St, *Limerick Leader*, 16/4/1966. See also 'Fianna Fáil Deputy Dies', *Irish Press*, 14/4/1952; See also Seamus Fitzgerald, WS 1737.

23 Desmond Ryan, *Remembering Sion, A Chronicle of Storm and Quiet*, A Barker, 1934, 182.

24 Desmond Ryan, *The Man called Pearse*, Maunsel and Company, 1919, 66.

25 William Feeney, *Drama in Hardwicke Street, A History of the Irish Theatre*, Associated University Presses, 1984, 104-105.

26 Desmond Ryan, *Remembering Sion, A Chronicle of Storm and Quiet*, A Barker, 1934, 104, 186-188. Ryan mentions Willie 'ag caoineadh' ('crying') about the lack of a bed in a letter to his father.

27 Ibid, 190.

28 Ibid, 103-104; 192-193.

29 'O'Donovan Rossa's Funeral; Scenes in Dublin; Speech at Graveside', *The Irish Times*, 2/08/1913.

30–31 'Funeral of O'Donovan Rossa, Impressive Procession to Glasnevin', *Freeman's Journal*, 2/8/1915.

32 O'Donovan Rossa's Funeral; Scenes in Dublin; Speech at Graveside', *The Irish Times*, 2/8/1915.

33 David Sears, 'Some Impressions of Willie Pearse', *Cuimhní na bPiarsach*, Coiste Cuimhneacháin na bPiarsach, 1958, 25-30, 26.

34 According to a bill preserved by Fr Senan Moynihan, MS 8265, TCD.

35 Image of original programme for 'Aeraíocht and Volunteer Display at Grounds of St. Enda's College, Sunday September 5th'. Reprinted in Brian Crowley, *Patrick Pearse, A Life in Pictures*, Mercier, 2013.

36 Mobilisation order in O'Rahilly Papers, UCD archives.

37 Cited by William Feeney, *Drama in Hardwicke Street, A History of the Irish Theatre Company*, Associated University Presses, 1984, 112, 119-120.

38 William Feeney, *Drama in Hardwicke Street, A History of the Irish Theatre Company*,

Associated University Presses, 1984, 112, 117, 119-120.

39 'Ghosts', Tracts for the Times, Whelan's, Dublin, 1916.

CHAPTER NINE

1 F. X. Martin and Eoin MacNeill 'Eoin MacNeill on the 1916 Rising', *Irish Historical Studies*, Vol. 12, No. 47, March 1961, 226-271, 234.

2 Florence O'Donoghue, 'Plans for the 1916 Rising', *Irish University Review*, Vol 3, No. 1 Spring 1963. 3-21, 7.

3 As recalled by former student E. O'Boyle. 'Donegal association in Dublin, Visit to St Enda's School', *Donegal News*, 4/3/1944.

4–5 David Sears, 'Some Impression of Willie Pearse', *Cuimhní na bPiarsach*, Coiste Cuimhneacháin na bPiarsach, 25-20, 25.

6 Eamon Bulfin, WS 497. David Sears, 'Some Impression of Willie Pearse', *Cuimhní na bPiarsach*, Coiste Cuimhneacháin na bPiarsach, 1958, 25-20, 26.

7 Fintan Murphy WS 370.

8 Senator Margaret M. Pearse, 'St Enda's ', Easter Week 1916, Capuchin Annual, 1942, 227-230, 227.

9 Royal Commission on the Rebellion in Ireland, Report of the Commission, Presented to Both House of Parliament by Command of his Majesty, London, 1916.

10 As recalled by Desmond Ryan, 'The Story of a Success', in *The Story of Success* and *The Man Called Pearse*, Phoenix Publishing Company, ND, 98.

11 'Echo of Executions', *Irish Press*, 4/4/1932.

12 'Pearse Letters in San Francisco', *Irish Press*, 27/11/1952.

13 *The Singer*, in Róisín Ní Ghairbhí and Eugene Mc Nulty, eds, *Patrick Pearse Collected Plays/Drámaí an Phiarsaigh*, Irish Academic Press, 2013, 201-231.

14 Desmond Ryan, *The Man Called Pearse*, 73.

15 'Pearse Letters in San Francisco', *Irish Press*, 27/11/1952. It is possible that *The Singer* was produced privately on the night of the Tullamore affray and the *céilí* at St Enda's; in Mrs Pearse's recollection the play was produced privately a few weeks before the Rising. Seamus Brennan recalled a play taking place that night (WS 48).

16 Oscar Traynor, WS 340.

17 Patrick Egan WS 327; Thomas Mc Carthy WS 307.

18 As recalled by Desmond Ryan in conversation with WR Rodgers, in WR Rodgers, 'Old Ireland Free', *Irish Literary Portraits ... WR Rodgers's Broadcast Conversations with Those Who Knew Them*, BBC, 1972, 209.

19 Desmond Ryan WS 725.

20–21 Áine Ceannt, WS 264; 'Dead March in a Garden Before the Rising', 'The Ceannt Papers', *Irish Press*, 11/1/1949.

22 Mary Brigid Pearse, *The Home Life of Pádraig Pearse,* Browne and Nolan, 1934, 15.

23 'Patrick Pearse's barber', *Irish Independent*, 28/3/1973.

24 Fintan Murphy WS 370.

25 Mary O'Sullivan, WS 465.

26 Information courtesy of Archives of Mount Argus.

27 Father Eugene Nevin Cp, 1605; Margaret Pearse, 'Patrick and Willie Pearse', Capuchin Annual, 86–88, 1943.

28–30 Máiréad Ní Cheallaigh, WS 925.

31 Seán T. O'Kelly WS 1765; Seamus Ó Buachalla, *The Letters of P.H. Pearse*, Gerrards Cross/Smythe, 1980.

32 Senator Margaret M. Pearse, 'St.Enda's', Easter Week 1916, Capuchin Annual, 1942, 227–230, 228.

33 Personal Recollections by the late Father Aloysius, O.F.M. Cap., Capuchin Annual 1966, 280–291, 280.

34 Máiréad Ní Cheallaigh/Máiréad O'Kelly, WS 925. Seán T himself did not recall meeting Patrick on the Sunday. Seán T. O'Kelly WS 1765. Seán T admitted his recollections of the Sunday were unclear.

35 Fintan Murphy and Eamon Bulfin recalled seeing 'Pearse and his brother' at four o'clock. Eamon Bulfin WS 497; Fintan Murphy WS 370.

36 Desmond Ryan,

37 Maria Perolz, WS 246.

38–39 Máiréad Ní Cheallaigh, WS 925.

CHAPTER TEN

1 Seán McLoughlin, 'Memories of Easter Week', *The Camillian Post*, Spring 1948.

2 CD 95/2/3 Bureau of Military History, accessed on http://dh.tcd.ie/letters1916/

diyhistory/scripto/transcribe/1141/3034 5/10/2014.

3 'Willie Pearse Bridge', *Irish Press*, 30/4/1943.

4 Fintan Murphy believed that he remembered seeing Eamon Bulfin and Willie Pearse hoist a 'second tricolour' at a flagpole on the Princes Street side of the GPO. Bulfin recalls hoisting the green Irish Republic flag that Willie had brought to the roof. 'The GPO flags in 1916', *Irish Press*, 22/4/1966. The article cites a piece written by Bulfin himself for the *Midland Tribune*. Michael Staines also claimed he hoisted both flags, WS 284.

5 Desmond Ryan WS 724.

6 Dick Humphries, 'A Rebel's Tale', *The GPO and the Easter Rising*, Irish Academic Press, 2006, 140–156, 143.

7 As repeated in account published in Desmond Ryan, *Remembering Sion, A Chronicle of Storm and Quiet*, A Barker, 1934, 204.

8 Information provided to author by journalist Mr Dave Kenny, Gypsy's grandson.

9 Desmond Ryan, WS 724.

10 Desmond Ryan, *The Man Called Pearse*, 70.

11 Piaras F Mac Lochlainn, Last Words, Kilmainham Jail Restoration Society, 1971, 77.

12 Recalled by Desmond Ryan who was in the process of bedding down behind the counters in the centre of the GPO, Desmond Ryan WS 724.

13–14 Dick Humphries, 'A Rebel's Tale', *The GPO and the Easter Rising*, Irish Academic Press, 2006, 140-156.

15 Patrick Caldwell WS 638.

16 Seán McLoughlin, 'Memories of Easter Rising', Camillian Post, 1948.

17 Desmond Ryan, WS 724.

18 In a statement to Piaras Mac Lochlainn. Piaras F. Mac Lochlainn, Last Words, Letters and Statements of the Leaders Executed after the Rising at Easter 1916, Kilmainham Jail Restoration Society, 1971, 163.

19 Desmond Ryan, WS 724, Séan Price WS 769.

20 Fintan Murphy, WS 370.

21 Sean Mac Entee, WS 1052; See also Sean Mac Entee, Pages from a Record of Easter Week, Easter Fires, Pages from Personal records of 1916, St Carthage Press, Waterford, 1943, 9-31, 18.

22 Eamon Bulfin, WS 497.

23 Ryan himself stated that his assertion that Plunkett is the second man was later disputed. Desmond Ryan, WS 724,

24 Seán McLoughlin, 'Memories of Easter Rising', Camillian Post, 18.

25 Ibid, 19.

26 Michael William O'Reilly, WS 886.

27 Patrick Rankin, WS 163.

28 As recounted by Dominic O'Riordan to WR Rodgers. O'Riordan was recalling a story told to him by Sean McGarry. 'Old Ireland Free', in WR Rodgers, *Irish Literary Portraits ... WR Rodgers's Broadcast Conversations with Those Who Knew Them*, BBC, 1972, 227. It is not clear when or where the alleged incident took place but a certain plausibility is lent to the story by the fact that Seán McGarry was in close proximity to Willie in Richmond Barracks and they were also court-martialled together.

29 Liam Ó Briain, Cuimhní Cinn, An Chéad Chló, Sairséal agus Dill, 1951, 156-161.

30 Charles Saurin, WS 288.

CHAPTER ELEVEN

1 Letter from Patrick to Mrs Pearse 1.5.16, Seamus Ó Buachalla, *The Letters of P.H. Pearse*, Gerrards Corss/Smythe, 1980, 376-77.

2 According to Piaras F. Mac Lochlainn the text of the poem did not come to light until a typed copy was found amid Asquith's papers in 1965. 'To My Brother', *Last Words, Letters and Statements of the Leaders Executed after the Rising at Easter 1916*, Kilmainham Jail Restoration Society, Dublin 1971, 21, 23.

3 Letter from Patrick Pearse to his mother (and siblings), 3/5/1916, Ms 49, 154/21 NLI.

4 Margaret Pearse only received a copy of this note in 1946. Piaras F.Mac Lochlainn, *Last Words, Letters and Statements of the Leaders Executed after the Rising at Easter 1916*, Kilmainham Jail Restoration Society, Dublin, 1971, 31. Margaret Pearse only received a copy of this note in 1946.

5 'My experiences in the 1916 Rising by Father Columbus OSFC', 29 July 1916, Irish Capuchin Provincial Archives.

6 John McGallogly, WS 244

7 Michael Staines, WS 284.

8 Leon O Broin, *Dublin Castle and the 1916 Rising: The Story of Sir Mathew Nathan*, Helicon, 1966, cited by Mac Lochlainn, 78.

9 John McGallogly WS 224.

10 JJ Walsh, *Recollections of a Rebel,* The Kerryman, Tralee, 1944, 40–41.

11–12 Bound typescript memoirs in two volumes of Brigadier General Ernest William SK Maconchy, 1860-1920, British Army Museum, 456. Cited by Brian Barton, *Behind A Closed Door: The Secret Court Martial Records of the Easter Rising*, Blackstaff, 2002, 34.

13 Maxwell Memorandum, Asquith Papers MS 43 26–33, Bodleian Library, Oxford University, cited by Brian Barton, *The Secret Court Martial Records of the Easter Rising*, The History Press, 2010, 178.

14 Clemency to prisoners, House of Commons debate, 8/5/1916.

15 Seán McLoughlin, 'Memories of Easter Rising', Camillian Post, 21.

16 Personal Recollections by the late Father Aloysius, OFM, Cap., Capuchin Annual, 1966, 280-289, 289.

17–21 Senator Margaret M Pearse, 'St Enda's, Easter Week 1916, Capuchin Annual, 1942, 227-230. The detail about the cell being in the more modern part of the prison is in Father Columbus's account: 'My experiences in the 1916 Rising by Father Columbus OSFC', 29 July 1916, Irish Capuchin Provincial Archives.

22 'My experiences in the 1916 Rising by Father Columbus OSFC', 29 July 1916, Irish Capuchin Provincial Archives.

23 'How the Men of Easter Week Met Death', *Freeman's Journal*, 19/6/1919.

24 'My experiences in the 1916 Rising by Father Columbus OSFC', 29 July 1916, Irish Capuchin Provincial Archives.

25 Father Augustine, OFM, Cap. WS 920; also 'How the Men of Easter Week Met Death', *Freeman's Journal*, 19/6/1919.

26 Father Augustine OFM, Cap. WS 920.

27–30 'My experiences in the 1916 Rising by Father Columbus OSFC' 29 July 1916, Irish Capuchin Provincial Archives.

31 See entry for An tAthair Tomás de Bhál on www.ainm.ie and letter from Dr Patrick McCartan dated 28 June 1928, Military Service Pensions Applications, DP 1910.

32 'Policy of repression (Treatment of Rebels)', House of Commons Debate, 04 May 1916, Vol 82, c125.

33 Brian Barton, *The Secret Court Martials of the Easter Rising*, The History Press, 2010, 51.

34 As told to Ryan by Willie's sister Margaret. WS 725. Mentioned also in *Remembering Sion, A Chronicle of Storm and Quiet*, Arthur Barker, 1934, 126.

35 John Dillon, Speech in House of Commons, 11/5/1916. Retrieved at http://hansard. millbanksystems.com/commons/. This is the source for all subsequent citations from Commons debates.

36 'P.H and William Pearse', House of Commons Debate 15 May 1916 vol 82 cc1125.

37 'Executions', House of Commons Debate 25 May 1916 vol 82 c2263.

38 'The Rebellion, Questions in the Commons, The Case of William Pearse', *The Irish Times*, 26/5/1916.

39 Geraldine Plunkett Dillon, 'The Irish Republican Brotherhood (Continued)', *University Review*, Vol. 2 No. 9, Spring 1962 23-36, 24.

40 Sir Alfred Bucknill, WS 1019.

41 Letter from M Brennnan to Secretary Army Pensions Board, Certified Statement from Minister of Defence 19/1/1928 Captain Henry S. Murray, WS 300.

42 Thomas J Doyle, WS 186.

CHAPTER TWELVE

1 MS Asquith 43, Dillon to Asquith 24/5/1916, cited by Ruth Dudley Edwards, *Patrick Pearse, The Triupmh of Failure*, Victor Gollancz, 1979, 329, 360.

2 Desmond Ryan, *Remembering Sion, A Chronicle of Storm and Quiet*, Arthur Barker, 1934, 145.

3–4 Letter from Mrs Pearse to 'Geraldine', OPW.

5 Mary Brigid Pearse, *The Home Life of Pádraig Pearse*, Browne and Nolan, 1934, 49.

6 Eamon Bulfin WS 497.

7 'W Pearse's casts broken', *Irish Independent*, 10/4/1920.

8 Desmond Ryan, *Remembering Sion, A Chronicle of Storm and Quiet*, Arthur Barker, 1934, 144-145.

9 'Sixteen teachtaí continue ratification debate', *Freeman's Journal*, 5/1/1922.

10 Desmond Ryan, *Remembering Sion, A Chronicle of Storm and Quiet*, Arthur Barker, 1934, 145.

11–12 Notes made by Brian Crowley, Curator of Pearse Museum/OPW, from a conversation on 3 January, 2005 with Ms. Nina Jaglom, London. See also Senator Margaret M. Pearse, 'St. Enda's', Easter Week 1916, 227–130, 228 regarding the cups.

13–14 Information and description from Florence's son, Noel Scarlett, speaking with the author in 2014.

15 With thanks to Noel Scarlett and Alf and Fionnuala Mac Loclainn.

16 Arthur Pearse was the son of James Pearse Snr's brother Henry. With thanks to Tony Pearse, whose mother provided the cited information to him.

17 Letter from Mary Kate Shovelton to 3/5/1916, cited in Ruth Dudley Edwards, *Patrick Pearse, The Triumph of Failure*, Victor Golllancz, London, 1979, 329.

18 Obituary of Patrick Shovelton: senior civil servant and obituarist for *The Independent*, *The Independent*, 3/2/2012.

19–20 David Sears, 'Some impressions of Willie Pearse', *Cuimhní na bPiarsach*, Coiste Cuimhneacháin na bPiarsach, 25.

21 Information from Lorraine Peavoy, National Library of Ireland, grand-daughter of John Fleming.

22 TK Moylan, 'A Dubliner's diary 1914-1918 by T. K. M. [Thomas King Moylan]', bound typescript diary including an account of Dublin during Easter Week 1916, Ms 9620.

23 David Sears, 'Some Impressions of Willie Pearse', *Cuimhní na bPiarsach*, Coiste Cuimhneacháin na bPiarsach, 1958, 25-30, 26.

24 Desmond Ryan, *The Man Called Pearse*, 72.

25 Desmond Ryan, *The Man Called Pearse*, 79.

26 Desmond Ryan, *The Man Called Pearse*, 61.

27–28 David Sears, 'Some Impressions of Willie Pearse', *Cuimhní na bPiarsach*, Coiste Cuimhneacháin na bPiarsach, 1958, 25-28, 27, originally published in *The Cross*.

29 Desmond Ryan, *The Man Called Pearse*, 62.

30 Piaras F Mac Lochlainn, *Last Words*, Kilmainham Jail Restoration Society, 1971.

31 Patrick Pearse, Unfinished autobiographical fragment, OPW.

32 See 'Memorial Mass for the 4th Battalion', No I Dublin Brigade, 24.4.1949; 'Pearse Memorial Unveiled' 14/6/1932, *Irish Press*.

33 Liam Ó Briain, Cuimhní Cinn, Sairséal agus Dill, 1951, 161 (Translated by Ní Ghairbhí from Ó Brian's Irish).

34 Notes made by Brian Crowley, Curator of Pearse Museum, OPW, from a conversation

on 3 January, 2005 with Ms. Nina Jaglom, London.

35 Royal Hibernian Academy of Arts index of exhibitors and their works, 1826-1979, compiled by Ann. M Stewart with a summary history of RHA by C de Courcy, Manton, Dublin, 1985. See also the site 'Mapping the profession and practice of sculpture in Britain and Ireland 1851-1951 http://sculpture.gla.ac.uk/view/person. php?id=msib3_1205318341, accessed 12/1/201431.

36 Desmond Ryan, *The Man Called Pearse*.

37 Éamonn Mac Thomáis, 'Down Dublin Streets', *Irish Press*, 21/1/1987.

38 Pádraig Ó Snodaigh, 'William Pearse: Artist', Leabhrán Cuimhneacháin arna bronnadh ar Ócáid Bronnadh Eochair Scoil Éanna ar Uachtarán na hÉireann Éamon de Valera 23 Aibreán 1970, pp 17-18. Thomas Duffy, *Artisan Sculpture and the Stone Carving Firms of Dublin*, 1859-1910. Unpublished Thesis, National College of Art and Design Faculty of History of Art and Design 1999. Brian Crowley, 'William Pearse' in Paula Murphy, ed., *Sculpture, Art and Architecture of Ireland* Volume III, pp287-289; John Turpin, conversation with author 2014.

39 'Pádraig Pearse', newspaper clipping dated 20/7/1937.

40 William Feeney, *Drama at Hardwicke*, 96.

41 Desmond Ryan, *The Man Called Pearse,* 67-68.

42 Ruth Dudley Edwards, *The Triumph of Failure*, Victor Gollannz, 1977; Ruth Dudley Edwards, 'Is it unpatriotic to be honest?', *Irish Times*, 1/4/1991.

43 Desmond Ryan, *The Man Called Pearse*, 68.

44 David Sears, 'Some Impressions of Willie Pearse', Cuimhní na bPiarsach, Coiste Cuimhneacháin na bPiarsach, 1958, 25-30, 27, originally published in *The Cross*.

45 Mary Brigid Pearse, 'Two Brothers', *Irish Press*, 3/5/1940.

46 TK Moylan, 'A Dubliner's diary 1914-1918 by T. K. M. [Thomas King Moylan]', bound typescript diary including an account of Dublin during Easter Week 1916, Ms 9620.

47 Desmond Ryan, *The Man Called Pearse*, 1919, 75.

48–49 Mary Brigid Pearse, 'Two Brothers', *Irish Press*, 3/5/1940.

Sources

JOURNALS

Camillion Post, Capuchin Annual, Circa, Clogher Record, Donegal Annual, Dublin Historical Record, Fianna Magazine, Folk Life Journal of Ethnological Studies, Irish Arts Review Yearbook, The Irish Review, The Tablet, Irish Historical Studies, Studies.

NEWSPAPERS AND MAGAZINES

An Barr Buadh, An Claidheamh Soluis, An Phoblacht, An Sgoláire, Belfast Telegraph, Fáinne an Lae, Freeman's Journal, Freeman's Journal (Sydney), *Irish Freedom, Irish Citizen, Irish Independent, Irish Times, The Independent* (London), *Irish Press, Limerick Leader, The Leader, Sinn Féin, Donegal News, Irish Worker, Woman's World.*

MANUSCRIPTS, UNPUBLISHED MATERIAL

Archives of Passionist Community Mount Argus: Pearse file.

Bibliothèque Nationale de France: 'L'académie Julian', (magazine) as microfiche.

Bureau of Military History Witness Statements.

Irish Capuchin Provincial Archives: 'My experiences in the 1916 Rising' by Father Columbus OSFC' 29 July 1916.

Military Archives Pension Records (William Pearse DP 1910).

National College of Art and Design: Student Registers for Metropolitan School of Art; Oliver Sheppard Papers; Thomas Duffy, Artisan Sculpture and the Stone Carving Firms of Dublin, 1859–1910, unpublished thesis, 1999.

National Library of Ireland: Cuala Industries and Cuala Press Visitors Book c1908-1928; Coffey and Chenevix Trench family papers; Bulmer Hobson Papers; Joseph Holloway collection; Eamonn Martin Papers; Memoirs of John McGallogly; Máire Nic Shiubhlaigh. Additional Papers; Seán T O'Kelly Papers, Minutes of Cluichtheoirí na hÉireann (Theatre of Ireland) 1906-1907; Pearse family papers.

Office of Public Works/Pearse and Kilmainham Museum: Pearse and St. Enda's Collections.

Public Record Office, Kew: CO 904, PRO 30/89, PRO WO71/358.

University College Dublin, Archives: O'Rahilly Papers, Desmond Ryan letters in WJ Ryan Papers.

PROGRAMMES AND CATALOGUES

Cláracha an Oireachtais/Oireachtas Catalogues, incl. art exhibition catalogues. 1906-
1916, (NLI).

Catalogues for exhibitions of the Arts and Crafts Society of Ireland, (NLI).

Aonach na Bealtaine Catalogue (Irish Capuchin Provincial Archives).

Catalogues for Sinn Féin Aonach na Nodlag, and Aonach Art Exhibitions, 1908-1912 (NLI).

Royal Hibernian Academy of Arts, Index of Exhibitors, 1826-1979, compiled by Ann M.
Stewart with a summary history of the R.H.A by C De Courcy, Manton Publishing, 1985.

Cork International Exhibition Official Catalogue, 1902 (NLI).

Original programmes for St. Enda's productions (Allen Library, OPW, NLI); for Leinster
Stage Society productions (NLI); for Theatre of Ireland and Irish Theatre productions
(Allen Library, OPW and NLI); (limited) programmes for Met. School of Art produc-
tions in Oliver Sheppard Papers.

Irish International Exhibition Catalogue 1907, various editions and versions, NLI.

DIGITAL RESOURCES

www.rte.ie/doconone 'Pearse's People' and 'This man had kept a school' http://www.
nival.ie/collections/collections/collection/archive/college-student-registers/view/col-
lection Student registers of Metropolitan School of Art.

www.ainm.ie Database based on *Beathaisnéis* series about prominent Gaelic speakers.

http://sculpture.gla.ac.uk Mapping the Practice and Profession of Sculpture in Britain
and Ireland 1851–1951, University of Glasgow.

www.dia.ie Dictionary of Irish Architects.

http://dh.tcd.ie/letters1916 Letters of 1916 Project (incl mobilisation orders).

http:/hansard/millbank systems.com/commons House of Commons debates.

www.irishgenealogy.ie; www.findmypast.co.uk; www.census.nationalarchives.ie.

Other information to author as cited in Acknowledgements.

Select Bibliography

Annual Report and Distribution of Prizes [Met. School of Art] 1884-1915, bound series, NLI.

Brian Barton, *The Secret Court Martial Records of the Easter Rising,* The History Press, 2010.

Sighle Bhreathnach Lynch, 'Albert Power RHA', *Irish Arts Review Yearbook,* 1990-91, pp111-114.

Colum, Mary, *Life and the Dream,* Doubleday and Company, NY, 1947.

Crowley, Brian, 'I am the son of a good father: James and Patrick Pearse', in Róisín Higgins and Regina Uí Chollatáin, eds, *The Life and After-life of P.H. Pearse,* Irish Academic Press.

Crowley, Brian, *Patrick Pearse, A Life in Pictures,* Cork, Mercier Press, 2013.

Crowley, Brian, 'William Pearse', in Paula Murphy, ed, *Sculpture, Art and Architecture of Ireland,* Volume III, 2014.

Dudley Edwards, Ruth, *Patrick Pearse, The Triumph of Failure,* London, Victor Gollancz, 1977.

Enright, Seán, *Easter 1916: The Trials,* Kildare, Merrion, 2014.

Feeney, William, *Drama in Hardwicke Street: A History of the Irish Theatre Company,* Associated University Presses, Rutherford & London, 1984.

Gefen, Gérard, *Jean-Marie de Moral, Paris des Artistes 1840-1940,* Paris, Editions de Chêne, 1998.

Gordon Bowe, Nicola and Cumming, Elizabeth, *The Arts and Crafts Movements in Dublin and Edinburgh, 1885–1920,* Dublin, Irish Academic Press, 1998.

Higgins, Róisín and Uí Chollatáin, Regina, eds, *The Life and After-life of P.H. Pearse,* Dublin, Irish Academic Press, 2009.

Mac Entee, Seán, *Episode at Easter,* Dublin, Gill, 1966.

Mac Lochlainn, Piaras F. ed., *Last Words,* Dublin, Kilmainham Jail Restoration Society, 1971.

Liam Mac Piarais, Taispeantas ina omós, Áth Cliath, Músaem an Phiarsaigh, (sic), 1981.

Martin, F.X., ed., The Howth Gun Running and The Kilcoole Gunrunning, recollections and documents, Browne and Nolan, 1964, 156-159

McLoughlin, Seán, *Memories of Easter Rising,* Killucan, Camillian Post, 1948.

Murphy, William, 'William Pearse', *Dictionary of Irish Biography,* Cambridge, 2009.

Mc Nulty, Eugene, *The Ulster Literary Theatre and the Northern Revival,* Cork, CUP, 2008.

Ó Buachalla, Séamus, ed., *The Letters of PH Pearse,* Gerrards Cross, Colin Smythe, 1980.

Ó Briain, Liam, Cuimhní Cinn, Baile Átha Cliath, Sáirséal agus Dill, 1951.

Ó Conaire, Pádraic Óg, 'Cuimhní Scoil Eanna', *Cuimhní na bPiarsach,* Coiste Cuimhneacháin na bPiarsach, 1958.

Ó Conaola, Dara, *Albert Power, Saol agus Saothar*, Ceardshiopa Inis Oírr teo, 1996.

O'Donnell, Ruan, ed, *Among the Nations*, Dublin, Irish Academic Press, 2008.

Ní Ghairbhí, Róisín and McNulty, Eugene, eds., *Patrick Pearse, Collected Plays/Drámaí an Phiarsaigh*, Dublin, Irish Academic Press, 2013.

Nic Shiubhlaigh, Máire, *The Splendid Years*, James Duffy and Co, 1955.

Ó Buachalla, Séamus, ed., *The Letters of PH Pearse*, Gerrards Cross/Smythe, 1980.

Ó Snodaigh, 'Willie Pearse: Artist', Leabhar Cuimhneacháin, Arna Fhoilsiú ar ocáid bhronnta eochair Scoil Éanna ar Uachtarán na hÉireann, Éamonn de Valera 23 Aibreán 1970.

Pearse, Senator Margaret M. 'St. Enda's, Easter Week 1916', *Capuchin Annual*, 1942.

Pearse, Margaret, 'Patrick and Willie Pearse,' *Capuchin Annual*, Dublin, 1943.

Pearse, Mary Brigid, *The Home Life of Pádraig Pearse*, Dublin, Browne and Nolan, 1934.

Hilary Pyle, *Cesca's Diary 1913-1916, Where art and nationalism meet*, Dublin, Woodfield, 2005.

Reddin, Kenneth, 'A Man Called Pearse', *Studies*, Vol. 34, No. 134, June 1945.

Ryan, Desmond, *The Man Called Pearse*, Dublin, Maunsell and Company, 1919.

Desmond Ryan, *Remembering Sion,* London, Arthur Barker, 1934.

Sears, David, 'Some Impressions of Willie Pearse', *Cuimhní na bPiarsach*, Coiste Cuimhneacháin na bPiarsach, 1958, (and *The Cross*, Mount Argus, 1917).

Sisson, Elaine, *Pearse's Patriots: St Enda's and the Cult of Boyhood,* Cork, CUP, 2004.

Turpin, John, *A School of Art in Dublin Since the Eighteenth Century; a History of the National College of Art and Design*, Dublin, Gill and Macmillan, 1995.

Turpin, John, *Oliver Sheppard 1865–1941, Symbolist Sculptor of the Irish Cultural Revival*, Four Courts, 2000.

Walsh, J.J. *Recollections of a Rebel*, Tralee, The Kerryman, 1944.

Index